Also by Greg Kot
Wilco: Learning How to Die
Survival Guide for Coaching Youth Basketball

RIPPED

How the Wired
Generation
Revolutionized
Music

GREG KOT

Scribner
New York London Toronto Sydney

SCRIBNER
A Division of Simon & Schuster, Inc.
1230 Avenue of the Americas
New York, NY 10020

First Scribner hardcover edition May 2009

For information about special discounts for bulk purchases,
please contact Simon & Schuster Special Sales at 1-866-506-1949
or business@simonandschuster.com.

The Simon & Schuster Speakers Bureau can bring authors to your
live event. For more information or to book an event, contact the
Simon & Schuster Speakers Bureau at 1-866-248-3049 or visit our
website at www.simonspeakers.com.

Text set in Stempel Garamond

Manufactured in the United States of America

10 9 8 7 6 5 4 3 2 1

Library of Congress Control Number: 2008040839

ISBN-13: 978-1-4165-4727-3
ISBN-10: 1-4165-4727-4

For Deb, Katie, and Marissa

CONTENTS

INTRODUCTION

Chaos and Transformation

Peter Jenner is a man who knows his "freak-outs"—sixties termi-
nology for an intense, drug-induced emotional experience. He was
Pink Floyd's first manager, after all, and he has remained one of the
industry's most forward-looking thinkers for forty years. So when
he spoke to a room full of music executives in the fall of 2006 at the
Future of Music Policy Summit in Montreal, his assessment of their
business resonated.

"We are in the midst of a technological freak-out," he said. "The
business is broken. . . . Digital technology is fundamentally changing
our business in a way that no development of the last two hundred
years equals, except the onset of electricity."

Jenner described a worst-case scenario for people who had made
a lucrative living as middlemen in the twentieth-century music business, the conduits between musicmakers and consumers. The Internet was making them obsolete.

"We're trying to force a nineteenth- and twentieth-century business model into twenty-first-century technology," he said. "I'm not
surprised we're in chaos."

Peer-to-peer file sharing had turned consumers into distributors. CD burners had turned them into manufacturers. This shift
in responsibilities left the industry with only one role: as "police-
man . . . hostile to consumers . . . [and] stopping progress."

In a report prepared that same year, *Beyond the Soundbytes,*

Jenner expanded on his disdain for this shortsighted response: "The flagrant spread of 'Internet piracy' in developed countries is a reflection of the failure of the industry as a whole to develop an appropriate copyright response to the distribution and remuneration options made possible by the new technologies."

He mocked the industry's response to the new challenges posed by Internet distribution and peer-to-peer file sharing: hand-wringing, followed by litigation, in which "the endless predictions of victory reminds one of the Vietnam War."

We were back in the sixties again, when Rock 'n' Roll Inc. was still in its infancy. Now four decades later, it was looking like a relic.

"When five percent of the artists are making ninety-five percent of the money, the system is broken," Daniel Levitin, a McGill University music professor, proclaimed.

Through the breach rushed a new generation of bands and fans empowered by personal computers and broadband Internet connections. Willy-nilly they forged a new world of music distribution that seized control from once all-powerful music and radio conglomerates.

In less than a decade, a new Internet-savvy music hierarchy had been created. Commercial radio, MTV, retail stores, and record companies lost their exclusive tastemaker status, while consumers morphed into de facto music programmers who shared information and music via message boards, Web pages, e-zines, and MP3 blogs.

In the process, more people than ever were creating and consuming music. Without a physical product to sell, costs sunk for recording and distributing music. At the same time, opportunities to be heard increased. In this world, the fringe players could more easily find and build a dedicated audience, and a musical ecosystem encompassing thousands of microcultures began to emerge.

"We're moving into an era of massive niche markets rather than a mass market," Jenner said. This was bad news for people awaiting the next Beatles or the new U2—a band that could unite the masses in a whirlwind of hits and hype. For everybody else, this was an opportunity for more music to flourish in more places than ever.

In this broader, more diversified world, bands such as Montreal's Arcade Fire, Seattle's Death Cab for Cutie, and Omaha's Bright Eyes rose to prominence. They were viral success stories, selling out shows around the world before they were selling albums in the kind of numbers that would make the majors take notice of them.

It was enough to make Death Cab for Cutie's Chris Walla proselytize like a digital evangelist: "This is the golden age of the Internet. The laptop kids have clued in everybody else to what's going on: radio, television, the record industry—they're all following the Internet's lead. Because those kids know their laptop can make their cultural existence more fulfilling than any media corporation."

Who knew a laptop could be so empowering? The music industry sure didn't. But the Internet turned fans into gatekeepers. It also gave bands an independence they never had: the ability to communicate directly with their fans in ways their predecessors never could have imagined.

Consider that when the nineties roared to a close with CDs generating millions in profit, the industry consisted of six multinational record labels, and a single corporation (SFX, soon to be bought out by Clear Channel) that dominated the concert and commercial radio businesses. The primary decisions about what kind of music most of America would hear and how consumers would access that music (through radio, retail, and touring) were essentially being made by a few dozen key executives at a handful of companies.

But that power structure, the by-product of a century's worth of empire building, started to crumble the instant the first music file was ripped onto a computer hard drive and shared online. Metallica and the major labels took the rogue file-swapping service Napster to court in 2000 and held back the Internet tide for a few months. But as independent producer Steve Albini said, "It's like trying to hold back the ocean, like trying to keep the sun from rising every morning. It's a whole new era, except the music industry doesn't know it yet." It would find out soon enough.

In the fall of 2000, Radiohead's *Kid A* was a Napster-fueled hit on the Internet long before it arrived in record stores. The esoteric album barely registered on commercial radio; but it was in heavy rotation on the Net months before its release. The result was a number one album, an extraordinary confluence of underground taste and mass popularity.

The industry responded not with vigorous new ideas, but with strong-arm tactics and threats. It served fans not with digital innovation but with lawsuits—more than twenty thousand in a span of four years, in an attempt to intimidate consumers away from file sharing.

Seven years after *Kid A*, Radiohead released *In Rainbows* through its website, without the aid of a record label.

The cost to fans? "It's up to you," Radiohead told them.

In contrast to the major labels, the band embraced one of the fundamental principles of good business: the customer is always right. It was a moment of clarity, a moment in which the future finally overtook the past. The following pages contain the story of that transformation.

I

Consolidated to Death

In February 1999, Sheryl Crow found herself in the strange position of having won a Grammy Award for an album put out by a record label that no longer existed.

In the weeks before the Grammys, A&M—the record label that had signed her, nurtured her career, and overseen her rise from Los Angeles studio singer to international rock star over the previous decade—was gutted and folded into the Interscope label as part of the newly formed Universal Music Group. The demise of A&M was the result of a $10.4 billion purchase of the PolyGram music companies by Seagram.

As the rest of the industry celebrated itself at the Grammys, Crow saw trouble ahead. In her acceptance speech, the singer delivered something of a eulogy for her old label. She was the only artist at the nationally televised ceremony to publicly acknowledge the huge toll exacted by the wave of consolidation that had washed over her profession.

Up until a few months before, she had been working for one of the smaller major-label companies, headed by veteran music executive Al Cafaro; now Cafaro and A&M were gone and she found herself under contract to the world's largest record company, headed by Edgar Bronfman Jr. The immediate costs of the merger were easy to quantify: besides Cafaro, more than twenty-five hundred employees lost their jobs and 250 bands lost their deals with labels such as A&M, Geffen, Mercury, Island, and Motown.

But in the long term, the effects of consolidation would be even more profound, and usher in a decade when the twentieth-century music industry would suddenly find itself fighting for its life, undone by its single-minded pursuit of profit at the expense of the cornerstone principle that had allowed it to thrive for decades: artist development, as nurtured by savvy executives who not only knew their business but knew their music.

Now Cafaro, a music lifer, was out, and Bronfman, a longtime liquor magnate, was in. He'd soon head the biggest music corporation in the world. Bronfman was heir to the Seagram fortune and was running the family business in the nineties when he sought to diversify the company's holdings by branching out into music. As with the other moneymen taking power in the consolidation-heavy nineties, music was not central to his vision but rather a piece in a larger portfolio of products.

Cafaro was one of Crow's champions; he had signed her to her first record deal in 1991 and had allowed her to rerecord her debut album because she was dissatisfied with the initial results. Cafaro's faith was rewarded with a hit: *Tuesday Night Music Club* established Crow as an artist to be reckoned with in 1993. It went on to sell more than 4 million copies and her career flourished; her 1999 Grammy was her sixth.

Yet she wasn't in a particularly celebratory mood in the days after the '99 ceremony.

"It's a frightening time as far as the music industry being an artist-nurturing industry," she said. "Now everything is so numbers-oriented and new artists get one shot, maybe two, to get a hit, and that's it. They sign two-album deals now. I was signed to seven albums and I was given a chance to get on the road and hone my craft. You want artists who have a strong point of view, who have the potential to grow into something wonderful, like Jackson Browne and Joni Mitchell, who found themselves by touring and continuing to write, and their album sales slowly grew. But now artists aren't getting that opportunity because there's pressure to have instant hits."

Consolidation was the era's trendiest business strategy. It caught on because it enabled companies to claim bigger market share, streamline operations by cutting overlapping positions and payroll, and explore new revenue streams. By the late nineties, Wall Street was rife with merger news, and deals that further centralized power in the record, radio, and concert industries were brokered. Power was concentrated in fewer hands than ever: the PolyGram-Universal merger left five multinational conglomerates to run the $14.6 billion-a-year record industry. Ten conglomerates accounted for 62 percent of the gross revenue in the $10.2 billion commercial-radio business, and one company—SFX Entertainment—dominated the $1.5 billion concert-touring industry.

One side effect of this strategy profoundly affected consumers: the price for music spiked. Compact disc prices approached a record $19, even though the manufacturing cost had actually declined since the discs came into the marketplace in the early eighties. Tickets for major shows skyrocketed. Indirectly, an even steeper price was being paid: concerts were being transformed into marketing opportunities for a vast network of products.

Enter New York–based SFX, which bought more than a hundred major concert venues nationwide and then began acquiring tours by major artists underwritten by national advertisers. In 1999, SFX had a hand in producing 60 percent of the two hundred biggest revenue-generating shows; the concert industry had its biggest year ever, with $1.5 billion in sales. The reason? Ticket prices had increased a whopping $10 a ticket, a 30 percent increase over 1998, to an average of $44.

With consolidation came pressure to produce profit. The multinationals were effectively run by their shareholders, who wanted a steady flow of quarterly returns to justify their investment. But in an industry supposedly devoted to creating a highly volatile and unpredictable product—music—this was hardly a sound strategy. How to reconcile the whims of creativity with the need for producing profit on a prescribed schedule?

"That's a big problem because Wall Street is looking for stability—quarter-over-quarter growth—in an industry that is dependent on artists," whose creativity can't be doled out in quarterly spurts, said Michael Nathanson, a New York investment counselor.

His words—delivered in 1999 at the South by Southwest music conference in Austin, Texas—brought silent "Amens" from a roomful of music executives, many of whom must've felt like they were attending their own wake. Each of their jobs was in jeopardy as longtime record labels were folded inside Godzilla-sized multinational corporations.

"Every day the corporation became more and more powerful inside of the company and suddenly it was our total focus, rather than the consumers, or the artists," said Howie Klein, a longtime old-guard executive who ran Reprise Records until he was deemed expendable in 2000. "And at a certain point, it wasn't even the shareholders we were serving, but the Wall Street analysts. We were there for the short-term needs of Wall Street, which is antithetical to the needs of a company that is supposedly founded on music. The industry was built on signing artists with a strong vision, and trusting that vision to do good work over a long period of time. Your job as a record-company man was to help them realize that. [Former Warner executive] Lenny Waronker once told me, 'If it's a real artist, you can never go wrong.'"

Klein's view of the industry he once knew is highly romanticized. There were always plenty of bloodsuckers in it for a quick buck. But Klein had his priorities straight. In the eighties, he had started a fine independent label, 415 Records, in his San Francisco bedroom. When he was able to finally pay himself $100 a week, it was a big deal. "I'd never seen a three-figure salary before," he says now with a laugh. Later he was mentored by some of the best minds in the business, including Sire's Seymour Stein and Warner Bros.' Mo Ostin, and he'd help nurture the careers of artists and bands such as Romeo Void, Lou Reed, and Depeche Mode.

To a large extent, those artists built a career by being different. It was their idiosyncrasies that made them interesting and gave them staying power. But the industry of the late nineties didn't want idiosyncrasy. The long-range, career-building view was out. Instant payback was in. In the late nineties the acts dominating the charts were marketing triumphs more than creative ones: Britney Spears, 'N Sync, the Backstreet Boys, Ricky Martin, and Will Smith. They were the kind of telegenic, cross-format acts that could be sold quickly through a variety of mediums.

"There is so much pressure on the people at the label to generate profits that the music isn't allowed to breathe and artists aren't allowed to develop," said Moby, who had just signed a deal with an independent label, V2 Records, and released what would be his biggest record, *Play.*

"It makes bad creative sense, and it makes bad business sense. Under the circumstances of the music business right now, Bruce Springsteen and Fleetwood Mac would have been dropped long before they had a hit because their first few records didn't do that well. Prince's first few records were not huge sellers. So the major labels in the pursuit of quarterly profits are shooting themselves in the foot by putting out lowest-common-denominator music that works on the radio but doesn't generate any loyalty. There's no room for idiosyncratic artists. You have to fit the mold, and radio defines that mold. Right now, if you're not a teen pop star, an R&B artist, a hip-hop artist, a generic alternative rock band, or a female singer-songwriter, you might as well not even think about making records."

That mold was set largely by two monoliths: MTV and commercial radio. To get the word out about its latest music, record companies had to do business with both. And both were becoming increasingly narrow outlets for only the most heavily budgeted music. Though MTV launched in 1981 by playing music videos round the clock, it was now much like any other cable television station. Nonmusic programming dominated its schedule, and videos were confined to a select few superstars. Commercial radio was still the kingmaker as far as hits were concerned, and in the consolidation era it was all about centralized decision making. The playlists at commercial stations across the country became increasingly difficult to tell apart.

The trend was accelerated by the 1996 Telecommunications Act, the first major overhaul of U.S. telecommunications law since 1934. It eliminated most media ownership laws. Section 202 of the act, in particular, would prove to have a major impact on music; it required the Federal Communications Commission to eliminate "any provisions limiting the number of AM or FM broadcast stations which may be owned or controlled by one entity nationally."

That decree quickly led to the rapid near monopolization of the radio industry by a handful of corporations, most notably Clear Channel Communications. In 2000, the San Antonio, Texas–based radio conglomerate further expanded its interests by acquiring SFX. It was a move hailed by the company as a triumph of synergy that would enable Clear Channel stations to promote concerts in Clear Channel concert venues. By 2002, the company owned more than twelve hundred radio stations, covering 247 of the nation's top 250 markets, and controlled the biggest concert venues nationwide.

"I think that putting stations in the hands of people who are committed to public service and who are top broadcasters is good for the public," said Randy Michaels, the CEO of Clear Channel from 1999 to 2002. "When we were in the mom-and-pop era, half the radio stations were owned by people who were as interested in playing what they liked as opposed to really serving the public. When you have professional management, who is focused on serving the listener, then of necessity we are obsessed with what the public wants, and we work every day to give them what they want."

But the numbers told a different story. At the time Michaels was interviewed, Arbitron surveys showed that the average time spent listening to radio by consumers twelve years old and older had dropped 9 percent since deregulation. The young especially were tuning out: teenage listeners were down 11 percent, and listeners between the ages of eighteen and twenty-four had declined 10 percent. From 1998 to 2008, the average share of Americans listening to radio at any given time declined 14 percent.

Indeed, the real story was not that radio stations were trying to give listeners what they wanted so much as fretting about chasing them off with new, unfamiliar music. In this environment, taking chances on unproven artists supported by underfunded independent labels was considered bad business.

Clear Channel's Michaels argued that listeners didn't want adventuresome music chosen for reasons of taste; they wanted familiarity. His argument wasn't particularly new; corporations had always put making a buck ahead of aesthetics. But now that philosophy was integral to the corporate culture. "We all have nostalgia for the way things were, but radio is experiencing the same kind of consolidation that every other business has seen," Michaels said. "I love to visit small towns and eat at the mom-and-pop restaurants. But more and more it's getting harder to do, because there are a million choices and the chain restaurants are nudging out the mom-and-pop places. There are people, including me, who think that's bad. But people want to eat at the chain restaurant for some reason."

A handful of locally owned stations, such as WMPS in Memphis, were hanging tough by reviving some of the adventurousness and eclecticism of FM radio's free-form golden age in the seventies. WMPS's playlist blended Ben Harper, R.E.M., and Ani DiFranco with hard-core country acts (Rodney Crowell), Tex-Mex roots groups (Los Super Seven), and independent local artists.

"We play records based on gut instinct," said WMPS program director Alexandra Inzer, an adventurer marooned in an ocean of Clear Channel vanilla. "The problem with radio today is that corporations have paid a tremendous amount to buy these properties, so they can't afford to take a risk, which makes for really boring radio. Our approach is risky, and our audience is smaller because of it. But the ones who do like it stick with us. They have the station on for long periods because they're not going to hear the same songs over and over."

A similar philosophy prevailed at locally owned WWCD, an alternative rock station in Columbus, Ohio, that worked records by indie artists and local rockers into its rotation in a town where rigorously programmed playlists by Clear Channel and Infinity stations predominated.

"This conglomeration thing has totally ruined our industry," said WWCD program director Andy Davis. "I think people are listening to radio less and disappointed more when they do listen. We are fortunate to be owned by a local guy who loves music, who has a passion for new and progressive sounds. But always lingering in the back of my mind is that the next quarter could be our last, because there aren't many of us left."

Indeed, no comment summarized commercial radio's attitude toward music more succinctly than one made by Clear Channel chairman Lowry Mays to *Fortune* magazine in 2003.

"We're not in the business of providing news and information," he said. "We're not in the business of providing well-researched music. We're simply in the business of selling our customers products."

People weren't going to buy music unless they could hear it. That's what college radio and MP3 blogs were for. It's to the bands' benefit for people to hear their music because we're in a day when nobody buys music unless they've heard it. Because we don't trust anyone, really.

—Garrison, e-zine editor and satellite-radio programmer in Texas, born 1982

2

Payola Blues

No matter where I go / I never hear my
record on the radio.

—"Payola Blues," Neil Young, 1988

For most of the last sixty years, middlemen ran the music industry.
These anonymous, deeply entrenched record company lifers "discovered" the music and then figured out ways to buy, sell, promote,
market, and distribute it. Their accomplices included radio and video
station programmers, retailers, and magazine editors. Hundreds of
artists and bands made it big in that time; a few got rich and famous.
Many, many more did not. At the major-label level, the failure rate
was about 90 percent. Translation: fewer than 10 percent of the bands
signed to major labels actually made money off record sale royalties.
Most were dropped from their deals, owing their labels hundreds of
thousands of dollars.

But the middleman's life was relatively stable. There were rough
patches when the industry would cut back and lay off employees,
but for the most part, music was a growth industry, and working
for a major label was a decent, well-paying job—far more stable
than playing bass in a fledgling rock band. The traditional contract
with a major label ensured that the middlemen would always get
paid before any band actually did, with profits split 90–10 in favor

of the label, and then only after the artist had recouped expenses for recording and promotion.

The key to any band's success, and by extension any record label's success, was held by radio. Throughout the rock 'n' roll era, commercial radio (and later its video equivalent, MTV) was the main outlet for exposing music.

There were exceptions, of course—records that would find an audience through relentless touring, word of mouth, and critical acclaim. But for most major-label albums, where the aim was to sell at least five hundred thousand copies, airplay was like oxygen. Without it, a record would die unnoticed.

By the turn of the twenty-first century, the pipeline to commercial radio was as narrow as it had ever been, open only to the wealthiest and best-connected middlemen.

Four radio groups controlled the top-40 music heard by 63 percent of the 41 million listeners nationwide. Playlists at stations across the country continued to shrink, with only about twenty songs a week played with any regularity. In one week in 2002, the forty biggest modern-rock stations in the country opened a total of sixteen slots for new records, and the forty-five biggest top-40 stations added a total of twenty. Every one of those records was underwritten by one of the five majors.

The intimate connection between the major-label artists and corporate-radio airplay was no coincidence. Commercial stations had been receiving upward of $100 million a year in big-label money funneled through independent radio promoters, a legal variation on the old pay-for-play payola that was stamped out by a federal inquiry in the eighties.

Consider the plight of *Veni Vidi Vicious*, an exuberantly hard-hitting garage-rock album by the Swedish band the Hives. Initially released in 2000 on the Burning Heart label, a subsidiary of California indie Epitaph Records, it was ignored by commercial radio stations across America. The album sold forty thousand copies, a modest success by indie label standards but hardly a hit.

No matter that the album was flat-out brilliant, sprinting along the fine line that separates insanity from celebration. The list of great albums that have gone down in commercial flames, ignored at the time of their release only to be lionized long after the band had broken up, was a long one. But in 2002, the two-year-old Hives album avoided that fate.

Reprise Records, then a subsidiary of AOL Time Warner, licensed *Veni Vidi Vicious* from Epitaph, and soon after a track from the album, "Hate to Say I Told You So," zoomed into the top 10 of the modern-rock singles chart. Suddenly, the Hives were no longer anonymous; their album began selling at a fifteen-thousand-copies-a-week clip and cracked the top 100 of the Billboard pop chart.

Why did commercial radio ignore "Hate to Say I Told You So" for nearly two years, only to jump on it when Reprise licensed the album from Epitaph? The record hadn't been remixed or rerecorded—but connecting with a label that could afford the new payola got it on the radio and exposed it to an audience who would otherwise never have known it existed.

Reprise funneled at least $100,000 to commercial radio stations through middlemen known as independent promoters to ensure that "Hate to Say I Told You So" would get airplay.

"We're pushing a boulder up the hill, being an independent label playing the radio game," said Christina White, the Epitaph executive in charge of radio promotion at the time the Hives broke. "The Hives made a great record that people loved when they had a chance to hear it. But there was no way in hell we could have spent what Reprise did to get that record on radio. If the Hives stayed with us, no way they'd have the profile they have now."

An indie label such as Epitaph didn't have the budget to throw that kind of money into promoting a record, especially with no absolute assurance that it would be added to a station's regular rotation, much less become a hit. It was not unusual for a label to spend more than $1 million in promotion costs for a single by a major artist, which is why the marketing expenses—including radio promotion money—for multiplatinum albums by singers such as Alicia Keys and Jennifer Lopez could range upward of $14 million.

Throughout the nineties, the acknowledged master of this legal-ized pay-for-play system and quintessential middleman was a Chicago-based independent promoter, Jeff McClusky.

"This," said McClusky, riffling through a stack of fifty Backstreet Boys concert tickets on his desk during the height of his power, "is Record Promotion 101."

In 1999, these were among the most coveted prizes in the enter-tainment world, and McClusky had paid $2,000 for the premium seats to a Buffalo, New York, show out of his own pocket. The seller was the Backstreet Boys' Los Angeles–based management company, the Firm, with which McClusky had a long relationship. Now he hoped to forge another long relationship with the program director of a top-40 station in Rochester, New York, and he would use his new prizes to wedge the door open.

"Somebody else committed fifty Backstreet Boys tickets to the station and couldn't deliver," McClusky said. "This is how relation-ships develop—somebody needs tickets to a big concert, and I'm going to send them the tickets, gratis. So maybe they'll remember me in three or four months when their present relationship with another independent promoter is not going where it should be going. I spent $2,000 of my own money to prove a point."

In an industry of power brokers and tastemakers who were all but invisible to the music-buying public, McClusky was the man with the widest reach, the most clout, the ability to anoint a song or bury it. At its height, Jeff McClusky & Associates was a thirty-six-person operation based in Chicago's gentrifying Bucktown neighborhood, with satellite offices in Atlanta and Los Angeles.

Each record company had its own radio promotion department, but the independents were often hired to work high-profile records because of their long-standing relationships with the most influen-tial radio programmers. This was the music-industry equivalent of the smoke-filled room at which high-stakes political decisions are brokered.

The price commanded by McClusky and other independent pro-moters was steep because the major labels had such a narrow window of opportunity: if a record wasn't a hit within a few weeks of its release, it was often shelved. Competition was fierce for a handful of airplay slots, and McClusky's ability to pick up the phone and personally pitch a program director made him the first high-priced option at many record companies. Hiring McClusky didn't guarantee a hit, or even airplay, but it improved the odds considerably.

At a station with a playlist of thirty songs, maybe two or three underperforming songs are removed each week and two or three new ones added. Competition for those "adds" is fierce: perhaps twenty songs pitched by record labels and promoters.

"Of those, five or six might be really good," said a Portland commercial radio programmer, Dennis Constantine. "One of those good songs is being promoted by an indie [independent promoter] who happens to be offering a package to your listeners to see a Bruce Springsteen concert in Paris. The indie is throwing some promotional value on the table and that does have an effect on programmers' thinking."

McClusky's livelihood depended on finding a way to make himself indispensable. He armed himself with information—from regional sales figures to programmers' personal tastes—and he was savvy in sprinkling money and gifts around to grease the industry relationships critical to his livelihood.

"He's a guy that if you only meet him once, even in the most casual circumstances, you'll get a little reward later," said one major-label promotion executive. "I met him for the first time at a music conference, and a week later there was a Yankees jersey sitting in my office, sent by McClusky. I thought to myself, Wow, I feel like Don Henley. I just got schmoozed big-time."

Such forget-me-nots were a daily part of business in an industry where the major labels routinely spent hundreds of thousands of dollars on radio promotion for records deemed worthy of a commercial push. The hotter a song got, the more it cost: if a song hit the top 40, an independent promoter got paid an additional $2,500 from the label; if it went top 10, that ratcheted up the price to $5,500. Even something as trivial as boosting a song's profile by adding five to seven spins a week could cost the label an additional $500 per station.

"It's obscene," said longtime major-label executive Howie Klein. "We empower these independent promotion people to spend our money on what basically comes down to bribes."

So why did the industry keep rolling out the cash carpet every time a new record came out?

Fear. In a backroom world where money opens all doors, if a label doesn't spend serious cash to push a record, it sends a signal to other programmers and labels that it's not taking the record seriously.

"Major labels are like drunken pirates, spending way too much money on indie promotion," Epitaph's White said. "But it's the only way to get a record played in the corporate radio world."

The independent promotion system that McClusky helped build put a premium on a song's monetary value; a great song with no promotion budget had almost no chance of getting airplay.

The quality of the song—the art itself—was often irrelevant. "Art?" scoffed one commercial radio programmer, Dave Benson of Colorado. "Whoever brought that word in?"

Eventually, the system designed to help record companies get their records played was co-opted by the new, more centralized radio conglomerates, who worked out exclusive deals with certain independent promoters. The record-label money flowed through the independent promoters to corporate radio headquarters and trickled down to individual stations. In exchange, program directors gave the promoters exclusive information about what songs their stations added each week and why.

"You can't have a pop hit without spending enormous amounts of money in payments to independent promoters," said Trey Anastasio, a singer-guitarist whose band Phish is one of the few acts to have sold millions of albums in the nineties without significant radio airplay. "Even that doesn't guarantee you'll have a hit. But if you don't spend the money, you definitely won't have one. It has nothing to do with the quality of music and everything to do with the money spent on promoting it."

The biggest losers of all were the listeners. "When all a young audience hears on the radio is pop groups backed by businessmen willing to spend hundreds of thousands of dollars to get their songs on the radio, they're being ripped off," Anastasio said.

"We have to spend tens of thousands of dollars just to even get to the starting line with most radio stations," said Donovan Finn, head of radio promotion for Matador Records, an independent label that nurtured the careers of artists such as Liz Phair, Yo La Tengo, and Pavement in the nineties. Like most indie labels in 1999, Matador hadn't had a song get significant commercial airplay in years.

"It's rarely worth it," Finn said. "Maybe four or five years ago it was financially viable for a smaller label like us to get airplay on commercial radio, but not anymore."

The radio playlists that determined hits were controlled by fewer hands than ever under the new payola. It worked this way: A radio conglomerate signed a consulting deal with an independent promoter, with the promoter agreeing to pay $125,000 or more annually to individual radio stations in the form of promotional services (concert and sports tickets, vacation trips, T-shirts, even office supplies like fax machines) in exchange for exclusive access to information about programming decisions. The independent promoters then billed the record companies for songs that were added to a station's playlist. These fees could range anywhere from $250 for a small record to more than $1,500 per station per song for a major artist like Britney Spears or U2.

By funneling the payments through a middleman, money was never directly exchanged for playing a record, insisted John Gehron, a regional Clear Channel vice president at the time. "The stations have no direct encouragement to add records based on any kind of a payment."

But Clear Channel revenue swelled by at least $40 million a year thanks to the deals with the independent promoters. And the promoters, with their exclusive access to information, in effect made themselves the sole conduit between the record company and the radio programmer. As expenses mounted for radio airplay, the labels started to cry foul—and the irony didn't escape Clear Channel. "They've lost control of a system they created," Gehron said of the major labels. Some radio executives also insisted they'd welcome a complete overhaul of the new payola system (they preferred to get their record company cash in the form of paid ads), but the labels were too chicken to change.

Gary Briggs, a former marketing director at Reprise Records, agreed: "We've created a monster that we couldn't kill. If you don't hire an independent promoter to push a record, it's perceived within the industry that you're not serious about a record."

By 2002, the record industry was turning to the U.S. Congress for help in killing, or at least declawing, its own creation. The Recording Industry Association of America, the political arm of the major labels, joined a coalition representing artists, broadcasters, and retailers in signing a statement calling on the federal government to revise payola laws and to investigate the growing monopoly that a handful of corporations held over the radio industry. The statement called the effects of the 1996 radio deregulation "anti-artist, anti-competition, and anti-consumer."

A few weeks later, radio listeners had their say in a nationwide poll conducted by the Future of Music Coalition, a Washington, D.C., advocacy group. It found broad dissatisfaction with the state of commercial radio, with the vast majority of respondents favoring congressional action to put a cap on consolidation of the industry, expanded playlists that repeated fewer songs, and tougher restrictions on payola.

U.S. Senator Russell Feingold, a Democrat from Wisconsin, then introduced federal legislation that would drastically curb the power of the radio industry, including restrictions on the new payola.

"As a senator, you can't pursue every single consumer complaint, but the range of negative things I've heard about the radio business makes me feel this deserves serious attention," Feingold said. "It's time to expose this as a national problem for consumers and a national problem of concentration of power in a few hands, and to expose the abuses. I am troubled in particular by what I've heard about the tone as well as the tactics that Clear Channel apparently uses. They appear to be bullying people."

U.S. Representative John Conyers, the Michigan Democrat, called the payola issue a fundamental violation of democratic principles: "The average citizen and consumer of music hears a song being played constantly and assumes it's on the air because it's better than all the other music out there, when in fact it's being played because the artist has an agent who pays to get it played. That distorts the whole process. It creates a playing field that isn't level. I'm not saying everybody too poor to pay under the table would be a famous artist; all I'm saying is we don't know who really deserves to be famous under the present system. I do know that some of these artists who are now famous wouldn't be if they didn't have agents backing them up with big bucks."

While attacking a broad array of issues on the radio consolidation front, Feingold's initiative was singled out for praise by the record industry for its tough stand on payola. But some artists and managers, who suddenly found themselves on the same side of an issue with the record labels, were skeptical.

"It's a hot-button issue in the industry now, because the record industry is having trouble getting airplay and breaking new artists," said Bert Holman, manager of the Allman Brothers, one of the most successful touring acts of the last two decades. "The labels created the system, and now they're trying to cast blame somewhere else. They're certainly capable of that. If it was only the artists getting screwed by payola, they couldn't have cared less."

Clear Channel president and CEO Mark Mays said as much in a response to Feingold's bill: "For years the record companies . . . have complained about paying the promoters but have also refused to stop paying them. Instead of disciplining themselves to break the pattern, they are asking Congress to do it for them."

Once again, the music industry found its integrity in question, and with good reason. After being pushed out of the business he once loved, Howie Klein could only laugh at the mess he left behind: "Payola corrupts the industry, so we wind up with worse and worse music on the radio, which means worse and worse artists are being signed and developed. It reminds me of American politics, in that money has corrupted the entire process."

In 2004, the attorney general (and future disgraced governor) of New York, Eliot Spitzer, began an investigation of the new payola that produced significant results. Over the next few years, Warner Music Group, Sony BMG Music Entertainment, EMI-Capitol, and Vivendi Universal all acknowledged paying radio programmers to play specific songs and paid fines totaling nearly $31 million. In 2007, the Federal Communications Commission used evidence gathered in the Spitzer probe to extract fines and concessions on payola from four major radio companies: Clear Channel, CBS Radio, Citadel Broadcasting, and Entercom Communications. The radio conglomerates agreed to pay $12.5 million in fines and to allow closer scrutiny of their dealings with record labels.

Had the Spitzer investigation taken place a decade sooner, the shock waves would've been significant. But by 2007, commercial radio had long since lost its impact as a tastemaker, the medium to which consumers turned for new music. Payola was as much a dinosaur as the medium it once helped underwrite.

As radio companies narrowed playlists and soaked up record-industry revenue, bored music fans were tuning out.

"The next generation is not interested at all in radio," said Jerry Del Colliano in 2002. Del Colliano was a radio veteran who published an industry newsletter, *Inside Radio,* and lectured at the University of Southern California in Los Angeles. "They don't need radio to find out about music anymore."

They had something far better: an unlimited playlist, and a tool that put access to all of it just a click away.

"The Internet is here," Del Colliano said. "That's this generation's radio."

Before Napster I was hard-core listening to the radio all the time, figuring out what songs I liked and then going out and buying CDs, then making tapes and mix CDs for myself and my friends. So it was a pretty big jump going from buying CDs to Napster. I was getting money babysitting, but I liked way more music than I could afford at $13 a CD. As soon as I could get it for free, that was over. My [older] brother showed me how to use Napster and it became pretty addicting.

—Emma, college student in Washington, D.C.,
   born in 1988

3

Napster vs. Metallica

The Internet was conceived as a utopian ideal, designed by nonprofit researchers in 1990 as an undiscriminating conduit for information. Within a decade, however, it had morphed into a threat to the biggest entertainment industry in the world.

In the summer of 1999, an eighteen-year-old college dropout became the most feared pirate in the music industry. Huddled for weeks in an office in Hull, Massachusetts, with his Dell notebook, Shawn Fanning had feverishly tapped out the source code for a free download tool called Napster. Within months, his software had attracted 50 million users. It enabled them to log on to Napster's server and search for specific music files among a worldwide network of Napster users. Within seconds, Napster could find a match, and a file would be exchanged. Fanning's software wasn't the first digital file-sharing service, but it was by far the easiest and most efficient to use; it made the need to run to a record store to buy an album seem like a quaint twentieth-century custom. If a music fan wanted to hear all or part of his favorite band's latest album right away, he could have it within a couple of mouse clicks.

Before Napster, downloading music on MP3 files was a relatively esoteric pursuit reserved for only the most dedicated music geeks. MP3, a digital format that compresses a song to one-twelfth of its original size, had been around since 1987 but didn't start coming into vogue until a decade later.

Benn Jordan was an aspiring musician and computer technician living in Illinois when a friend turned him on to MP3s in the mid-nineties. Soon he and a community of music lovers were downloading digital albums, burning the files onto recordable compact discs, or CD-Rs, and trading them. But dial-up modems made the process slow, and the audio quality of the files was wildly unpredictable, and sometimes downright unlistenable.

Surely nobody is going to spend forty hours downloading an album at a horrible audio quality, Jordan thought. But the onset of Napster and faster-speed broadband connections conspired to turn this relatively insular pursuit into a worldwide phenomenon.

"I was the first guy on my block to be using Napster," Jordan later wrote in his blog, theflashbulb.net. "Digital piracy existed before this time, but Napster made it so damn easy. I'd get into my girl's car and see a backseat filled with marked CD-Rs. Now you could buy CD-Rs at Walgreens. It became impossible to find a portable CD player as the market flooded with MP3 players. Every software developer in the world was making a shareware CD ripper and encoder. America stopped buying music, and there was a brand-new industry to collect on the money everyone was saving while stealing their favorite band's new albums."

At first, the music industry tried to ignore Napster. The future was bearing down, and the industry's first instinct was to stand and fight for an older, safer, more profitable, and more easily controlled way of life. It had lobbied for passage of the Digital Millennium Copyright Act in 1998, which applied intellectual property laws to the Internet. Yet many music executives only vaguely knew what an MP3 file even was, let alone what it could mean for their industry.

Many of the artists the industry purported to represent knew better. Like Shawn Fanning, they saw the Internet as a new tool for communicating directly with their fans, one that didn't involve massive publicity or marketing campaigns cooked up in the high-rises of Manhattan or in luxury cars clogging the freeways snaking into West Hollywood. In the summer of 1998, the music industry was already enlisting some of its star performers to speak out against the rising tide of digital piracy. Instead, the Beastie Boys cast their lot with the insurrectionists. In August, the hip-hop trio began giving away digital files of songs from their summer tour on their website. Their parent label, Capitol Records, shut down the promotion, but not before the Beasties had collected more than a hundred thousand e-mail addresses.

In March 1999, Tom Petty uploaded a free version of his hard-hitting garage-rock single "Free Girl Now" on the website MP3 .com. More than 150,000 fans downloaded it in fifty-six hours, before his label, Warner Bros., shut down the giveaway. Rather than seeing an opportunity to e-mail those listeners about the new Petty album they were about to release, which included "Free Girl Now," the label issued a statement that said, "Warner Bros. Records Inc. does not endorse the dissemination of its copyright through any unsecured digitally distributed format."

Like the Beastie Boys, Petty hadn't asked for his label's permission before making the track available. "I understood why they might've been upset," he said with a laugh a few months later.

"It was a huge concern at the label," said Bob Merlis, a senior vice president at Warner Bros. at the time. "We all saw everybody's assets flying out the window. When you have a forty-one-year catalog of music, and suddenly it's being given away by a career artist like Tom Petty, it's hugely troubling. It's not that we're against this technology, but this is about self-preservation."

Petty had been playing music with his band, the Heartbreakers, since the eight-track era in the early seventies. He was not by any means computer savvy. But he saw the future of the music industry more clearly than some of the executives running his label.

Those 150,000 e-mail addresses enabled Petty's management to better promote his 1999 summer tour, which pulled in nearly $27 million in revenue, despite an average ticket price under $40 (the Rolling Stones, also on tour that year, were asking more than $100 per ticket).

"I'm not sure it did me a lot of good with my record company," Petty said of his MP3 end-around. "But I thought this is what would happen anyway eventually with music, so let's get 'em used to it. The industry is probably going to have a lot to do with the Internet in the next few years. It's not a phase."

Artists such as Petty and the Beastie Boys embraced Internet distribution, problematic as it was as a revenue stream for recorded music, because they saw no way of stopping it. It made no sense to fight the inevitable. But the labels with which these artists had recording contracts saw the Shawn Fanning gang as interlopers, intent upon shoehorning their way into a business they had dominated for a century. Fanning, in their eyes, was a thief, pure and simple. The key issue came down to one of control: the industry wanted to control digital distribution, just as it had the distribution of CDs, vinyl records, eight-track tapes, and cassettes. The only problem was, it had no system in place for selling music digitally, much less one that was as sleekly efficient as Napster.

"Napster demonstrated just how important music was to a generation of kids," says Mark Kates, who was running the Beastie Boys' boutique label, Grand Royal, during the Napster era. "Shawn did not seek to bring down the modern record business. He was a music lover and he wanted to share music with his friends. I kept telling people, 'We have to follow the audience. They're going to tell us what to do, because they need it more than we do.' It was the ultimate example of the audience leading the way. When the audience is actually creating the technology, the business has to adapt."

But the industry saw no reason to adapt to anyone's new technology because it was enjoying an unrivaled run of prosperity: nearly two decades of continual growth, fueled by the introduction of CDs in 1983, which enabled the big labels to resell customers records they already owned—by the Beatles, the Rolling Stones, Stevie Wonder, and countless other marquee artists—for double the price of a vinyl album or cassette. There was no economic reason to change when things were going so good. The notion of giving away music seemed absurd when demand for compact discs was higher than ever. In 1999, the total revenue from all music sales (albums and singles) was a record $14.6 billion.

"When MP3s started circulating, you had certain artists think ing like drug dealers in the way they used the Internet: Here's a little taste of my music for free, and then if it's good, it gets you hooked that you go out and buy more, whether it's a CD, a concert ticket, a T-shirt," says Michael Ackerman, a Los Angeles entertainment attorney who has represented countless record labels and artists in his two decades in the business.

"But the record companies never seemed to get that with the Internet. They never got the idea that if you expose someone to music they might otherwise never have heard, it could've been good for everyone. You didn't have to deal with radio or retail. You could control it and expose it on your terms. But they were building walls to keep people out instead of inviting them in."

The record industry's reticence to embrace the new technology was predictable. It had recoiled in horror each time a new technical innovation had come along. Phonographs were seen as threats to live music at the turn of the twentieth century: if consumers could get music at home, what incentive would there be to go out and see a show or an opera? Radio was going to kill the phonograph in the 1930s: if listeners could access music for free over the broadcast airwaves, what need would they have to buy records? The introduction of the cassette and home taping was going to undermine the business in the 1980s: Why buy an album when you could record your friend's copy?

"Home Taping Is Killing Music," the industry declared in an advertising campaign, and it branded home recording a form of piracy. The cassette recorder posed a threat because even technophobes could copy and own any album with the push of a button.

None of the sky-is-falling scenarios came to pass. The Copyright Royalty Tribunal, a five-member commission created in the seventies by the federal government to oversee copyright rates, found in a study that home tapers were actually among the most active record buyers. As with each technological advance before it, home taping gave more people access to more music than ever before, and their appetite for music only increased.

One of the many bands who benefited from the home-taping boom was the then-unknown Metallica.

James Hetfield and Lars Ulrich were barely out of high school when they entered the recording studio for the first time in 1981. They imagined themselves as California's answer to the new wave British metal of Diamond Head, Motorhead, and Iron Maiden.

Ulrich had given up tennis to play drums, and in the two-man band's first sessions, his inexperience became immediately apparent. One of his cymbals kept falling over, so frustrating Hetfield that he walked out. Hetfield himself sounded adrift, like he couldn't decide whether he wanted to be Ozzy Osbourne or a castrato-voiced opera singer. But by the next year, they'd gotten their act together, with the addition of lead guitarist Dave Mustaine. They recorded seven songs steeped in speed and violence, slapped them on a cassette dubbed *No Life 'til Leather,* and began mailing or handing them out to a network of headbangers.

"I gave the tape to about five people, and by the end of the week fifty people had it, then a hundred more, and it just kept mushrooming," Ulrich said backstage at a Metallica concert in Peoria nine years later. "I mean, the idea of writing our first song was unbelievable. Getting a regular gig was beyond our wildest dreams. It went from me playing air drums to all my favorite metal songs to doing the real thing. We had no idea how big we were going to become."

The tape-sharing network turned Metallica into underground stars, and it landed them a record deal. A copy of *No Life 'til Leather* found its way to Jon and Marsha Zazula, who ran a New Jersey record store that specialized in metal and underground music. In 1983, the couple released Metallica's first album, *Kill 'Em All,* on their Megaforce label. The album went on to sell three hundred thousand copies, and several hundred thousand more when reissued by Elektra a few years later.

Metallica was selling out arenas by the end of the decade. But they hadn't yet forgotten how they'd built their audience. They encouraged concertgoers to record and circulate tapes of shows, and they lingered before and after shows to sign thousands of autographs.

"Respect is the word," Ulrich said while in the midst of a two-year tour after the band had released its commercial breakthrough album, . . . *And Justice for All*, in 1988. "We were fans once, too. Just because we're the guys onstage now doesn't entitle us to have an attitude. Other bands may take things for granted, but I think people appreciate how straightforward we are, that we're not larger than life."

But all that changed a decade later. By then, Metallica was one of the biggest bands in the world. Its fifth, self-titled album had sold more than 14 million copies. Over their career, they had become multimillionaires, the epitome of rich rock stars living in mansions who could afford multimillion-dollar art collections, Serbian hunting trips, and a $40,000-a-month "performance enhancement coach" in the recording studio, never mind a producer.

Their rise coincided with the industry's CD-era expansion, culminating in blockbuster sales by pop artists like Britney Spears, the Backstreet Boys, and 'N Sync as the Napster era dawned. When Napster—and by extension the Internet—began to take off as a viable force for distributing music, the five conglomerates dominating the $14 billion-a-year business went into a collective panic and responded with a flurry of lawsuits.

The emergence of websites such as MP3.com, which linked listeners to tens of thousands of MP3 files, and file-sharing services such as Napster, which connected file sharers to one another, were viewed not as an opportunity to further expand the industry but as a threat that needed to be dealt with harshly.

In December 1999, the Recording Industry Association of America—the trade group that represents the major record companies—filed suit against Napster in U.S. District Court, charging that "nearly every hit song by every significant recording artist can be found on Napster." The suit focused on two hundred songs, seeking $100,000 in damages per infringement: $20 million.

The suit was great for business—Napster's business. The publicity tripled the site's users in a month to 150,000, and the number of songs available quadrupled, to 20 million. In February 2000 the site reported 524,000 unique visitors. Four months later it had leaped a phenomenal 768 percent, to 4.6 million. The growth was especially acute on college campuses, where the increased availability of high-speed Internet connections in dormitories made downloading a snap.

David, a freshman at Southern Illinois University in Carbondale in 1998, says the transition to high-speed broadband from dial-up modems was dramatic. "I had to pay $50 a semester for a 56K [56,000 bits per second] dial-up modem in my dorm and it took about fifteen minutes to download a single MP3," he says. "So I went to the computer lab, which had a broadband connection, and started downloading from there. I was able to get songs in a minute or two, fit eighteen to twenty-five songs on a zip disc, and go back to my place, where it would take me twenty-five minutes to transfer them to my hard drive.

"I was the first person from my group of friends to get MP3s, and I was getting them from sites whose names I can't even remember. They were not there for more than a couple of weeks. They were in weird file formats and a lot of stuff didn't work. So when Napster came along, it was huge. All those other sites fell to the wayside because Napster was a search engine that allowed you to move and search for more things easier than ever. With faster Internet connections, Napster got very, very big very quickly."

Eric Grubbs, a student at Texas Christian University in Fort Worth at the time, first read the word "Napster" in the fall of 1999 on an Internet discussion list devoted to the punk band Jimmy Eat World. Posters on the list touted the site as a great source for finding rare Jimmy Eat World music, and Grubbs immediately checked it out.

"I was into the band and wanted to find out everything I could about them, and get all their music," he says. "I downloaded the Napster software and immediately started finding all sorts of other songs I wanted. I thought, Wow, this is a good supplement to buying records. You can download stuff that is really impossible to find or just really expensive."

But it soon spiraled into something different. "A feeding frenzy," Grubbs called it. In the same way teenagers could sit in front of a television screen for hours at a time playing video games, college students became hooked on Napster.

"I lived with three guys at the time," Grubbs says, "and in a few weeks I saw Napster go from this obscure thing to something that was everywhere, at least on my campus. I had one roommate who was a passive music fan; he listened to only country pop music, but he was pretty casual about it. But when he got Napster, he spent the rest of the semester on his laptop downloading songs from every type of band. He'd download them and burn them onto CDs. Dozens of CDs. I saw how fast everything went. It spread like wildfire and it was really exciting, but I also was thinking, This could be a problem."

Within months, hundreds of colleges, including TCU, banned Napster, either because they were pressured by the recording industry or because the increased traffic was unduly taxing their servers.

In May 2000, Metallica added its muscle to the recording industry's fight when the band sued Napster for copyright infringement. Lars Ulrich showed up at Napster's office in San Mateo with thirteen file boxes filled with names of hundreds of thousands of Napster users who were making Metallica songs available on the Internet. Within a week, Napster had barred more than 335,000 users from the service for ripping off Metallica.

But the suit also marked a turning point in Metallica's career. The band settled with the free file-sharing website, but the backlash from some of Metallica's most ardent fans—not coincidentally, the very fans the band was trying to bar from the website—diluted any feelings of triumph. The band instantly became public enemy number one in the file-sharing community, and was trashed even on its own Internet message boards, its reputation as a "people's band" shattered.

Some fans called for a Metallica boycott.

One of the 335,000 named by Metallica was Mark, of St. Charles, Illinois. "This is how I've used Napster in the past: I would download a song or two of a band," he said. "If I liked something, then I would fork over the money for the CD. The funny thing is that if it weren't for Napster I would not have bought [the 1999 Metallica CD] *S&M*. My punishment for doing this is to be banned from Napster. Metallica's punishment is that I'll never buy another one of their CDs, and my friends also will not be buying any either. My question to Lars is: Was this really worth it?"

Another fan, Nina Crowley, offered a broader perspective on her Mass Mic website: "The recording industry has consistently paid musicians as little as possible for their art, striving to keep as much of the profit as they can for the company," she wrote. "For many, many years we, the fans, have paid full price for concert tickets, CDs, tapes, posters, T-shirts, etc. If anyone needs to be penalized for their actions, it's the record labels, not the fans."

Crowley's point was amplified only days later when the Federal Trade Commission announced that consumers had overpaid millions of dollars for CDs because of "illegal arrangements" between record companies and retail stores. An antitrust settlement with the five major U.S. record companies put an end to a long-standing practice in which major labels withheld advertising money from record stores that sold CDs below minimum prices.

The trade commission estimated that consumers may have paid as much as $480 million more than they should have for CDs the previous three years because of the Minimum Advertised Price program. In the fall of 1999, just as Napster was taking off on college campuses around the country, compact disc prices hit an all-time high of $18.98. Yet most artists still were making less than $2 for every CD sold, and then only after repaying their record label for recording and promotional expenses. The label, distributors, and retailers split the rest.

A few days after Metallica's legal action, hip-hop's most powerful producer, NWA founder Dr. Dre, filed his own suit against the software company. He provided Napster with nearly 240,000 names that he said were illegally trading his songs.

"The issue is basically this: they're stealing my money," Dre said at the time. "They are hi-tech bootleggers. When I started making music I had a dream to do something I really love and make a living from it, and feed my family from it. This is a job. Free downloading is a good thing for new artists who want to get their music heard. But for a person like me, who makes a living from it, it's a different story."

Other bestselling bands, such as Limp Bizkit and the Offspring, came out in defense of Napster. Limp Bizkit even launched a free tour underwritten by Napster in the summer of 2000. Dr. Dre's peer as a hip-hop innovator, Public Enemy's Chuck D, laughed when he heard the music industry's argument against Napster.

"Piracy? The biggest pirates have been the record companies," he said. "The people running the record labels are lawyers and accountants, and they could be selling Brillo pads for all they care. It's not about the art at all. What has that got to do with music? So when people download a song, if it's a good song, people want the artist. People worship Eric Clapton or Ray Charles. What they do is bigger than any song. Downloading music gives people a chance to be exposed to an artist, not just a Brillo-pad manufacturer."

Chuck D's forward-thinking approach was echoed by Prince, in a long essay posted on his website in the summer of 2001 (complete with typically creative spelling drawn from his Paisley Park dictionary). While not exactly endorsing Napster, he saw file sharing as a long-overdue democratic response to an industry that had built a business on exploiting artists: "From the point of view of the real music lover, what's currently going on can only b viewed as an exciting new development in the history of music."

In July, Ulrich and Napster squared off before the Senate Judiciary Committee. The Metallica drummer called for government intervention to stop Internet "piracy." Hank Barry, Napster's chief executive officer, insisted that the file-sharing service "is helping, not hurting, the recording and music publishing industry and artist."

His testimony came at a time when record sales were still climbing, up 8 percent in the first half of the year. "Like other advances in technology, what Napster shows is that more access to music leads to more interest in music," Barry insisted.

"That's just a bunch of hooey," said RIAA chairman Hilary Rosen a few days after Barry's testimony. "Napster is successful because they're giving away new music. If I flung open the doors of Tower Records and said, 'Take what you want,' I'd have a real popular store."

But Napster kept right on rolling, relying on word of mouth and generally favorable media coverage to stay afloat. It continued to attract users, with 26 million registered by February 2001. That same month, the Ninth Circuit Court of Appeals in California upheld an injunction against the company that ordered Napster to remove all unlicensed content from its directory. In response, Napster presented a $1 billion compromise to the five major record labels. It would turn into a subscription service, charging customers $2.95 to $9.95 per month, and pay the labels $150 million per year over five years for nonexclusive licenses to their catalogs, to be divided up based on file-transfer volume. Another $50 million would be set aside to pay indie labels.

But the majors, satisfied that Napster was all but dead, declined. It was the turning point in the file-sharing wars, the moment when the record industry walked away from a compromise that could've turned their adversarial relationship with millions of music downloaders into a lucrative revenue stream. They walked even though they had no viable Internet strategy of their own; by late 2000, fewer than a thousand paid tracks had been downloaded by consumers from major-label websites.

"It's embarrassing," said Epic Records executive Mike Tierney at the time. "The way we're doing it is definitely not the future."

The labels were still fixated on CDs, and the infrastructure of retail stores and distributors that sold them. Napster represented a threat to all of those institutions. What's more, most of the labels' contracts with their artists didn't even address digital distribution of music. Virtually every one of those contracts would have had to be rewritten. It could have been done, but it would have taken more time.

It would be the major labels' last, best chance to harness digital distribution under a centralized server.

Napster shut down in July 2001 and declared bankruptcy the next year. Even more than the RIAA litigation, the Metallica suit effectively marked the beginning of the end for what had been the fastest-growing application in the history of the Internet. It was one thing for the industry to play bad cop, quite another for a major band to come knocking on Napster's door in a foul mood.

"Metallica are my heroes," said the RIAA's Rosen soon after the band filed suit against the file-sharing service. "It was a turning point in the issue when they jumped in. For Lars it's about respect and creative control, not money."

But that's not the way the public saw it. At a time when countless news accounts played it as Napster's David against the music industry's Goliath, Metallica was portrayed as the guys who stole David's slingshot. They may have been trying to protect their creative rights, but they were perceived as greedy rock stars.

Nor was Napster entirely pure. It had quickly turned into a business that was selling advertising on its website, and was either incredibly ignorant or incredibly arrogant about its potential liability under the 1998 Digital Millennium Copyright Act. According to the law, Napster could be held liable if it were warned that a user was infringing a copyright and failed to act. At a certain point, the Napster brain trust must have believed that an artist or band would never resort to naming names as Metallica and Dr. Dre had. Posting on his blog in 2005, former Napster vice president Don Dodge said the company got too big too fast, and was instantly perceived as a threat rather than a potential business partner: "We had a plan. We just didn't get a chance to make it work."

Five years after Napster's demise, the major labels were reaping damage claims. Paying the bill was Bertelsmann AG, which had invested $85 million in Napster even while it joined the other major labels in suing the company. When Bertelsmann settled the last of the claims in September 2007, it had paid out $400 million to its

major-label peers—Universal Music Group, EMI Group, and Warner Music—as well as the National Music Publishers Association.
Napster eventually reemerged as a legal online music service but
never regained its central place in the file-sharing culture. By 2008,
the onetime rebel Fanning had been reduced to shilling for the music
industry in a TV car commercial. "Your thing is legal, and trust me,
legal is cooler," he confessed to a talking Volkswagen.

At least Fanning could laugh about it. In 2003, Ulrich looked
back and called the Napster episode "a bad dream."

"That didn't really happen, did it?" he said with a rueful laugh,
waving his hands as if wishing he could make the whole thing disappear. "I think I dreamt all that. It was just a weird time. For eighteen
years till that point we always stood up to protect our shit. When
someone fucked with us, we fucked back with them. One day I got
a phone call telling me that this song we were working on ['I Disappear'] for this movie soundtrack [*Mission Impossible 2*] is being
played on thirty radio stations in America, and I'm like, 'We haven't
finished it yet. How did that happen?'

"The leak got traced back to some company called Napster. So I
thought, OK, let's go put them out of their misery. That went sort of
slightly askew. I didn't see that one coming. We're definitely guilty of
taking the leap and asking the questions as we're falling. That would
be the ultimate example of that. We were all pretty Internet-ignorant
at that time. It all came out of us protecting our shit. It was a weird
time. A lot of people were coming up and whispering in our ear telling us how cool we were for going after them. So we're the cavalry,
but nobody followed. It was a lonely time."

Ulrich sighed. He understood how the fans saw it as a contradiction. "There was some abstract stuff going on. It was almost like
there were two Metallicas. There was the Metallica that I knew and
that I was in, and then there was the Metallica that everyone was
accusing of being anti-bootleg. We'd been selling tickets to people
who tape our shows for twenty years. We'd been allowing bootlegs
for years. We were accused of being the band that was pro–record
company. But we were the band who never let the record company

in the studio till our records were done. It was surreal. The problem is, when you're out in the thick of all that shit, you have to put your game face on. Two years later, I'm finally at the point where I'm comfortable talking about it. When you're out in the thick of it, you pretend it doesn't bug you, but it was tough.

"We spent a career being control freaks. 'Yes, Your Honor, guilty as charged.' But we did that because we're proud of what we put our name on. We'd never been in a situation where someone took that choice away from us. That choice was never taken away. The point everyone missed is, we're not against downloading. We're against someone taking our choice to do that away from us. I'm proud of the fact we jumped in. It puts us in some awkward places, but there is some purity of that."

It was a passionate argument but one that was being made quickly irrelevant by a legion of faster, better Napsters.

When Shawn Fanning got sued I pretty much went cold turkey off downloading. I was terrified of Napster. It felt wrong to me, at least at first. Then I got Lime Wire and my objections sort of went to the wayside. I started downloading again, and have been ever since. I never really liked Metallica, so I felt pretty justified in screwing them over.

—Jake, college student from California, born 1988

I don't justify [downloading music from the Internet]. I know it's stealing. It's definitely a copyright violation, but a lot of things I have, I wouldn't have heard of them or I wouldn't have them in my collection if it weren't for file sharing. I have 3,648 songs on my hard drive. I listen to more music and more varieties of music than I have at any other point in my life, yet I don't pay anything for it.

—Sarah, college student from Boston, born 1988

4

Customers or Criminals?

It soon became apparent that Napster's demise was just the beginning of the record industry's problems.

"Who's going to control digital distribution?" said Steve Albini, a guitarist in the indie band Shellac and the producer of albums by Nirvana, PJ Harvey, and countless punk bands. "That's like asking who's going to control the sunlight. The Internet exists like the air, and I and everybody else have very little control over its direction. The record industry is making a fundamental mistake by thinking they can lasso this thing and make it work for them."

At the same time, Albini was not impressed by Napster's clumsy rise and fall. "I cry no tears over the demise of Napster. It's an absurd business model. Pull up their Web page, and they're selling ads. I have no fondness for that corporate thinking. But the procedural element, that people at home can make free copies of music that they otherwise couldn't get ahold of, is valid and will survive this territorial urination fest going on now."

David Loundy, a law professor in Chicago, said Napster had no one to blame but itself for its demise. "Napster was dumb, stupidity in action," he said. "They were advertising with screen shots that showed infringing music. They tried to make money by keeping their finger on every transaction, and that involvement produced liability."

Even as Napster was being slowly extinguished by lawsuits,

Internet file sharing only expanded as decentralized file-sharing networks such as Morpheus, Lime Wire, Gnutella, Kazaa, Grokster, and Soulseek began to proliferate. These applications allowed users to communicate directly—peer-to-peer—rather than through a centralized server, which was the Napster model.

"Now there was no single point of control," Loundy said. "Music could be uploaded from anywhere in the world."

The most popular of the services, Kazaa, averaged more than 9 million users a month in 2002.

"With Napster you could cast a shallow net looking for music, because you were restricted to how many other people were using Napster," says David, a student at Southern Illinois University in Carbondale when Napster died. "There was a limited number of fish you could catch. With these other programs, you weren't just restricted to people using that program. You could look all over the world at all these different files from different programs. It was an exponential increase in what you could do and how much music you could get."

CD burning proliferated, as CD-R sales doubled to 1 billion in 2000. By the end of 2001, the number of burned CDs worldwide (2.5 billion) had matched the number of CDs sold in retail stores, according to the International Federation of the Phonographic Industry. Meanwhile, music industry revenue had plunged to $12.6 billion in 2002, down from an all-time peak of $14.6 billion in 1999—a 13.7 percent decline.

In 2003, the recording industry got more bad news, as a federal court handed the business its first significant legal defeat on the Internet front. Judge Stephen Wilson ruled that StreamCast Networks Inc., the company behind Morpheus and Grokster, could not be held liable for copyright infringement by those who use its peer-to-peer software.

Wilson ruled that unlike Napster, the peer-to-peer companies "are not significantly different from companies that sell home-video recorders or copy machines, both of which can be and are used to infringe copyrights." Unlike Napster, which required users to connect to its servers to download files, the new breed of file-sharing companies only created software but had no control over user activity.

The record industry thought it had neutralized its biggest threat when it shut down Napster, but the effect was exactly the opposite: it opened the way for decentralized software that only made file sharing far more efficient. Napster could have been controlled by the music industry; it was a central resource with the names of everyone who downloaded music. The proliferating peer-to-peer networks made that sort of containment impossible.

"There are legal and illegal uses of such software, and the only way to shut it down is for the RIAA to sue the people who use it illegally," one college student, Prasad Arekapudi of the University of Michigan, observed as early as 2000. "It would have to sue students, average working people, and such—basically a very unlikely move."

Unlikely at the time, perhaps, but by 2003 the industry was desperate. By the time of the StreamCast ruling, there were an estimated 57 million people sharing music files in the United States. About 2 billion music files were being downloaded monthly.

If there was a silver lining in the Morpheus decision for the recording industry, it was the judge's assertion that "individual users are accountable for illegally uploading and downloading copyrighted works off publicly accessible peer-to-peer networks," RIAA chairman Hilary Rosen said. "Individual infringers cannot expect to remain anonymous when they engage in this illegal activity," she warned.

This meant that tens of millions of Americans were, by the recording industry's definition, criminals. The Recording Industry Association of America said as much in a full-page ad published in *The New York Times* in June 2003. It wagged an intimidating finger at practically every household with a personal computer in it: "Next time you or your kids 'share' music on the Internet, you may also want to download a list of attorneys. . . . Some folks ask us, 'How can you sue your customers?' Well, the same question can be asked of retailers who prosecute shoplifters."

In September 2003, the music industry filed its first major round of lawsuits, naming 261 consumers who had shared more than a thousand songs each on music-swapping websites. Under federal law, those consumers were liable for damages of $750 to $150,000 per song.

"Nobody likes playing the heavy and having to resort to litigation, but when your product is being regularly stolen there comes a time when you have to take appropriate action," said RIAA president Cary Sherman.

In tandem with the litigation blitz, the industry offered an amnesty program to people who had downloaded copyrighted music but had not yet been sued. It required that individuals delete all the songs from their hard drives and sign an affidavit in the presence of a notary public that said they would never do it again.

The lawsuits made front-page news around the country, most of which painted the recording industry as a bully. The *New York Post* featured the story of one lawsuit target: twelve-year-old Brianna LaHara, who lived in a housing project. "I got really scared," she said upon being notified that she was being sued for copyright infringement. "My stomach is all turning." Her family eventually settled the suit for $2,000. As part of the settlement, the girl was required to publicly confess her sins: "I am sorry for what I have done. I love music and don't want to hurt the artists I love."

The strong-arm tactics were in character with an industry used to having its way, but the moral posturing was a laughable new wrinkle. Here's an industry that had instituted payola, routinely manipulated shady contracts to take away publishing from songwriters, and engaged in questionable accounting practices to deny royalties from record sales to the vast majority of its artists. For a century it had controlled the recording, manufacturing, marketing, and distribution of virtually every album, and operated like a monopoly. Artists knew they were being ripped off, but most couldn't afford an audit. The industry was in a different position than most of its artists, however; it had a $12 billion bank account, and it was going to war against file sharing to protect its most valuable asset—the compact disc—and by extension the retail industry that had grown around it.

When it was introduced to the U.S. market in 1983, the compact disc revived the music business. Domestic sales of the new technology zoomed from eight hundred thousand copies in 1983 to 288 million by 1990, and continued to surge by the hundreds of millions through the nineties, a period of unprecedented growth. By 2000, the recording industry was selling nearly 1 billion CDs a year.

CDs had become so lucrative that the industry virtually phased out every other kind of music product. The single, for decades the affordable entrée into music consumption for young fans, became practically extinct.

"Ten years ago, the record industry said, 'Screw the young kids— we're not going to put singles out anymore,'" said Joe Kvidra, who had been general manager of a Tower Records store in Chicago as the Napster era dawned. "That's the entry-level purchase everyone makes; when I was young, you could buy two singles for a dollar. People would still come into the record store requesting singles [during the late nineties], but those singles didn't exist."

Even the RIAA's Rosen complained that the industry was not offering its customers enough choices. "The consumers are telling us they want music in different sizes at different price points," she said. "They want a twelve-ounce can, but we keep insisting on selling it to them in the sixty-four-ounce bottle."

By the time the CD turned twenty in March 2003, its commercial allure was fading. Compact disc shipments in the United States plunged nearly 9 percent in 2002, to just more than 800 million.

But it was disingenuous of the industry to blame its slump on file sharing without acknowledging the role played by rising CD prices. The average retail price of CDs had increased more than 19 percent from 1998 to 2002. Peak price was $18.99, with middlemen getting the vast majority of the split: 29 percent to the label, 29 percent to retail, 15 percent for marketing and promotion, 6 percent to the distributor, 5 percent to publishing royalties, 5 percent for packaging, 1 percent to the musicians' union, and 10 percent to the artist (against recoupable expenses such as recording costs and touring).

Even artists who were losing sales could understand why the fans had stopped buying. "While I've complained about artists being ripped off," singer Sinéad O'Connor said, "the people who have been ripped off the most by the music industry is the audience. Because it costs record companies fuck-all to make a CD. Yet they charge kids $20 for them. Every dog has its day. I think it's great that the record companies are losing their control."

"Consumers feel they're being gouged," said law professor David Loundy. "Historically, everything technology-related—TV's, videocassette players, computers—drops in price. Why aren't compact discs? If the industry had addressed the price of CDs, it might have been able to get people to see downloading its way. But it never did."

Peer-to-peer offered consumers the opportunity to select exactly the song they wanted at an unbeatable price: free. It was convenient and portable, and most consumers didn't think twice about grabbing songs online. As the teenage son of former EMI Records executive Ted Cohen told him, "It doesn't feel wrong." But the opportunity to stick it to the Man appealed to some downloaders.

"My CD buying habits the last two years have dropped to ten percent of what they were, and the industry has only itself to blame for that," said Thomas, thirty-five, a Detroit graphic designer who had downloaded thousands of files by 2003. "It's an evil institution that has been screwing consumers with high CD prices for two decades."

"If I like the band and respect the artistry—like Wilco or the Strokes—I will buy the album," said Russ, a nineteen-year-old Northwestern University premed student in 2003 with $1,000 worth of music on his hard drive, most of it obtained from Morpheus and Audiogalaxy. "But what's the point of spending $18 for a CD with only one or two good songs on it?"

There were other factors the industry ignored in its campaign to deter file sharing. Other entertainment media were competing with the record industry for the consumer dollar. With nearly $16 billion in revenue in 2002, the video game industry had eclipsed the music business. And DVD sales had soared more than 700 percent in four years by 2002, to more than $8 billion. Both these industries were exploding creatively. The same could not be said of the mainstream music industry, which at the end of the nineties was riding the teen-pop trend as hard as it could, then found itself gasping for air when those performers could not sustain their success.

"There has been an effect on sales because of all the free music on the Internet," said Chris Blackwell, founder of Island Records, for which artists such as Bob Marley and Traffic had recorded. "But the bigger problem affecting sales is that there is very little new and fresh in the music business. There was a very similar situation in 1979–80, when everyone was blaming home taping for the drop in record sales. But when something is exciting and vital, people want a piece of it, they want to hold it in their hands. I don't think I'm being too much of a dinosaur when I say that's still the case."

Many file sharers knew that what they were doing was, at a minimum, morally shaky. "You're either disgusted or curious about how I justify doing this," said Detroit downloader Thomas. "Well, I'm not sure I do justify it." But the industry's strong-arm tactics made their decision to break the law a no-brainer.

"The lawsuits only engendered more hatred toward the RIAA," said John, of Chicago, who had eight thousand files acquired on Soulseek stored on his hard drive. "It drove people to more secure peer-to-peer networks, where they can mask their location. I think they underestimated the savviness of the generation they are dealing with."

The industry's efforts to rein in consumers were exacerbated by the lack of a viable alternative to the rogue file-sharing services. After considering but ultimately rejecting a last-ditch Napster plea to turn itself into a music subscription service, the record industry eventually began rolling out its own Internet subscription services. These tried to induce consumers to pay a monthly fee for a relatively small pool of songs that did not include many major artists readily available on peer-to-peer networks. In addition, these downloads were loaded with digital-rights management restrictions, which meant they could not be copied or shared easily. These legitimate services included AOL's MusicNet, Liston.com's Rhapsody, Pressplay, and Full Audio; by early 2003, they had attracted fewer than five hundred thousand subscribers and generated only $25 million in revenue.

"How we compete with 'free'" is the big question facing the music industry and its nascent subscription services, said Pam Horovitz, president of the National Association of Recording Merchandisers. "The solution is to make something better than free."

Then along came Steve Jobs. The cofounder, chairman, and CEO of Apple Inc. opened iTunes, an online music store, on April 28, 2003. It attracted more than a million sales in its first week by offering downloads at a rate of ninety-nine cents per song. Five years later, the store had sold 4 billion songs, accounting for more than 70 percent of worldwide online digital music sales. But the store didn't so much revive the music industry as fuel sales of another Jobs creation: the iPod, a sleek, 6.4-ounce digital music player. By October 2003, Apple had sold 1 million iPods. By the end of 2005, it had sold more than 42 million of the devices, at prices ranging from $99 to $599, which accounted for 75 percent of the U.S. market in digital music players.

Yet the volume of illegal downloading continued to dwarf the legit industry. A consumer could pack an iPod with thousands of songs, but how many of them were actually paid for? Even Jobs acknowledged that only about 3 percent of the music in every one of the 141 million iPods he had sold by 2008 was purchased from iTunes.

The flurry of industry lawsuits was designed to scare consumers and steer them toward legitimate downloading. The hottest-selling single at the end of 2003 was OutKast's "Hey Ya!" At its mid-November peek, it registered eighty-five hundred paid downloads in a single week. During the same period, the song was swapped 317,000 times on peer-to-peer networks, according to BigChampagne, a website that tracks file sharing. That's a ratio of about one legit download per every thirty-seven unsanctioned ones.

Maggie, a sophomore at Marquette University in 2003, said that at the start of the fall semester the university sent letters to students threatening expulsions, suspensions, and fines if they participated in illegal file sharing. The students had been reading about the wave of record industry lawsuits, and they took the letter seriously.

"A lot of people got scared because, 'Oh, man, I have four hundred songs and I paid for none of them,'" she recalls. "And then nothing happens. Nothing. I never heard of one incident where someone got caught. I think it was more to scare us. A lot of us stopped file sharing for a few days. For a week after the letter I didn't touch Kazaa. But nobody got in trouble, and people went back to downloading."

Garrison was a residence adviser at a Texas State University dormitory in San Marcos when the RIAA campaign began. "There is a certain anonymity that I think was naïvely assumed by a lot of the students," he says. "People weren't processing the news like, 'I could be next.' In a college environment, the kids think they can outsmart the professionals, and kept right on downloading."

Yet the record industry persisted in trying to squash file sharing through litigation. In June 2005, the Supreme Court swung a big blow in favor of the major labels by ruling that peer-to-peer companies such as Grokster could be held responsible for copyright piracy on their networks. Even though Grokster was not actually hosting any sort of infringement on a central website, the way Napster had, the court unanimously ruled that the company had created software to "foster" infringement, reversing a 2003 federal court ruling that held Grokster blameless.

A year later, recording industry association CEO Mitch Bainwol said illegal song swapping had been "contained."

"The problem has not been eliminated," he said. "But we believe digital downloads have emerged into a growing, thriving business, and file trading is flat."

Bainwol's statement smacked of false bravado. A few observers were reminded of President George W. Bush strutting across the deck of an aircraft carrier in May 2003, less than two months after the U.S. invasion of Iraq, beneath a banner that read, "Mission Accomplished." Bainwol believed the tide had turned in a war that was far from over, and in many ways was only getting worse.

The International Federation of the Phonographic Industry estimated that a year after the Grokster ruling, 20 billion illegal downloads had taken place. That same year, the iTunes store finally cracked 1 billion sales.

While the high court ruling effectively shut down file-sharing companies such as Grokster and BearShare, the infringing software was still easily accessible on the Internet. And consumers were already gravitating toward even more convenient technologies to share files, such as instant messaging and BitTorrent.

BitTorrent was created by twenty-six-year-old programmer Bram Cohen in 2001, and eventually caught on as the fastest, most efficient file-sharing method ever invented. Cohen's software enabled consumers to download files from many different sources, which sped up the download rate; the more popular the file, the faster the file could be downloaded by everyone.

"So now it became ridiculously easy not just to get one song or one album, but full discographies from people," says one BitTorrent user, David, of Chicago. "I downloaded thirty-two Beastie Boy albums—imports, remixes, B sides, basically everything they've done—in one all-encompassing file similar to a zip file. It was 3.5 gigs, a huge file, and it took me just an hour and a half to download."

David had been downloading illegally since the late nineties, accumulating seventy thousand MP3 files, and had never suffered the music industry's legal wrath. The wave of lawsuits, he says, "made me think about it a little bit," but not enough to stop trading files. "I have software on my computer that cancels my Internet connection, assigns me a new IP [Internet Protocol] address, and logs me back on to my downloading software. So that more or less gives me a new mailing address on the Internet. It's not like they can't get me. It's all there on my hard drive. But you can make it a lot less traceable."

Still, some less savvy file sharers were getting caught. By 2007, the number of lawsuits against file sharers was approaching twenty thousand. As legal costs mounted, the RIAA peppered college campuses with settlement letters, designed to forestall costly litigation. These listed IP addresses of infringing computers and directed the colleges to identify the users and pass along the letters to them.

"We represent a number of large record companies, including EMI Recorded Music, Sony BMG Music Entertainment, Universal Music Group and Warner Music Group . . . in pursuing claims of copyright infringement against individuals who have illegally uploaded and downloaded sound recordings on peer-to-peer networks," the letter read in part. "We have gathered evidence that you have been infringing copyrights owned by the Record Companies."

The recipients were directed to a website, www.p2plawsuits.com, where they could "settle this matter immediately" to avoid a lawsuit and pay "significantly reduced" fees, usually $3,000 to $5,000, instead of damages ranging upward of $750 per song, plus legal costs.

"If we do not hear from you within 20 calendar days," the letter concluded in boldface type, "then we will file suit against you in federal court."

At the University of Nebraska in Lincoln, a version of that letter went out to eighty students in the first four months of 2007. That raised the total number of warning letters sent to students at the campus to more than a thousand; the campus had been identified by the RIAA as the third-biggest source of infringing activity among American universities, behind only Ohio University and Purdue.

David Solheim, the student body president, didn't deny that infringing activity was going on. He said the eighty students named in the letters were hardly exceptions on the campus of twenty-two thousand. "The majority of students engage in some kind of file sharing with illegal media, either songs or movies or something similar," he said. "I think you could safely say that well more than ten thousand students in a half a mile of me are probably downloading music sometime this week."

According to the RIAA's logic, that made universities the gangster capitals of the file-sharing era. But Jimmy Sammarco, one of twenty-four hundred college students to receive a settlement letter in 2007, doesn't have an ounce of gangster swagger about him. On the contrary, he says, once he found out what the rules were, he was more than willing to play by them. But the RIAA never gave him the chance. The nineteen-year-old Northern Illinois University student dabbled in file sharing, just like all his friends, and he never thought of it as a big deal. When the authorities told him to stop, he did, but he still got his knuckles cracked and his wallet lightened.

"I got a warning [from the RIAA] back in January," he said. "My Internet was shut off and the school said my Internet address was caught downloading illegal files from Lime Wire. So I went into the Internet abuse officer's office and signed an agreement saying I wouldn't download anymore. I also had to bring my computer into the technical office at my school and they took Lime Wire off my computer and all those music files.

"After that date in late January I never downloaded any music files and I didn't reinstall the program. But right before spring break my computer was shut off again. The Internet abuse office said I was caught downloading again. And I said, 'No, I wasn't.' He showed me the complaint from the RIAA and what they were accusing me of was downloading the music that I had downloaded prior to signing that agreement in January. He agreed with me that the matter had been settled, that we had a signed agreement, but there was nothing he could do. I was caught in the middle. Obviously, being a college student, and not knowing what to do, I gave in. The letter is very threatening, claiming they can sue you for millions. Obviously I didn't want to risk that. So I settled for $3,000."

Sammarco didn't have that kind of money. He spent the summer working construction jobs for his father in the western suburbs of Illinois, and was able to pay off the fine in six $540 monthly increments, with interest.

What's puzzling to Sammarco was that he didn't download much music, especially compared to his peers on campus. He had 290 songs on his hard drive when he received the legal notice. "I knew people on my floor in the dorm that had thousands of files and didn't get in trouble at all," he said. "I'm not denying what I did was wrong, but I feel the punishment didn't fit the crime. It seemed I was chosen at random. I didn't download thousands and thousands of songs. I ended up paying more than $10 a song."

There were thousands of Jimmy Sammarcos in the country, college kids and other consumers who'd gotten smacked by the industry for trading music files. Most of these cases were settled quietly before they became a matter of public record.

But one consumer went down fighting, noisily.

In October 2007, Jammie Thomas—a thirty-year-old single mother of two children with an annual income of $36,000—became the first accused infringer to take the RIAA to trial. She was accused of uploading twenty-four major-label recordings to her hard drive and making them available for peer-to-peer file sharing on the Kazaa network.

Besides presenting another one of those underdog showcases so beloved by the media, the federal trial in Duluth, Minnesota, offered a muddled portrait of the record industry's thinking on the issue of file sharing.

That Jennifer Pariser, the head of litigation for Sony BMG, testified that "stealing" was killing her industry was nothing new. But how she defined stealing was eye-opening. In response to a question from an RIAA attorney, she testified: "When an individual makes a copy of a song for himself, I suppose we can say he stole a song." Copying a song is just "a nice way of saying 'steals one copy.'"

A few weeks later, the RIAA said Pariser misheard the question; she apparently thought she was being asked about illegal downloading, not ripping physical copies. The record industry didn't really hold that a consumer who copied his CD collection onto his hard drive was guilty of stealing. But the damage had been done.

Pariser further testified that the labels had spent millions of dollars pursuing the copycats, and had "lost money on this program." Their overhead included payments to SafeNet, to investigate file sharers, and to attorneys, to prosecute them. Settling for $3,000 to

$5,000 per case apparently wasn't enabling the RIAA to break even.

The stakes were higher for Jammie Thomas. After receiving her prelitigation warning from the RIAA, she refused to settle. According to the Copyright Act, she faced punitive damages ranging from $750 to $150,000 per song.

"We did not have a crusade in mind," said Thomas's attorney, Brian Toder. "She came into my office and said, 'I didn't do this and they're not going to bully me.'"

Toder argued that Thomas's screen name and Internet Protocol address had been hijacked and that she hadn't made the twenty-four copyrighted songs—including tracks by Journey, AFI, Aerosmith, and Guns N' Roses—available for other Kazaa users to download. But to no avail. After only four hours of deliberation, the jury found her guilty of infringement and awarded the record industry an astonishing $9,250 per song, a total of $222,000.

This for songs worth less than $24 on iTunes. As outrageous as the damages seemed to be, the guilty verdict itself was widely expected. Thomas's case proved to be not much of a case at all. Though she claimed she wasn't responsible for uploading the songs, the user name and screen name on the Kazaa account were the same ones she'd used for a decade.

Two rulings during the trial undercut the defendant's case, while exposing the limitations of copyright law in dealing with the new digital reality. U.S. District Judge Michael Davis instructed the jury that downloading copyrighted recordings on a peer-to-peer network violated copyright, and that merely making copyrighted files available on a peer-to-peer network constituted infringement. In other words, the prosecution didn't have to prove that anyone had actually downloaded Thomas's files, only that she put them on a network where unauthorized downloading could take place.

Davis's interpretation of copyright law was exactly that, an interpretation. By the judge's logic, anyone throwing a party at home for twenty-five people and putting out an iPod loaded with songs or a handful of CDs on the coffee table could be found guilty of infringement. Davis also applied the Copyright Act to peer-to-peer file sharing, even though the law posits that in order for distribution to take place, a physical copy has to change hands—and no physical music copies were distributed by Thomas.

"The copyright laws came from a day when there were mimeograph machines and vinyl records," Toder said. "Now, in the electronic age, nobody knows exactly what infringement is or is not, and frankly, I believe, this is something that Congress is going to have to fix."

For a few weeks in late 2007, Jammie Thomas was the latest poster child for peer-to-peer file sharing. Of course, she had a website (freejammie.com), which briefly shut down due to high traffic. Within six weeks she had accumulated more than $17,000 in donations for her continuing legal defense.

Soon after the verdict, Judge Davis had second thoughts and asked for briefings on whether Thomas deserved a new trial. A year later, he concluded that she did. In a forty-four-page ruling, Davis acknowledged that he made a mistake in his instructions to the jury, which "substantially prejudiced Thomas's rights" and likely turned the case against her. Thomas may have made music files available in a shared file on her computer, Davis said, but that wasn't enough evidence to constitute copyright infringement.

The Thomas trial exposed the inadequacy of current copyright law in dealing with the new digital reality. Davis urged Congress "to amend the Copyright Act to address liability and damages to peer-to-peer network cases . . . [because] the damages awarded in this case are wholly disproportionate to the damages suffered by the plaintiffs."

Though Davis did not go so far as to defend file sharing, he said, "Thomas acted like countless other Internet users. Her alleged acts were illegal, but common."

Indeed, they were becoming more common by the day. Her high-profile case did nothing to slow down file sharing. It only brought the RIAA more ridicule. Despite higher traffic at digital download stores in 2007, forty songs were being downloaded illegally for every legal download, according to the International Federation of the Phonographic Industry.

The state of affairs left at least one prominent member of the recording industry lamenting lost opportunities.

"We used to fool ourselves," Warner Music Group CEO Edgar Bronfman said at the GSMA Mobile Asia Congress in November 2007. "We used to think our content was perfect just exactly as it was. We expected our business would remain blissfully unaffected even as the world of interactivity, constant connection, and file sharing was exploding. And of course, we were wrong. How were we wrong? By standing still or moving at a glacial pace, we inadvertently went to war with consumers by denying them what they wanted and could otherwise find. And as a result, of course, consumers won."

The record industry suing file sharers is like the railroad
industry trying to shoot down airplanes.

—Ken Waagner, digital guru for Wilco, born 1961

All of us are standing back to see what happens. If the
bands and artists could get more control, rather than the
record companies, free downloads could be a great thing.
The potential is unbelievable.

—Jeff Ament of Pearl Jam, born 1963

5

Is Prince Nuts?

In 1996, Prince ventured where no music superstar had gone before: he walked away from the mainstream industry that made him a multimillionaire so he could run his own label and release as many albums in as many different ways as he desired.

Such self-contained operations were already common among underground artists: folkie Ani DiFranco and punk rockers Fugazi had run their own labels for years. But the stakes were lower for these performers. Neither had been major-label stars with $100 million recording deals. Prince became the first mainstream rock star near the height of his powers to buck the system, turning his back for a few years on the multinational music companies and their distribution and marketing muscle, then returning to them for distribution deals in which he held the upper hand (and the master tapes). He presaged the do-it-yourself artists of the twenty-first century with his single-minded devotion to one concept: recording whenever, whatever, and wherever he wanted and sending the results to his fans as quickly and directly as possible. Prince was among the first artists to successfully exploit Internet distribution of his music, and certainly the most prominent.

The story is all the more remarkable in light of what Prince left behind to author it. The diminutive multi-instrumentalist singer-songwriter-producer had been a crown jewel in Warner Bros.' musical empire for most of the eighties; his 1984 album, *Purple Rain*, was one of the biggest sellers in history, and he signed a major deal with Warner in 1992 (Prince claimed it was worth $100 million, though Warner downplayed that figure). But by that time his relationship with the label had already soured. Prince had wanted to release *Sign o' the Times* as a triple album in 1987; Warner whittled it down to a double. Prince wanted to release two or three albums a year, Warner insisted that more than one would flood the market. As it was, Prince managed to release thirteen albums between 1978 and 1992, including two double-disc sets. In the nineties, he started to let his feelings about the label affect his work, releasing uneven albums in what looked like a blatant attempt to finish his contract as quickly as possible. He toured North America only once between 1988 and 1996. In further protest, he began writing the word "slave" on his cheek in black marker.

Was Prince nuts? The artist did little to dispel the notion. In the early nineties, he had changed his name to an unpronounceable symbol (a combination of the symbols for male and female). For most of the decade he insisted upon being referred to in print as the "Artist Formerly Known as Prince." Given his erratic musicmaking and his even more erratic behavior, Prince was cast as the ultimate "difficult" artist, draining patience and cash from Warner Bros.

The image was, at least in part, true. "Nobody—his managers, his record company—could tell him what to do," said Alan Leeds, Prince's former road manager and business associate. "He never took advice well. Management's attitude was that they were desperately holding on to the reins of a wild horse. If they didn't, he'd run from one thing to the next. He was so prolific, but he had little appreciation for setting things up with radio, press, or the public to build awareness. None of that mattered to him, but it mattered a lot to the label."

Prince had always been a constellation of genuine eccentricity in a galaxy of pop stars who claimed to flout the rules but rarely did. This was the same guy who tossed an androgynous curveball at funk's masculine prototype by appearing clad only in bikini briefs and lingerie on the cover of his 1980 breakthrough album, *Dirty Mind.* He employed a multiracial coed band that played both rock and R&B with equal authority as he became one of the few pop stars who transcended racial and genre lines on radio and the concert circuit. He ping-ponged from style to style and from persona to persona, and indulged his artistic whims. He once pulled a finished work (*The Black Album*) only days before it was to be released, at considerable expense to himself and his record label (the album was eventually released in 1994 as Prince rushed to fulfill his Warner contract).

When Prince finally negotiated his release from Warner, he quickly released a three-CD album, *Emancipation.* He celebrated with a postmidnight concert in November 1996 at the Park West, a one-thousand-capacity club in Chicago. Prince, dressed in white lace pants and a turtleneck halter top, rolled out a sleek new five-piece coed band. He unleashed an epic guitar solo on "Purple Rain" and cut short "The Most Beautiful Girl in the World" to play a grinding blues, with his fire-breathing guitar again at the forefront. The performance was heavy on loose, funk jams, with Prince directing the band like Duke Ellington—with better dance moves.

"Freedom," he crowed, "is a beautiful thing, y'all."

In his first twenty months as an indie artist, Prince released no fewer than nine CDs' worth of new and archival material on his NPG imprint: the three-disc *Emancipation*; *Crystal Ball*, which was released in four- and five-disc configurations; and the single-disc *New Power Soul.*

The music was an up-and-down mix of gems, experiments, and half-baked demos. But it was done on Prince's own terms, and these terms had nothing to do with the far different agenda of the music industry he had just left.

In those first post-Warner months, Prince lived in the studio. He had always been prolific, but now his musicians and engineers at Paisley Park Studios, his longtime home in the hilly suburbs outside Minneapolis, could barely keep up. One week, his in-house engineer, Hans-Martin Buff, put in 112 hours. Prince didn't smoke, inhale, or drink anything stronger than coffee. On the contrary, he expressly banned booze and drugs from the studio. He was running on something else.

"Energy, adrenaline, creativity," Buff said. "He works long hours, but he accomplishes a lot. No one works more quickly. I've been at sessions [with other artists] where it takes half a day to bring in a keyboardist or bassist to play a part, but if something's missing in one of his arrangements, he just does it himself and moves on."

Leeds said Prince's work ethic as a musician informed his attitude as a businessman: "For him, music is like a newspaper, and his attitude is, 'What's the point of reading last week's paper?'"

Prince's more-is-better campaign culminated with *Crystal Ball*, a bulky box set of new and archived material, which he sold directly to fans through his website or directly to retailers, often bypassing music distributors who made their money as middlemen taking records from labels to the stores. There were problems filling orders. Some fans had to wait weeks, or even months, to receive a copy of the box set after ordering it from the website. They were not happy. Websites with off-color names (The Artist Currently Known as Asshole) sprang up as gathering places for the disgruntled to vent. Retailers griped that they couldn't get copies of the release after supporting Prince's career for two decades.

"What he's doing is a pure ego thing, running a label without really knowing how," said Rick Swenson of Bayside Entertainment Distribution, at the time the nation's largest independent distributor. "I'd say he's succeeding at his little end run around the music industry about as well as Pearl Jam did in their fight against Ticketmaster."

Swenson was referring to Pearl Jam's 1994 appeal to the U.S. Justice Department seeking an investigation of what it called monopolistic practices by the nation's largest concert-ticketing company, Ticketmaster. At the time, the band charged fans $18 for a concert ticket and wanted to cap Ticketmaster fees for processing the ticket orders at $1.80. The suit marked a major breach of music-industry etiquette: a major band trying to change the business practices of a key cog in the lucrative touring industry.

The next year the band boycotted concert venues with exclusive Ticketmaster contracts. But the Justice Department ruled in Ticketmaster's favor, and Pearl Jam eventually began touring at Ticketmaster venues again. By the next decade, 25 percent service fees were routinely tacked on to the price of concert tickets—more than double the rate when Pearl Jam filed its appeal.

Pearl Jam had the right idea, but they nearly cost themselves a career. Eddie Vedder said the band was on the verge of breaking up in 1995, in part because it was having difficulty finding non-Ticketmaster venues to play. "What lessons did we learn?" Vedder cracked a few years after the debacle. "I suppose we learned how to accept a good butt kicking by the powers that be. There are some things that are just beyond the power of one band to change."

Prince also found himself very much alone when it came to challenging practices that had guided the marketing, distribution, and sales of music for decades.

"Prince is bungling it," said Joe Kvidra, then a general manager at Tower Records, one of the most powerful record chains in North America. "I know little local bands selling records out of their car trunk who look like sophisticated multinational corporations compared to the way Prince runs his business."

Distributors were aghast that Prince demanded cash on delivery of new albums, instead of extending the traditional sixty-day billing period. "He has no clue how the industry operates," Bayside's Swenson groused.

Instead, Prince created his own rules as he went along. *Crystal Ball* sold out its 250,000-copy pressing in 1998, at prices ranging from $30 to $50, with Prince keeping up to 95 percent of the profit on copies he sold through his website. With Warner Bros. he would have kept 10 percent, and then only after recoupable expenses had been deducted.

"Prince never could understand why all those people had to be in the middle between him and the fans," Leeds said. "Long before the Internet came along, he was chafing at the bit, trying to figure out ways to get more music out faster. It was incredibly naïve and hypocritical in some ways. The business made him a superstar, and those middlemen laid the groundwork for huge successes like *Purple Rain*. But he always saw business as a means to an end, not a reason for being. The process frustrated him. He liked the money, but it was always ancillary to the music. He wanted to do creative things and do them right away. He would book shows on a Monday and play to a sell-out crowd on Saturday. He thought recording and releasing records should be the same way. The Internet made that goal realizable for him."

To make it up to fans who didn't get *Crystal Ball* in a timely manner, Prince cooked up a twenty-six-minute psychedelic funk jam, *The War,* and sent it to them gratis. He announced free shows at Paisley Park on his website, and hundreds of fans would show up at 3 A.M. to watch him preview new material. For Prince, forward motion and constant activity were his way of dealing with mistakes.

"Booking a show? I call up a few radio programmers, tell them I'm coming to town in a few days, and place a $5,000 ad—that's my idea of promotion," Prince said. "I call up the guy from Best Buy or the guy from Target and play them the record. 'Oh, you like it? How many you want?' That's distribution."

"The guy from Best Buy" at the time, Senior Vice President Gary Arnold, said the retail chain had to adapt to Prince's unconventional business strategies. But it did so willingly. "More artists than you might realize are watching him because he's breaking ground," Arnold said in 1998. "He's one of the first topics of conversation whenever I meet with people like Elton John. They're all very interested because he's maintained control of his product at a time when the record business is basically being run by five corporations."

Prince worked his free-agent status to the hilt, pumping out music on his website and then striking licensing deals with the big labels to release some of his higher-profile projects. In 2004, he licensed his studio album *Musicology* to a major label for sale in traditional retail stores, but also bundled copies of the disc with the price of tickets to his arena tour. Each fan who walked through the turnstiles at one of his concerts received a copy of the album.

Sitting backstage that summer at an arena show in St. Paul, Minnesota, across the Mississippi River from the city of his birth, Prince was putting up impressive numbers: $87 million in tour revenue earned and 1.4 million tickets sold. *Musicology* would go on to sell 2 million copies, his most popular release in more than a decade. Most of those transactions took place at a concert arena, not a retail store.

For Prince, an artist whose new music no longer mattered to commercial radio and MTV, it was a brilliant move: he hijacked the *Billboard* album chart and wound up with his first number one album in more than a decade. Record-label executives grumbled that the CD/concert tie-in was unfair double dipping, and shouldn't be counted as an album sale. *Billboard* eventually ruled that in the future it wouldn't count such two-for-one deals as an album sale unless consumers were given the option of not buying the CD. But Prince got what he wanted: a quick, efficient way of getting his new music directly to his most ardent fans.

"The music industry is a matrix that is counter to what is natural and right," he said in his candlelit dressing room while checking e-mails on his laptop. "I've wanted to do this for a long time, but I had to be free of record contracts to do it. To me, this is just another form of peer-to-peer [music file sharing]. It's a way of operating that has nothing to do with the charts, radio, or MTV."

The innovation was adopted by other bands and artists, including the Cure, Gomez, and Neil Young. "A revolution? Call it what you want, but something has changed," Prince said. "It's a new way of looking at things."

Three years later, in the summer of 2007, he struck a deal with the London tabloid the *Daily Mail* to give away copies of his studio album *Planet Earth* to its 2.8 million readers. Prince licensed the album to the newspaper for a discount rate of thirty-six cents per CD (instead of the customary $2). Though he lost about $4.5 million in potential licensing revenue, the stunt served as an ad for his twenty-one-show residency at London's O$_2$ arena, where he collected $22 million in revenue.

"It was like bus placard advertising," says R.E.M. manager Bertis

Downs, whose band once shared a label with Prince. "Ninety-five percent of the people reading it don't know what's being advertised. It's not targeted at all. But there was something to be said for the audacity of being the first to do something like that. It just got so many people talking . . . and that's real valuable at a time when everyone is trying to cut through the clutter."

As with most of Prince's unconventional moves, the stunt enraged music business veterans who didn't like the rules being bent—in this case, overseas retailers. Sony, the album's U.S. distributor, didn't even bother to release the album at retail in the United Kingdom. But what else was new?

"I'm not a businessman," Prince said soon after he went independent in the nineties. "I hate the word. Can't stand it. It's not a business what I do."

It was an odd statement coming from an artist who controlled every aspect of his career from the start. But he wasn't really anti-business so much as anticonvention. If an artist could reinvent himself and his music, as Prince had done for so many years, why not constantly reinvent the way the music is distributed?

"With everyone else I've been with," said Maceo Parker, the Prince saxophonist who had worked with James Brown in the sixties, "they pass on the business details to someone else, but with Prince, it surprised me how involved he is with every aspect of his operation."

Prince's innovations on the business and distribution side were rarely matched by his new recordings. After the overstuffed but still potent *Emancipation,* he began crafting albums that echoed his eighties masterpieces without coming close to equaling them. *Musicology* and *Planet Earth* came off as compendiums of the artist's best moves, undercut by the notion that we'd heard them all done better on previous Prince albums.

But in a way, the studio albums were just advertisements for the artist's renewal as a live performer. The son of a working musician, Prince has a deep appreciation not only for music history but for the work ethic and aesthetic of big bands, from Duke Ellington's to Sly

Stone's. The roots of his landmark *Musicology* arena tour could be found in the frequent theater tours he did in the years leading up to it, when he began assembling his band and honing their interplay on everything from jazz instrumentals to old soul covers. Then he ushered in his larger-scale ambitions by performing on the nationally televised Grammy Awards.

Even during sound checks on that 2004 tour, Prince was working his nine-piece band with cool yet firm purpose. Trailing cologne and charisma, he'd circle the arena in a white golf cart while the band rehearsed, frequently calling out adjustments or refinements. "The guitar sounds too brittle!" "Hit those harmonies a beat sooner!" Prince then would join the group and run down three or four songs, utterly at ease with himself, his musicians, and his place in the world: at center stage.

For saxophonist Mike Phillips, who at twenty-eight was young enough to be a son to the then forty-six-year-old Prince, it was like going to music school. Phillips had previously played with Stevie Wonder but said Prince has made him reconsider how he plays his instrument. "I get private lessons from the guy that have made me a better musician, and he doesn't even play the saxophone. When I first joined the band I played a solo, and he came up to me later and said, 'Think of it as if you're courting a woman. You're not gonna run up to her and start babbling. You're gonna take your time.' And he was right. I was trying to pack in every idea I had to wow the crowd, and he taught me how to talk to the crowd."

The shows were high-octane mixtures of soul-funk precision and thrilling jam-band looseness. He'd drop in bits of Beyoncé and OutKast between horn-drenched crescendos, hold the arena rapt with a thirty-minute solo acoustic set, and then roll out "Little Red Corvette" and "Raspberry Beret" amid homages to Ray Charles and Eddie Floyd.

After the flurry of recordings that ushered in the indie-Prince era, the singer focused his energies on his unparalleled prowess as a live act in 2006–7. In addition to the London showcase, he played an extended residency in Las Vegas, at $125 a ticket. Each night he juggled set lists, played requests, and did whatever the hell he wanted. It was high-level entertainment, delivered by a great band led by a genius maverick in Cuban heels.

"It was like a TV that had been playing for years suddenly got shut off and you realize, I can do whatever I want," he said in the relative stillness of his Paisley Park recording studio. "I heard, 'Prince is crazy,' so much that it had an effect on me. So one day I said, 'Let me just check out.' Here there is solitude, silence—I like to stay in this controlled environment and just create stuff. A lot of it may never come out, but a lot of it will—at my discretion. People say I'm out of touch, but I'll do twenty-five or thirty more albums. I'm gonna catch up with Sinatra. So you tell me who's out of touch. One thing I ain't gonna run out of is music."

Getting MP3 files over instant messenger is no different than me going to somebody's house and letting them listen to a CD. Within a week, I'll get four to five albums from friends like that. If I like the band, most of the time it leads to going to a concert. I will buy later CDs from the band or I'll buy previous CDs. You download the CD, but you end up supporting the band more. And none of it would've happened if I hadn't gotten the music for free initially. I never would have spent $10 for a CD by an unknown band.

—Adam, college student in Seattle, born 1988

6

"Do Not Insult Death Cab"

Death Cab for Cutie became one of the most talked about bands on the Internet through no fault of its own.

For years, bassist Nick Harmer and his bandmates—singer Ben Gibbard, guitarist Chris Walla, and a series of drummers—were too busy trying to make music to bother with logging on to a computer and communicating with their fans. "We're not Luddites," Harmer says with a laugh. "But communicating with people in that way about our band just was never at the front of the agenda. We were self-managed, we did everything ourselves. Making records and going on tours was pretty time-consuming for all of us. Participating in that [Internet] world was something we just let run in the background."

But while the members of Death Cab were being distracted by the day-to-day business of being a band, fans in chat rooms and blogs were transforming them into virtual stars. It was an MP3 world defined by kids who were bored silly by the constricted playlists of modern-rock radio and who lived in towns where Wal-Mart or Best Buy were the primary outlets for CDs. So they sat in their bedrooms after school staring at a computer screen, trolling for something, anything, to break the monotony. It created an opening for underground bands such as Death Cab for Cutie, an opening that really didn't exist five years earlier.

"I was thirteen, so I was hormonal and had so many sad problems. Eighth grade, ya know?" says Emma, a college student who grew up in the Chicago suburbs. "The big bands at the time like Limp Bizkit and Creed seemed abrasive to me. The music I found on sites like Napster and Audiogalaxy was something that wasn't being presented to me elsewhere and I thought it was really great. Pretty soon I stopped listening to radio and soon after that I stopped buying CDs. But I was listening to music more than ever, all on the Internet.

"When I discovered Death Cab, the lyrics really made me think about what a song could say in a new way. Death Cab was talking about things that most people wouldn't necessarily talk about, these small details of everyday life. Ben Gibbard would write songs about going to visit your parents once you're on your own and how weird that can be and how weird it is to drive home and not have it feel like home. You weren't hearing that kind of thing anywhere else."

Long before Emma and like-minded listeners entered the picture, Ben Gibbard's most prominent early fan was Nick Harmer.

When Gibbard began attending Western Washington University in Bellingham as an environmental-chemistry major he was playing in a band called Pinwheel. Harmer, a year older than Gibbard, was playing in a band of his own that included Jason McGerr, who would eventually become Death Cab's drummer. Harmer also was booking concerts on campus and gave Pinwheel an early shot; Harmer and Gibbard became fast friends and eventually roommates. At a party a year later, Gibbard met Chris Walla, an aspiring recording engineer with a newly bought eight-track tape recorder. Walla was eager to use his new toy, and Gibbard had a bunch of highly personal songs that just weren't working in Pinwheel.

"Right place, right time," Walla says, looking back. "I had some microphones and some equipment. I knew how to play guitar, and we liked hanging out together. I sort of ended up in a band with Ben by default. Death Cab was pretty much my first band. It's not like I was chosen or anything. But when I heard Ben's songs, I knew right away I wanted to record them. Being in a band with the guy was just a bonus."

Gibbard's songs were written in the aftermath of a breakup.

"They're all kind of devastating at that age, aren't they?" Gibbard says with a laugh. Gibbard played all the instruments, while Walla served as engineer and cheerleader. As precious as the songs might have been, they presented Gibbard as not only an oddly consoling singer who knew how to map the geography of a broken heart, but an inventive arranger and melodist.

"I really liked that there were lots of parts to each song and there were different melodies within each," Walla says. "He packed a lot into his songs without making any of it feel showy or extraneous. 'President of What?' is the perfect example of that, the way it moves around. There's not really a chorus, the structure of it is pretty atypical, and each verse is made up of these big, long, weird progressions. When I heard that I thought, There's a lot to work with here."

The eight songs Walla recorded, dubbed *You Can Play These Songs with Chords,* came out on a cassette released by the Bellingham label Elsinor Records. Gibbard dubbed the project Death Cab for Cutie, the name of a song performed by the Bonzo Dog Doo-Dah Band in the Beatles' *Magical Mystery Tour.*

"It wasn't even a band at that point, and the release of the cassette was kind of a joke, because there were only about a hundred copies around," Harmer recalls. "It was just a tape that Ben passed around to his friends, but the songs were great and everyone was kind of pushing him to take the next step: 'Is this a band you're going to do?'"

Josh Rosenfeld, the proprietor of a small Seattle-based label named Barsuk Records, heard the Death Cab tape and became an instant fan. "He was just a teenager when he wrote a lot of those songs, and I was blown away," he says. "We all were. My friends, people in Seattle. Everyone who heard it had the same reaction: 'Who is this kid?' He was writing about love and loneliness—the usual subjects—but he was doing it in this very moving, profound way."

Gibbard took the hint. He put Pinwheel down and enlisted Walla, Harmer, and drummer Nathan Good, a friend of Walla's, to play and record his songs.

"Soon after hearing that tape, we had our first practice," Harmer recalls. "It was one of those moments—I can still remember the very first time Chris, Ben, Nathan, and I set up and played in the living room of this house that we all lived in, 1138 Ellis Street in Bellingham. We knew it right away. 'Yes, let's make a record. Yes, let's go on tour.' I had filled out a bunch of applications for graduate school because I was going to apply for Ph.D. programs in English literature and push through some kind of professor track. I had gotten letters of recommendation and was ready to go, but the band and the songs felt too good to pass up. I gambled on Ben's songs."

Soon after, Rosenfeld signed Death Cab to Barsuk, and in 1998 released their debut album, *Something About Airplanes.*

It was all rather surreal to Gibbard. As a middle-class child of the eighties he was intimately familiar with Poison and Mötley Crüe videos, which quickly convinced Gibbard that people like him simply didn't have what it takes to become rock stars.

"I thought there was no way to be in a band unless you could play a ripping guitar solo," he says. "I thought it was a prerequisite that I would never be able to achieve."

By those standards, Gibbard still doesn't look or act like a rock star. He doesn't even look like a guy who would be allowed backstage, let alone onstage entertaining a few thousand people. His sole distinguishing feature is a pair of oversized glasses that speaks more to his inner biochemist than his ability to rock an arena.

Gibbard's modest songs didn't rock particularly hard, either, but they turned melancholy into a powerful muse. The first ones were preoccupied with what might've been, tucked inside a tangle of guitars and sometimes cloaked in reverb, like a fog rolling in from the Pacific on a drizzly afternoon. At their best, they honed in on emotional specifics, with Gibbard in the role of an older brother sharing his secrets with or offering his consolation to the person listening between the headphones.

For Rosenfeld, that sound helped turn Barsuk into a serious business. Like Gibbard's career, the label had begun modestly, a hobby for Rosenfeld while working as a clinical researcher in Seattle. He and a friend began putting out seven-inch singles by bands they liked. Then Death Cab came along, and the homemade business plan faced its first major test. Rosenfeld loved Death Cab so much he agreed to split profits with them sixty-forty in favor of the band. Gibbard actually had to talk him out of giving away an even bigger share.

Not that it mattered in the first few years of Death Cab's existence. The path out of poverty-level subsistence was painfully slow.

"There were tours from hell," Harmer says. "We started out doing six West Coast dates with another Seattle band that had had a hit, Harvey Danger, and we thought, This is fun. Then we went out on our own and we played to nobody. There was no money, no fans. I think that the muses were testing us at that point, saying, 'Are you really ready for this, boys? If you can get through this, you'll be all right. But if you can't, then this is where the path splits in the woods—go back to your day jobs.'"

That nearly became a reality in 1999, soon after drummer Nathan Good departed the band.

"It could've ended right there," Walla says. "At the very least, it was awkward for all of us. But what else were we going to do? Ben had a bio-chem degree, but that wasn't what he wanted to do. Nick had an English degree, which equals coffee shop job. I didn't have a degree at all, which equals coffee shop job. I had just quit my coffee shop job to go on tour, so what the heck? It's like I have no money and no job and I'm making a decision that is going to ensure that I have less money and no job for the foreseeable future. Ben was able to keep himself afloat with the money he made working at an oil refinery in Bellingham. I ended up moving back in with my parents. It was really a rotten year."

And in many ways a typical one for a struggling independent band with no major-label budget from which to siphon. On tour, the band was making $50 a night, barely enough to cover fuel expenses to get to the next town. Paying for a hotel was out of the question, so they'd shack up with fans, sleeping on floors and couches. That's when it became apparent that something else was going on, something they couldn't control but that was benefiting them in ways they couldn't quite yet fully grasp.

"When we were having these face-to-face interactions with people who were coming to our shows and letting us stay at their apartments, that's when we discovered what role the Internet was playing," Harmer says. "They'd say, 'A friend of mine e-mailed me a link or sent me a song of yours that I ended up really liking.' We were pretending to go along with it, 'Oh, sure, great.' But we had no idea."

At that point, the band wanted an audience—any audience. How the music got out there was beside the point, as long as people showed up at the gigs. Barsuk didn't have much of a promotion budget. It relied on word of mouth and a few sympathetic fanzine writers to spread the word. The Internet took those staples of indie promotion and gave them impact far beyond what Barsuk or Death Cab could've imagined.

"It seemed like magic; this thing was happening around us that we really couldn't control or really have any presence in, but that's how people were finding out about our band, and it allowed us to survive," Harmer says. "It was the equivalent of a big party chat line, where a lot of people were calling each other and you really didn't have any influence on shaping the conversation. You never asked for it, never did anything for it, it just popped up and started running."

Each Death Cab record sold better than the previous one, peaking just short of sixty thousand copies. Then *Transatlanticism* came out in October 2003.

The record sounded bigger, bolder than anything the band had attempted previously. As producer, Walla judiciously splashed reverb and primary-color guitar through Gibbard's typically wan, typically lovely songs. The music took on an epic quality; the bedroom vibe of the early records was replaced by a more grandiose, if no less bittersweet, vision. On the title song, the arrangement stretches to nearly eight minutes, with Gibbard patiently turning the plea "I need you so much closer" into an incantation over a softly churning ocean of guitars.

What remained constant was Gibbard's confiding tone: an underrated singer, he always sounds like he's sitting on the edge of the listener's bed, immersed in an intensely private 3 A.M. conversation. In the midst of the album's crashing opener, "The New Year," he is the one guy trapped at the party who wonders what he's doing there "as thirty dialogues bleed into one." Self-doubt amid celebration—classic Gibbard. How un-rock of him. And yet this guy with the melancholy glasses was now reaching an audience that only two years before seemed ridiculously out of reach.

It didn't hurt that the album's release coincided with the TV debut of the syndicated teen soap opera *The O.C.* The show starred Adam Brody as Seth Cohen, a southern California teenager who was a hard-core Death Cab for Cutie fan, as was Brody in real life.

Brody/Cohen became an unlikely star by reflecting his audience: nerdy, self-deprecatingly sarcastic, and militant about his music.

"Hey, do not insult Death Cab," Seth said in the middle of a heated argument with one of his friends during the first season.

These words still make Rosenfeld crack up in disbelief. "The idea that an indie-rock kid can be made into a TV idol, a heartthrob, is hilarious and gratifying to people in our world. If mainstream culture is driven by popular TV shows, the fact there is a Death Cab poster on Seth Cohen's wall had impact."

"I think if we ever had a moment where we thought, Oh, man, things are going to change, it was when Josh called and said, 'There's this television show called *The O.C.* and they want a song—is that cool?'" Harmer recalls. "And at that point we really had never been on television at all. Nobody had wanted one of our songs before. We hadn't even made a video. We didn't have any presence in that world. We thought some people might hear the song, and that would be a good thing."

The band got together at Gibbard's apartment in Seattle to watch their TV debut. "We were all sitting on the couch when the character says, 'Do not insult Death Cab,' and we're looking at each other like, 'Oh, no—this isn't what we signed up for,'" Harmer says. "We didn't know if it was a good thing or a bad thing. Then they kept putting us in the scripts. We became part of this character's life. It got ridiculous."

The show's creator, Josh Schwartz, and music supervisor, Alexandra Patsavas, were self-described music nerds and Death Cab fans too. The lower licensing budgets ($2,000–$3,000 per song instead of $20,000) of a fledgling show made it imperative to seek out music that wasn't on the mainstream radar—Patsavas's specialty.

"I had the bad haircut and saw the English Beat when I was still in junior high," Patsavas says. She booked underground shows at rock clubs while attending the University of Illinois at Urbana-Champaign in the late eighties, and in 1999 began licensing music for shows such as *Roswell* and later *Six Feet Under, The O.C.,* and *Grey's Anatomy.* These shows turned into a cottage industry for breaking new bands. *The O.C.* alone spun off a series of CDs spotlighting underground bands like Spoon, Death Cab, Of Montreal, and Interpol. If there was a single instigator for the mainstreaming of indie rock in the first half decade of the new century, it was Patsavas.

"The music that fits *The O.C.* the best has an indie sensibility: stuff that's innovative, different, that hasn't been overplayed and overhyped," Patsavas says. "It was the kind of music I grew up on, and I was fortunate to work with people who didn't have the same constraints that record labels have. I didn't need to find twelve good songs. I needed a great song to fit a scene, and it doesn't matter where it came from. There's a lot of freedom in that."

Sam Riback, the talent scout who later signed Death Cab to Atlantic Records, says the O.C. link was crucial because it played out not as a gimmick but as a mark of respect. "As someone who's pitched Alex before, I came to realize it's not about what's on any label's agenda, it's about what she likes as a music fan," Riback says. "Everything she's done, from *The O.C.* to *Six Feet Under,* is done with taste and respect for the music. It was a case of true music fans becoming gatekeepers of popular taste, and that translated to careers taking off for bands like Death Cab and Modest Mouse."

Maggie was a sophomore at Marquette University in Milwaukee when *The O.C.* debuted.

"Everyone in my dorm watched that show, and each episode had a really different range of music," she says. "As soon as the episode was over they had all the songs listed on the website, and a few minutes later you could be listening to it on your hard drive. You couldn't buy it or download it from their website, but you could obviously find it somewhere else. They played Death Cab. They played Spoon. They played Rooney, Phantom Planet. They played Modest Mouse before Modest Mouse was getting played on the radio. They had the Killers on before the Killers even started getting out there. It was stuff that really wasn't getting played a lot or at all on radio. That's how I know a lot of people got into Death Cab. It's kind of silly, but the way they used music was totally cool. Sometimes you'd watch and you'd tune out the scene. You were just listening to this song and it'd be like, 'Oh, God, what's that? I need this.'"

Jordan Kurland, a longtime friend of the band who had booked the first tour with Harvey Danger, came aboard as Death Cab's manager a few weeks before *Transatlanticism* was released. "I was sitting with Josh at the Barsuk office, and he had a staff of three people at that time," Kurland says. "Everybody was guessing the album would sell maybe six thousand copies the first week, maybe eight thousand at the high end. Everyone's goal was to sell seventy-five thousand total. And then it did fifteen thousand the first week. No one was denying the impact of *The O.C.* But even with the O.C. effect, the exposure wouldn't have mattered as much had it been released five years earlier because people wouldn't have been able to easily find the record. Now they'd hear the song, they'd go to the Internet, and there was instant gratification. It wasn't just about reaching a lot of people at once, but being able to really capitalize on it."

Within two years *Transatlanticism* had sold more than 325,000 copies—a massive hit by indie-rock standards. By 2007 it had gone gold, topping 530,000 sales.

The "*O.C.* effect" that swept along Death Cab for Cutie was just one of the more notable examples of a broader transition. While a new generation was using the Internet to track down music, the generation that had come immediately before had ascended into taste-shaping and decision-making positions at record companies, movie studios, radio stations, ad agencies, magazines, and television. It was a generation that included people like Kurland, Patsavas, Schwartz, and Rosenfeld, who grew up as indie-rock fans in the eighties and early nineties and were now championing new bands that reflected those tastes.

"There were two waves of this, the first being when all the big indie bands signed to the majors in the eighties," Rosenfeld says. "Hüsker Dü and Dinosaur Jr. were the progenitors of people at the majors wanting to take chances on Nirvana and Green Day in the nineties. People who have seen that good music can also be a foundation for a good business plan are in position to make that happen."

Harmer sees Death Cab's ascent not as an isolated event or a fluke but as "a larger shift happening in popular culture across the board. Our peers and people that we had all slept on floors with together, we were all on the same circuit: us, Bright Eyes, the Shins, Spoon. We were all scraping by, and then there was a demand for our music. You started seeing it in movies, car ads, television shows."

Gibbard concurs. "In the last two, three years, this type of music has really started to mold pop culture," he says. "Whether it's the Shins getting name-checked in [Zach Braff's 2004 hit indie movie] *Garden State* or *The O.C.* or whatever kind of other TV shows, movies, books, media, it's being determined by people who grew up on college radio when things blew up in the nineties. People who were in college when I was in college are starting to end up in places of power in the music industry. They'll say, 'I don't want to use that fucking Staind song for this part in that movie. I want to use a Shins song. That's my music.' I think it's fantastic."

Death Cab for Cutie's ascent got a boost from another unlikely hit, a side project called the Postal Service. It was indeed facilitated by the U.S. Postal Service, with Gibbard in Seattle and his friend Jimmy

Tamborello in Los Angeles mailing songs back and forth. Together they fashioned a modest, breezy, uptempo update of 1980s synth pop, with Tamborello's electronic treatments providing a bed for Gibbard's melodies. "Our version of a Human League record," Gibbard says. And like Human League, it was a hit. *Give Up*, the Postal Service debut, was released in spring of 2003 on Seattle-based Sub Pop Records and sold six hundred thousand copies in two years. By the end of 2007 it had sold nearly 1 million copies, the second-biggest seller in Sub Pop history, behind only Nirvana's *Bleach*.

Its release caused some friction in the Death Cab camp. Walla paused for several seconds before answering a question about whether the Postal Service success had helped Death Cab.

"I don't know," he finally answers. "I think we've gotten to a point where everybody is really comfortable with it now. There was a point where it was really awkward. There was a point at which Ben said, 'I have this one thing that I have to do and then nothing more,' and we were like, 'Cool, great.' Then it took off and that one thing became touring and singles and lots of other responsibilities. That got to be frustrating. I think that ultimately it's turned out really well."

Gibbard says there will be another Postal Service record but insists that Death Cab was always his first priority. "There was this initial kind of fear where I hoped that the Postal Service didn't totally overtake the importance of what I do in Death Cab," he says. "And there are some concerns in the band about how things were going to pan out, but there's no doubt Postal Service has turned a lot of people on to Death Cab."

It also helped put Gibbard and Death Cab on the path to a major-label deal: a wrenching, yearlong process in which the band had to cut the cord with Barsuk and their longtime benefactor Rosenfeld to sign with Atlantic Records. The band owed Barsuk more music, but Atlantic bought out Rosenfeld, who refused to stand in the way of his friends. Barsuk was hardly left bereft; it was compensated for the two albums Death Cab still owed the label, and it would continue to benefit from the sales generated for the band's back catalog.

"The majors had been buzzing around the band for years, and the band always said, 'No, thanks,'" Rosenfeld says. "But for bands who have achieved a degree of success like Death Cab, and have bargaining power, a major can be a great home. If they hadn't done it, they would always be wondering what their career would be like if they had."

But Rosenfeld had to acknowledge that after four albums and seven years, the move was "bittersweet."

"The resources of a major can take Death Cab from a well-respected name to a household name like Coldplay," he says. "But I'm scrappy, so I feel like it's totally possible that us or any number of indies could've taken them from selling a few hundred thousand records to a million or more. On one level, I'm sad because I won't know what would've happened if we put this record out on Barsuk. I feel we could've totally nailed it."

But the band's issues weren't in North America with Barsuk so much as in Europe, where it was signed to nine different deals. That chaotic state of affairs made touring overseas a nightmare, with labels squabbling over travel expenses. The Atlantic deal consolidated all of those expenses under one roof.

Kurland also said the band had to take a wider view of its career. There may be only one opportunity to make the leap to a major and its broader marketing muscle, and this was that time for Death Cab.

"Part of it was looking at it historically," the manager says. "Looking at Guided by Voices, Superchunk, Archers of Loaf, and other bands that came before Death Cab, and knowing when that window is open as wide as possible. Bands like Sebadoh and the Faint waited one album too long to do a deal with a major. Modest Mouse hit it right on the mark with [2003 major-label hit] 'Float On' and really started seeing things. So this window opens, and if we really want to try and be an R.E.M., who knows if this window is going to be open after we release our next record?"

Walla, as usual, was philosophical about the split. He was clearly torn about leaving Rosenfeld and Barsuk, a label that he held in high enough esteem to enlist it to release his solo debut album four years later. "But at the time when we signed with Atlantic [in 2004], the

Internet thing was still working itself out," he says. "The Internet was either a revolution or an apocalypse depending on which side of the fence you're on. For us, moving to Atlantic made sense because the revolution isn't complete yet. I think we're halfway through the transformation of the Internet becoming this all-powerful thing that flattens the playing field completely. But at the time we made the deal, retail distribution and physical record sales were still a huge part of how you make money, of how you get your records to the people who want to hear your records. Barsuk was doing the online thing amazingly well. But it seemed like they weren't able to generate demand as much as they were keeping up with demand."

Atlantic became an option because the band was late to the Internet game. Had it been more savvy about online commerce, it might have been in better position to strike out on its own and bypass the majors entirely. But like the record industry, the band was slow to see the advantages of controlling its destiny online. It wasn't until Kurland came aboard as manager that the band even bothered to set up a website, in 2004.

"Even when all that stuff was starting with *The O.C.,* they still didn't have a site," Kurland says. "It was one of the downsides of not having management. They were an independent band, and they just didn't have the time or the manpower."

Harmer picked up the slack within the band, working with Kurland to develop the website and keep it running. But Harmer wasn't an Internet junkie by any stretch. He saw the value of it, but also recognized its limitations, how it could become a distraction from the whole point of being a band.

"I remember hearing about Napster, but I never used it," says Harmer, who was born in 1975. Like his bandmates, he was just old enough to miss the college-dorm peer-to-peer wave. "For me, the exciting part of buying music and liking music is going to a record store and thumbing through the racks and talking to the record store employees. I never really looked at Napster or those kinds of things as a bad or good thing—it was just a different way to find music. And that's the most important thing: don't try to stop it. Figure out a way to work with it, because this is how people want music. I like being able to touch a physical medium, I like to look at artwork—but I wasn't raised in front of a computer screen, either. Kindergarten kids know more about some aspects of the Internet than I do now. Their whole lives are raised in front of a screen and that's how they'll love their music as well. What it comes down to, it's not how you're experiencing the music. It's what's in the music that has to be meaningful. Without an inherent value in the music itself, the whole argument of how you're experiencing it is pointless."

Atlantic let Death Cab make the record the band wanted to make, right down to allowing the quartet to work with its favorite producer: Chris Walla.

"I want blood. I want grit. I'm not a gritty producer, but I want to hear a human being making music, not perfect little chunks of sound with perfectly tuned vocals and the drums precisely lined up. I want to be able to hear the music coming from a human voice or a pair of hands."

Walla had just spent the winter of 2005 hibernating in a recording studio, working twenty-hour days laboring over every sonic detail in what would become his band's major-label debut album, *Plans*. He says he did not step outdoors once during the entire five-week process, walled inside a cocoon of wires, microphones, guitars, keyboards, mixing boards, and music. The technology was far removed from the early days, when it was just him and Gibbard and an eight-track, but the mission was much the same. Sometimes the best thing the engineer/producer could do in recording Gibbard's songs was to simply get out of the way.

Such was the case with the centerpiece of *Plans*, a song called "I Will Follow You into the Dark." It's a stark beauty of a lyric that insists that love can transcend anything, even death. The potentially schmaltzy idea is executed with sublime simplicity: a guitar, a single microphone, and a voice. That's why it works: a quiet, confiding, quintessential Death Cab moment.

"No blinding light or tunnels to gates of white / Just our hands clasped so tight, waiting for the hint of a spark," Gibbard sings with hushed conviction.

As lush and layered as much of *Plans* is, "I Will Follow You into the Dark" is Walla's masterstroke as a producer. It is in many ways a return to those first bedroom recording sessions in Bellingham, just two friends alone with their music.

"We were actually recording another song and the headphones weren't working properly, so it was just him and a guitar during this downtime," Walla says. "I told him to take a break, but he started singing this other song we were working on, just for the heck of it. It was like he was performing for himself. He wasn't performing for a microphone or singing to a piece of glass with a recording engineer behind it. It was totally unconscious, just a song that he would sing to another person on the couch. It was one take, one microphone. About the only thing I had to do was be smart enough to record it."

"I Will Follow You into the Dark" reminded Rosenfeld of that early innocence too. "It revitalized my belief in something," he says. "That song brings a tear to my eyes every time I hear it."

Gibbard wasn't sold on the idea that this off-the-cuff performance could be the definitive take. He wanted something more elaborate, more in keeping with how the rest of *Plans* was shaping up. "I turned in the demo of that song, and it was multitracked with a couple of other vocals and more instruments," he says. "I never felt like I could play well enough or sing well enough to pull that kind of thing off."

But he eventually opted for intimacy over elaboration. It's a language perfect for the Internet era, in which information is silently exchanged by solitary individuals in the privacy of their homes or dorm rooms.

When the music from *Plans* first surfaced on MySpace.com in the summer of 2005, it was played more than four hundred thousand times in the weeks before the album was released. The fan reaction on the band's MySpace message board was more like a sigh. Fans didn't just write blurbs, but awkward poetry:

no other band has ever given me chills like death cab
you make my heart hurt
in a good way
   —Kristie

This devotion crystallized on a mass scale in July 2005. *Plans* was still weeks from release, but Death Cab found itself headlining the Lollapalooza Festival on Chicago's lakefront. The performance demonstrated that the band's intimate music could easily translate to the bigger stage. At the end of a sticky, hot weekend with record one-hundred-degree-plus temperatures, Death Cab's music blew in at dusk like a refreshing Sunday night breeze for thirty-three thousand fans. In previous appearances in Chicago, the band had headlined a twenty-five-hundred-capacity theater and didn't even sell it out. This was a huge leap for the band and its audience, and the mood was one of dumbfounded celebration, as if the fans were saying to one another, "Can there really be this many of us?"

Gibbard and the rhythm section were businesslike and tried to act like professionals. They stuck tenaciously to the bones of the songs. Off in the shadows, Walla and his guitar were dancing with the ghost of U2's master of atmosphere, The Edge. Notes echoed and chimed inside unseen catacombs. There were no big power chords, no look-at-me statements of guitar prowess. But the halo of light thrown up by the nearby skyscrapers gave it all a serene, at times majestic glow.

"I'll always reminisce fondly about the shows in small clubs and basements, and those intimate shows," Gibbard said afterward. "But I'd be lying if I didn't admit that it's thrilling to stand up there in front of that many people and feel like the music's translating."

Death Cab shattered all kinds of expectations in its slow, steady climb to stardom. Their success was a combination of new technology (viral word of mouth) and old-fashioned grind-it-out artist development. Much like Prince, the Replacements, and Bruce Springsteen, Death Cab was several albums deep into its career before a significant audience caught on. When it skipped to a major on its fifth album, the tide of recognition pulled its previous albums along.

After debuting at number four on the *Billboard* pop album chart, *Plans* quickly went on to sell half a million copies, and was approaching 1 million two years after its release. In that time, *Transatlanticism* sold an additional two hundred thousand copies, while sales of the earlier Barsuk albums more than doubled. In the four years since the Postal Service debut, Ben Gibbard had been involved in albums that sold nearly 3 million, all but one of which were on indie labels. On tour through most of 2006, Death Cab pulled in $5.4 million in revenue; an average night's work for the band was $116,000 in revenue—a long way from the $50-a-gig dog days of 1998. One tour with Scottish rockers Franz Ferdinand alone pulled in $3.4 million.

Gibbard is as surprised by the numbers as anyone. "I was talking to a friend of mine at Sub Pop who actually signed the Postal Service, and he had been to see Death Cab in ninety-eight, when he was one of four people in the audience. He said we used to act like 'shoe gazers' onstage. So for us to get this kind of audience after eight years of being a band is kind of mind-blowing. It's not the kind of thing you'd expect from a band that plays the type of music we do."

For Walla, Death Cab's rise was a mix of "bizarre cultural coincidences" (hello, Seth Cohen) and "the golden age of the Internet."

"This is the place we'll be telling our grandchildren about thirty-five years from now," he says. "It's the goddamn Wild West. You can do anything. People keep trying to impose order and telling kids they can't do whatever online, but they're wrong. You can do whatever, and more. If you can dream it, you can do it on the Internet. It's completely lawless and insane. The kids are smart—thank God, for us. They found our music out there in the wilderness and kept us alive as a band. I don't know if we'd be here without them."

The whole marketing machine that was built on top of a song from the 1950s until now wasn't meant to last. It was kinda weird anyway, with the artist getting 3 percent and 23,948,572,093 people in an office with jobs with weird names getting 97 percent. Don't get me wrong, there are a lot of people doing a great job out there, but if you look at the whole picture, it wasn't in balance. I like both songs and albums, and with the Internet you don't have to pick one over the other. If you like both, you can have both. I feel music will always win in the end. People need music. That won't go away.

—Björk, Icelandic avant-pop singer, born 1965

7

Conor Oberst: "He Was Thirteen and Kicking Our Asses"

Mike Mogis grew up in a small town in western Nebraska, where he and his brother, A.J., taught themselves the intricacies of home recording. After a brief, unsatisfying flirtation with college in Arizona, Mogis returned home in 1993 to attend the University of Nebraska in Lincoln, where he didn't know a soul. He was hanging out on campus one day wearing a Mr. Bungle T-shirt when a curly-haired student approached him needing a light. The student's name was Matt Focht, and he and Mogis started talking music.

"I'd see these Omaha kids on campus, all music lovers, and ended up getting involved with this loose group of friends," Mogis says. In addition to Focht, there was Robb Nansel, Ted Stevens, Chris Hughes, Tim Kasher, and a handful of others; all would end up in bands. The oddest member of this musical menagerie was a kid not even old enough to drive, let alone attend college.

"He had slightly longer hair, he was thirteen years old, and he'd come to the campus and play guitar," Mogis says. "He sounded like a kid, but the songs were really intelligent, even then. If any of us were to think about what we were doing at thirteen years old, we'd be embarrassed. This guy was in a different category altogether. I had my first electric guitar and some recording equipment, but I wasn't doing anything near his caliber. People like Ted Stevens, Tim Kasher, and Todd Buckley—these were some strong musical characters. But this kid was not intimidated. He was hanging with us. In fact, he was doing more than just hanging with us. He was kicking our asses."

The ass kicker was Conor Oberst. On campus, he'd stay with Stevens and Nansel in their dorm room, and he already had his first record out: a cassette of low-fi songs recorded by Stevens and released on a custom label, Lumberjack Records.

Born the youngest of three sons to a middle-class family in Omaha, Oberst attended private school and grew up around music. Both his father, who worked in the insurance business, and his oldest brother, Matt, played in rock bands. Once they taught Conor a few chords, he started writing songs. He was all of ten years old when he dashed off the first one.

"I didn't learn scales or Metallica riffs, and I didn't really learn a lot of cover songs either," Oberst says. "I was immediately interested in putting words together and singing. Once I learned two or three chords, writing songs was everything to me. At times it felt like I was writing a song a day."

His brother Matt steered him toward bands that weren't getting commercial radio airplay. "The Pixies had this timeless quality to their songs, where they seemed intensely modern and yet traditional," he says. "It's like they were deconstructing the pop song for you to hear. They were aggressive, angry songs, but they still had memorable hooks. With Fugazi, it's like I got my marching orders listening to them about what a song could say, and what it could do. I can remember being twelve, thirteen, and listening to Fugazi and realizing what they were saying meant something more than just 'la-la-la.'"

Oberst poured some of those ambitions into his first band, Commander Venus, which included a future Who's Who of Omaha music: Kasher, who would go on to front Cursive; Matt Bowen, later of the Faint; and future label owner Nansel.

Another of the Lincoln music mafia, Ted Stevens, collaborated with Mogis in a band called Lullabye for the Working Class. They recorded their first record in Mogis's parents' house in North Platte, Nebraska, then later signed with a small East Coast label, Bar None, to put out their records. But the rest of the fledgling Nebraska bands hit a dead end with their demos. "No one cared, so by default we kept it very close to home," Mogis says. "We liked what we were doing, even if nobody else did."

As a class project in 1993, Mogis and his dorm buddy Nansel put together a business plan for an imaginary record label, Saddle Creek, named after a street cutting through downtown Omaha. "We got an A, by the way," Mogis says. Their professor proved a prescient judge of talent.

Mogis and Nansel took the label out of their entrepreneurship class and into their house, eventually bringing Oberst and his Lumberjack recordings into the fold. Mogis became Saddle Creek's in-house producer when he opened a studio in Lincoln with his brother.

Though the Nebraska bands sounded nothing alike, they shared a certain aesthetic: they set desperate, heart-pounding arguments with fate, God, the world, and themselves to crudely played, slightly overheated music. For these bands, there was no time to waste on halfhearted gestures. Every one of life's disgraces was treated like the end of the world. The musicianship may have sometimes been suspect, but the conviction never was.

"We didn't have any money to get radio play or press, but we had strength in numbers," Mogis says. "We'd sell a few hundred records, then a few thousand. Getting to two thousand was a huge milestone. That enabled us to promote the next releases a bit harder. Lullabye went out there first and booked a tour, and then I'd pass the info on to the Faint, and they'd book their own tour. Everyone contributed to the greater cause. We networked and helped each other."

Among those who benefited was Oberst, who saw Saddle Creek less as a business venture than as an extended family.

"Saddle Creek was our house for a while—it was our friend's apartment, and it felt like home to me," he says. "I didn't think about this at the time, but art needs some sort of organization behind it, whether it's a management company or a record label or just a group of friends. A lot of creative people, left to their own devices, would end up spinning their wheels and not doing anything without that kind of support. Saddle Creek was like having a group of friends and confidants you could rely on as much as people who could manufacture and distribute your records. I don't think you can underestimate the value of that to an artist."

Commander Venus gave Oberst a national platform, but it wasn't a good fit; the band's original label, Grass Records, was bought by Wind Up Records, future home of hard-rock hacks Creed and goth-balladeers Evanescence.

Oberst was still learning on the job as a songwriter, but his solo demos exuded a disarming intimacy with their plaintive melodies and confiding vocals. Mogis wasn't all that impressed with Commander Venus, but once he heard Oberst's acoustic performances, on the Saddle Creek release *A Collection of Songs Written and Recorded 1995–1997*, he was floored.

"When you're ready to record more songs in this style, I'll bring over my gear and we'll do it," Mogis told Oberst. A week later, Oberst was ready to go with five new songs.

The engineer dragged his gear over to the Oberst household, set up in the laundry room, and let the kid roll. The recordings became the basis of *Letting Off the Happiness*, the 1998 album that would turn Saddle Creek into a national entity.

"There wasn't a stringent code to the recording," Mogis said. "The prior record was filled with technical inaccuracies, which is what gave it so much love, for lack of a better word, and I wanted to preserve that casualness, but refine it to the point where it would be more tolerable to the average listener. I wanted to keep it informal, sincere, but yet make sure things are able to be placed in more sonically and musically pleasing areas. My ability to play a variety of instruments in a half-assed manner helped decorate Conor's songs in a new way that he wanted to explore. That started our whole voyage into making songs really grandiose or not."

Mogis and Oberst have been joined at the hip musically ever since in the group Bright Eyes, surrounded by a constantly rotating cast of musicians drawn from their large pool of hometown friends. Bright Eyes tours habitually pile more than a dozen musicians into a bus, and sell out clubs and theaters across the country. No two touring lineups have ever been alike, and Oberst's songs have been fleshed out with everything from string sections to kazoos.

"We don't care about being perfect, it's more important to keep things fresh," says Mogis of the rotating lineups. He applies the same principle when recording Oberst. "A lot of things today are cut and pasted into perfection, but where's the expressiveness? Conor comes from the same school of thought: how to immediately convey a thought or feeling on tape."

Oberst's obsession with immediacy runs pretty deep. He's averse to repeating hooks or choruses, instead preferring to string verses together, sometimes for ten minutes or more. He rarely writes anything down, so that the songs feel new every time he steps to the microphone. He aims to capture that moment when "the whole fog of the day hasn't fully sunk into the brain, that spot between being asleep and being awake." The dreamlike cadences rise and fall between whispers and screams, and the instruments crest and tumble with him.

"My favorite moment is, honestly, still, that moment of conception when I finish a song," he says. "I make this thing out of nothing and I find some kind of value to it. To me, that's what gives my life meaning. It's the thing that makes me want to keep getting up every day."

Oberst's breakout years coincided with the Napster era. His music spread virally, and fans started coming to shows.

"I was aware of Napster coming into existence, not because I'm that computer-savvy—I'm not at all, actually—but because I had a friend that worked there," Oberst says. "It was amazing for my band at the time. The more people that heard the music, the more people started coming to the shows, and the more T-shirts I was able to sell. At that point, the struggle for me was to have anyone hear my music. I had no idea that anyone cared, not that it was going to stop me from writing songs. But Napster was a great tool for getting the music to people. And when they heard it, they came out. It changed everything."

The loose-limbed confessionals and rants on Bright Eyes' 2002 album sometimes sounded as awkward as the title: *Lifted or the Story Is in the Soil, Keep Your Ear to the Ground.* But it cracked the *Billboard* 200 and sold two hundred thousand copies, a remarkable figure for an independent album that received virtually no commercial radio or video airplay.

Pretty soon he was being touted by R.E.M.'s Michael Stipe and Bruce Springsteen, while *Los Angeles Times* critic Robert Hilburn anointed his 2005 album *I'm Wide Awake, It's Morning* "the most absorbing singer-songwriter collection since Bob Dylan's *Time Out of Mind* eight years ago."

Could a backlash be far behind? The *Riverfront Times*, a St. Louis counterculture weekly, named Oberst one of the "ten most hated men in rock": "Who wants to hear sad, sad songs about the day-to-day pathos of well-to-do suburban white kids?" it mocked.

It didn't help that *I'm Wide Awake, It's Morning* was released by Saddle Creek on the same day in January 2005 as another Bright Eyes studio album, *Digital Ash in a Digital Urn.* The records were markedly different in tone and sound, with *Digital Ash* built on electronic rhythms and *Wide Awake* focusing on acoustic songs drawing from the folk and country traditions. But the two-at-once gesture brought some uncomfortable comparisons, as if Bright Eyes were turning into the indie-rock answer to mainstream juggernauts such as Bruce Springsteen and Guns N' Roses, who in the early nineties had released two big-budget albums at once with decidedly mixed results.

The double dip fed the perception that Oberst was a talented but undisciplined artist who kept testing his boundaries at a prolific rate, as if he were racing time to release every lyric, melody, and sound in his head. But just because he could write a song a day, that didn't mean he had to release them all, did it?

Such questions only made Oberst squirm, in part because he knew the hype was just that: hype. Even Oberst knew he had a long way to go before he was writing songs on par with Dylan, despite the claims of respected critics. "I don't know if I ever have written a song that matches my standard for what a great song is," he says. "I have to feel a certain way about a song before I'll release it or perform it, but I never really thought, This is the one! I've got a hit on my hands! It's more like, I need to keep writing more songs and not judge them.

"For me, the songs are never done. They change every time I play them, or sometimes I wear out on them. There is no 'right' version of one of my songs, ever."

Mogis thought it was amusing that Oberst had become such a big deal. Not because he didn't think Oberst was talented, but because the recognition came almost in spite of the singer-songwriter's aversion to it.

"I'm surprised that Conor handles it so well," Mogis says. "He's aware of it. But when it comes to writing songs, he's not affected by it. In the studio he purposely tries to make himself unpopular. A lot of these songs on the *Digital Ash* record, he could have gone with a more traditional route of songwriting or arranging that would have made it easier to promote on MTV, and now would be the time if he ever wanted to get into a more commercial sound. But he wasn't interested. He didn't want to repeat the chorus, he wanted to do another verse instead. He never thinks about that sort of stuff. If someone said repeat the chorus, he'd ask, 'Why?' He goes against what you'd normally do to make a catchy song. It doesn't make sense to him to repeat words. Why say something twice?

"When we did *Lifted,* there was a guy who was going to make a video for 'Lover I Don't Have to Love,' which is probably the catchiest song Conor's written with a repeating hook, and they suggested that he double the chorus at the end, and he just laughed. He goes into this trance, the drums pick up double time, and the chorus just stops. He thought the repetition would've sounded boring and that the song would have lost its fire. The video never came out."

Wide Awake and *Digital Ash* sold a combined 640,000 copies in two years, another Saddle Creek landmark. Mogis, who produced both, saw them as groundbreaking moments, not just for the label but for Bright Eyes.

"Emmylou Harris came in to sing on *Wide Awake* and it was one of those moments where I thought, We're really way beyond anything we imagined here. People actually fucking care! She decided to sing on our record!" he says. "From that moment on, I felt we were entering a new territory of seriousness, where it wasn't just a bunch of kids playing at making records anymore. It's like Conor had become a genuine folk singer-songwriter because we have Emmylou on our record."

Cassadaga followed in 2007. It was only a single-disc release this time, but it was Oberst's most elaborately orchestrated concoction yet. Once noted for their low-fi, off-the-cuff shagginess, Oberst's songs were now swathed in dense, even elegant orchestrations. His quivering vocal histrionics were toned down, even if his lyrics were not. He was still prone to throwing around terms like "Great Satan" and "the whore of Babylon" in critiquing religious wars, media over-kill, and global warming. But Oberst's zealousness also is exactly what connected him to his audience.

In Oberst's world, creativity is the last line of defense, the best tonic there is. He's willing to overreach. The only thing he won't tolerate is not reaching at all.

As he sings on one of his best songs, "Road to Joy": "I could have been a famous singer / If I had someone else's voice / But failures always sounded better / Let's fuck it up, boys / Make some noise!"

Those ambitious, self-deprecating songs got noticed early on by Nate Krenkel, who was in a position to make Oberst a relatively rich man by the standards of most twenty-year-old college dropouts in 2000. Krenkel was a talent scout for the publishing division of Sony and signed Oberst to a deal that year.

"I bought [Bright Eyes'] *Every Day and Every Night* EP based on something I'd read and flew out to Chicago to see him perform in late ninety-nine," Krenkel says. "The publishing deal was a way for him to give his songs some exposure and make some money without losing his independence."

Oberst liked what he heard when he sat down with Krenkel. To stay financially afloat while recording and touring, he had to work day jobs. The publishing deal allowed him to buy a house in Nebraska and focus on music full-time. His parents stopped worrying so much about the son who had dropped out after only three semesters at the University of Nebraska.

The longer-range consequence was that it demonstrated to Oberst that there were more ways to making a living writing and playing music than he had previously realized. "I learned there were a lot of ways to make money with music that don't have to do with record sales," Oberst says. "I wasn't making money on record sales anyway. So the publishing deal kind of turned my career around in a way that enabled me to focus on the one thing I love the most, which is to write songs."

The relationship with Krenkel blossomed into a friendship and eventually a business partnership. Saddle Creek had evolved into a thriving record label, in large measure because Bright Eyes records began selling so well.

Yet Oberst was increasingly frustrated that Saddle Creek couldn't sign more bands that he was enthused about. The label had essentially become a collective, run by its business managers and key bands, but that ideal fostered its own bureaucracy of inertia. "I was frustrated that there were bands that I wanted to work with that Saddle Creek couldn't move quickly on," Oberst says. "Everything was a committee decision. To sign a band, there were about ten of us who had to agree—the people in Bright Eyes, Cursive, the Faint, Robb. All the signings took forever and we missed some opportunities."

At the same time, Krenkel was burning out on a Sony corporate culture ill-prepared for the downloading wave. Krenkel left Sony to manage bands in 2003, the same year the big labels started suing consumers for sharing copyrighted music on the Internet.

"Publishing was separate from the record company, but I didn't like the tone that was setting," Krenkel says. "The attitude was aggressive and hostile, rather than finding ways to work things out. And that was pretty alienating to fans. The assumption that I always thought was wrong was that if someone had twenty thousand songs on their hard drive, that equated to $20,000 in lost sales at retail. Whereas the reality is that I don't think anyone would've gone out and acquired that many songs if it cost that kind of money. The notion that downloading a song equated to a lost sale never made sense to me. After a while, I didn't want to be associated with that kind of behavior."

Oberst relocated to New York, where Krenkel lived. "We had daydreamed about forming our own label for a few years," Oberst says, and they launched Team Love in 2004 with releases from the Omaha folk-pop band Tilly and the Wall and teenage singer-songwriter Willy Mason.

In many ways, it was just another boutique label for a rising star to indulge his creative whims, in part aided by Saddle Creek, which handled distribution. But it was different from many other vanity projects in at least one significant way: the label would make every record it released available for a free, downloadable test run on its website. Fans were under no obligation to buy; they were invited merely to listen.

"We want you to take all the time you need before deciding whether or not to spend your dosh," read a note on the Team Love site. "Call it the Team Love Library."

Oberst was in a position to take a chance. He had built a successful career first on touring and then on a publishing deal. It wasn't until he had been recording and releasing albums for nearly a decade that he started seeing royalty checks from record sales. "I was able to make a living playing music because I found different ways to get my music heard," he says. "No one can buy your record if they don't ever hear it, if they don't know it exists. So when Nate and I talked about a label, we knew that the most important thing was to let people hear the music. And if they like it, we hoped that people would take the next step, which is to buy the record as a way of supporting the artist and enabling the artist to make more music for them to enjoy. We appealed to common sense: if you can afford something you like, you'll buy it because that benefits the person who created that thing you like."

The new label owners were intentionally flipping the major-label script 180 degrees. Instead of threatening consumers with lawsuits for listening to and sharing music, Team Love would encourage it: Go ahead, download all you want. Share the music. Talk up our bands. If people like it, they'll see fit to eventually pay for it.

"The main idea behind the label was first of all to acknowledge that it was futile to pretend that what consumers were doing on the Internet with music wasn't happening," Krenkel says. "We knew that peer-to-peer was enabling people to share lots of music without always buying it, so we might as well put everything on the site and use it as a promotional tool. I mean, here the record companies were aggressively chasing after consumers and we were reading all the stories about all the lawsuits. The whole thing was obnoxious and worth distancing ourselves from."

Four years and twenty-five albums after Team Love's inception, Krenkel says he's even more convinced the major labels got it wrong. The label's biggest coup was releasing the acclaimed 2006 debut solo album, *Rabbit Fur Coat,* by Rilo Kiley singer Jenny Lewis. It sold more than a hundred thousand copies in less than two years. In contrast, one album on the roster sold barely a hundred copies.

"At the time, people were saying to us, 'This is a business plan?' But we haven't been affected negatively by the free downloads," Krenkel said. "The tracks online that are downloaded the most are also the tracks that have sold the most for us. And the ones that have been downloaded the least are also the ones that have been sold the least. Additionally, we sell our music through online avenues— iTunes and Sony—and our percentage of online sales is consistent with any national average: ten to fifteen percent of our sales are from downloads. So it reaffirmed what we thought all along: everyone is freaking out over nothing, and the piracy issue was more of a scapegoat for other ills in the music industry, whatever those may be."

Lewis was surprised by the reception received by *Rabbit Fur Coat*. It was a deeply personal record that she made quickly, built on her vocal harmonies with twin sisters Chandra and Leigh Watson. But it was unlike anything she'd done to that point in her career, rooted in soul and country that transcended California singer-songwriter pop.

Lewis cherishes the experience, though she's not sold on Team Love's business plan.

"I was all for it, but I had mixed feelings," she says. "Music is worth paying for. I really don't think it should be free. You run the risk of lowering the quality if you don't pay for it. But it's their business model, and I went with it, because I trust Conor and Nate. I know that a lot of people probably shared the record and like it, and either they came later to support our live show or maybe they bought the record on vinyl. It turned out to be one of the best musical experiences of my life."

The success of *Rabbit Fur Coat* helped sustain the label, but barely.

"We lose money on a lot of stuff," Krenkel says. "Certainly, we're not doing this for the money. But I think that there is still a need for record labels. The notion of the MySpace, Clap Your Hands Say Yeah phenomenon, where a band bubbles out from the Internet and becomes a hit, is still a long shot. It requires constant refueling, because people burn out awful fast on a song or a band, and then move on. If we had a world where only the number of hits on a website determined popularity, it would be chaotic. Someone's got to say, 'I believe in this, I want to put money into this to market and promote it, and we'll take the risk on it.' It doesn't have to be a lot of money, but there needs to be that sense of believing in an artist and letting that artist develop over the long haul."

Much like Saddle Creek did with Conor Oberst?

"Yeah," Krenkel says with a laugh. "Exactly like that."

———

For Oberst, the label finances were secondary to providing a bridge between music he loved and an audience of attentive listeners. He was too busy making music to be an active part of the MP3 culture, but he fully understood the impulse to share music with friends. As a kid he was trading homemade mix tapes with friends.

"You make a pen pal in some other town and exchange some records and then they set up a show for you," he says. "It was a cool way of networking, much smaller and more archaic than it's done today, but for a kid just learning to play and appreciate music like I was, it was very exciting."

At the time, Oberst didn't realize the full implications of what that sort of cultural exchange would mean in his life. But now fourteen years later, he has a handle on it: "One of the great things about music is how you discover it and share it. It's based on friendships. I think most of the people I care about in the world I somehow met through music. It's just such a powerful force. I think all art is meant to be communicated to other people and it's hard to put a price tag on things like that."

The Napster era made that sort of exchange possible on a far larger and more rapid scale.

"The biggest downside of the whole peer-to-peer thing to me is the evaporation of the mystery," he says. "It seems that when I was first getting into music in high school, buying records and going to the record store, you might read something about the band, or you might see a video or something, but essentially you waited until the band came into town to know what they looked like. It was a little bit more magical. But now all the information's there and you can instantly know everything about someone just by looking them up on Google.

"It's almost too easy, but at the same time, you have the whole world at your fingertips. A lot of bands are discovered that way, especially for some kid in rural Nebraska who just doesn't have a record store in his town and no radio station playing underground music. How incredible is that for them to be able to discover all kinds of music from all over the world right there at their computer? That's kind of beautiful."

But one aspect of Oberst's life as a songwriter and musician remained immutable. He had grown up watching bands like Cursive play in Omaha, and they had changed his life.

"That's the one thing you can't download, you can't re-create even with YouTube," he says. "There's nothing that's going to replace seeing someone up on a stage, singing in the same room you're standing in. That's something people still want and desire, and it's a big part of what we do. There's a song as it exists in my mind when I write it, the words and the melody and what it means to me. And then there's the song as it exists on the tape when we record it. Then there's the song as it exists every time it's played and the way the individual standing there, receiving it, feels about it. That's never the same, it always changes."

Oberst chuckles self-consciously. He's not big on analyzing his music. But he can't resist one last big-picture pronouncement.

"It's really interesting—with all this technology, we've come back to the oldest form of musical communication there is—a person, the troubadour, going from town to town playing songs for people. I don't think that's ever going to go away, you know?"

Getting out and playing is the first step, and the last. I had a live thing going, an audience, before I had a record, or a record label. And I will still have it even if I don't make records anymore. You want international distribution and an office with curtains in the window, but first you have to go out and play. That's never going to change.

—Ani DiFranco, founder of Righteous Babe Records, born 1970

8

"Screw the Record Companies, Screw MTV, Just Go Out and Play"

In the February gloom of Chicago, 2002, Jeff Tweedy was chain-smoking cigarettes in Wilco's loft space on the North Side and singing the praises of Jerry Garcia. Tweedy's band had just come off the most tumultuous year in its history, and not only survived but somehow emerged as media folk heroes for their righteous battle against the Big Bad Wolf of the post-Napster music industry.

Wilco had amped up its Internet profile after making an album, *Yankee Hotel Foxtrot,* that the band's longtime label, Reprise Records, didn't much like. It was a time of massive consolidation in the record business and unprecedented pressure to buff up quarterly profit statements with instant hits (in 2000, Reprise's parent company, Time Warner, was purchased for $164 billion by Internet giant AOL). The adventurous *Yankee Hotel Foxtrot* left key Reprise decision makers unimpressed. Wilco got dropped, but as a parting gift, the band got to keep the album.

In the fall of 2001, Tweedy and his bandmates decided to take matters into their own hands. Instead of waiting around for another label to release the album, the band decided to stream the entire album on its website. No band of Wilco's stature had tried something like that before, essentially turning wilcoworld.net into a radio station that played nothing but Wilco's new album.

This strategy went against a half century of major-label marketing principles. Why would any band "give away" its album? Why would any consumer later want to pay for an album they could listen to for free?

But Wilco had more immediate issues: a fall tour. For Wilco, selling records was only a small part of what a band does. Playing for people was what kept the band alive artistically and financially. So sitting around at home waiting for a label to put their record out just seemed silly.

"The record leaked as soon as we turned it in to Reprise," says Wilco manager Tony Margherita. "So why not put it up on the website instead of freaking about it? It was impossible to control it, so let's give people who want to hear the record a chance to hear it. The fall tour had already been planned, in anticipation of Reprise releasing the record in September. We had a new band lineup, a new vibe, and a new record—except we didn't have a record out. So let's do it ourselves."

Yet no one in the band's camp could have predicted just how popular the log-on-and-listen strategy would become. Traffic to wilcoworld.net quadrupled, to 250,000 visitors a month.

"We were suddenly in over our heads," says Ken Waagner, who runs the band's website. "We were on a $29.95-a-month website, and as soon as we started streaming the album, we got buried. I woke up the next morning to an e-mail from my Web hosting company saying, 'You can't do this.' If you exceeded your allotment of server space you were penalized. At the time, we were allowed ten gigabytes a month, but as soon as the album came online we did fifteen gigs overnight. In 2001, it was $12 for every additional gig. I get up in the morning, and I tell Tony [Margherita], 'We gotta figure out what we're gonna do, because if we keep giving it away, our bill is going to be $4,000 at the end of the first month.'

"It was new territory for us, and for any band, and we were getting tens of thousands of visits a day and hundreds simultaneously. Fortunately, Apple stepped up and hosted the files for us. We knew a guy there who is a fan. And he put the files on his server and hosted them for us. That's the only way were able to do it, and it worked beyond our wildest dreams."

The publicity windfall had labels approaching Wilco about a deal. Within months, Wilco signed a two-album deal with Nonesuch, like Reprise a subsidiary of Warner Bros. Getting the same company to pay for the same record twice was quite a feat. In the next year, *Yankee Hotel Foxtrot* would double the success of any previous Wilco album, surpassing half a million sales.

But on this gray afternoon in 2002, Tweedy wasn't thinking about numbers or websites. The band's sold-out fall tour had been rejuvenating. "It was a rare opportunity to remind ourselves that making CDs is not our only reason to exist," he says. "It reminded us that we're not just a band to make records. We're a band because we like to play together, and feel good about doing it, and have people respond to that in a way that is immediate and unfiltered."

And it reminded Tweedy of the Grateful Dead. The Dead were a template for the Internet-era band, even though the Internet didn't really become a factor until after the Dead's forty-year run ended with guitarist Jerry Garcia's death in 1995. Yet the intensely loyal relationship they developed with their fans through touring and direct marketing anticipated the culture and community fostered by the Net.

"The whole notion of a band existing to make a product once a year or once every two years will go away," Tweedy said. "In some weird way everything will be like the Grateful Dead. They didn't need to make records. They were a real band and they were heard, and became part of people's lives, without making a lot of records. But their music reached everywhere, and now it has a life of its own."

The Dead grew from a hippie lark into a fifty-person, multimillion-dollar enterprise, Grateful Dead Productions Inc., over four decades. Though the band had a reputation as improvisers, both in terms of musicianship and lifestyle, their career was sustained by sound business practice. They treated every show as an event, outfitted with the best sound system in the business. Nearly a year before each touring season, the band and its staff of seasoned campaigners would plot each concert date. Architectural drawings of each concert site were sent to the band's sound man, who then fed them through a computer and designed a sound system specifically for each show with the group's state-of-the-art equipment. Then, a few months before the show, the road crew would meet with promoters and local officials to discuss security, crowd control, and parking.

In the last decade of the band's career, after it had a huge and hugely unexpected hit with "Touch of Grey," its audience exponentially expanded, and the Dead and its well-lubricated road-warrior organization found itself momentarily overwhelmed. But the band quickly adapted to its larger following, and glided into stadiums as if nothing had changed: seven schlubs dressed for a long evening of lounging on the couch, playing an off-the-cuff mix of rock, jazz, country, blues, soul, folk, and bluegrass. The idea that anything could happen, including complete collapse, was embraced. The new generation of fans, increasingly forgiving or simply less discerning than veteran Deadheads, ate it all up.

The band's pace of studio recording slowed to a trickle. In their last seventeen years, the Dead released only four studio albums. Yet the Dead became more popular than ever, while controlling every aspect of their music; Grateful Dead Productions sold concert tickets directly to fans, booked tours, released a steady stream of archival albums, and allowed fans to tape shows with increasingly high-tech recording equipment. These tapes spread through the community of Deadheads worldwide with the band's encouragement, and the Dead became the most obsessively documented ensemble in rock history. Long before Internet file sharing, the Dead were building and broadening their fan base by giving away the intellectual property rights to their music.

Garcia, despite massive health problems that eventually killed him in 1995 at age fifty-three and effectively broke up the band, was the guiding light behind this philosophy. By the early nineties, a new batch of "baby Dead" bands such as Phish, Blues Traveler, and Dave

Matthews had emerged, and each adopted the Dead's laissez-faire attitude toward fan taping.

"They're like us," Garcia said of the new jam bands. "They're following the Grateful Dead tradition of screw the record companies, screw MTV, just go out and play to real humans. And it's working for them. That's the story. If you want to survive in this business, you go out there and pick up your audience, you recruit 'em. That's who you're working for. If you're a performer, that's where it's at. Not playing to a microphone in a studio or a TV screen."

For these bands, Garcia's sole advice was this: it's the process, not the destination, that matters.

"That's one of the reasons why we don't write a set list," he said. "Because when you go out there you want to feel what the situation is like organically, because each place has its own personality, each day has its own personality. And you want to be able to play into the moment. You play it in real time. You don't try to force the experience through some kind of sieve or template. You cut a new template for each moment."

No post-Dead band better exemplified that ethos than Phish. The quartet never had a top 40 hit (one fewer than the Dead) and its music was rarely heard on commercial rock radio. The band members lived in the woods of Vermont, physically and psychologically far removed from industry epicenters such as New York and Los Angeles.

From the start, the band understood that it would not be for everybody. "We were very good at polarizing our audience," said keyboardist Mike Gordon. "It was love us or hate us, but not much indifference."

Like the Dead, Phish favored the type of long instrumental jamming that teetered between transcendence and self-indulgence, and the group's convoluted songs and oddball stage demeanor caused some observers to write them off as a novelty. Here was a band, after all, that was liable to encore with an a capella barbershop quartet version of Lynyrd Skynyrd's "Free Bird" or play guitar solos while jumping on a trampoline.

Yet in 1995–98, they filled the Grateful Dead void with tour revenue of $53 million, and—unlike the Dead—they recorded steadily for a major label, Elektra Records, a subsidiary of Warner Bros. But the record company figured into the band's affairs for only one reason: to distribute albums. The band did everything else for itself.

The Phish organization, based in downtown Burlington, Vermont, had expanded by the late nineties to more than twenty full-time employees and a half dozen corporations that handled everything from merchandising to touring.

"They are their own little company within a company," said Mike DePippa of Elektra's marketing department. "We find we don't need to promote them on a touring level, because their shows always sell out. When we come up with promotional ideas for them, like doing interviews at radio stations, they always turn them down. We basically just put their records out and let them do what they do."

Guitarist Trey Anastasio acknowledges he was never very good at taking orders anyway.

"We don't do much in the way of operating like a traditional band signed to a major label; we're just not interested in making videos or releasing singles or glad-handing radio stations," he says. "Maybe that has something to do with why we're successful. Maybe people are just tired of being spoon-fed trends."

Phish was antitrend from the start. Formed in 1983 when Anastasio, Gordon, and drummer Jon Fishman met at the University of Vermont (keyboardist Page McConnell came aboard in '85), the band was content to work out its music for five years before even attempting to tour outside the Northeast. They forged their sound playing free shows at a club called Nectar's in Burlington, three nights a week, three sets a night.

"That had a big effect on the band, because we could experiment and try anything," Anastasio recalls. "It was so relaxed as opposed to being a band in a premier club in Chicago or New York with just a short set once a month to prove themselves."

That attitude carried through the band's stadium years.

"Living out in the woods in Vermont, I don't even have a computer," Anastasio said in 1998. "I have a wife and two daughters, and I have a lot going on in my life outside of the band, so I can't get caught up in the trends because I don't even know what the trends are."

The band's touring base only got bigger. By the time the band called it quits in 2004, it was pulling in gross revenue of $2.2 million a night. Concerts for a 2009 reunion tour sold out months in advance.

Even as digital distribution threatened to make the CD industry and retail stores obsolete, the most old-fashioned distribution system of them all was in great shape.

David Byrne, founder of the Talking Heads and a successful multimedia artist, testified to that at the 2006 Future of Music conference in Montreal. No artist was more Internet-savvy than Byrne, with his forays into digital music distribution and blogging, but he still made his living on the road.

"Taking music from town to town and playing it for people has been around for centuries," Byrne said. "It was thriving before we were alive, and it will be around long after we're dead. It's an experience that cannot be digitized."

Wilco wasn't a jam band and it wasn't pulling Phish-scale numbers on the road. But by the time *Yankee Hotel Foxtrot* came out in 2002, it was making a comfortable living, with annual tour revenue in the millions. It had developed a loyal following worldwide, and could easily sell out two-thousand-seat theaters in major cities across America. Whenever Tweedy needed a few bucks to cover his monthly costs (a wife, two kids, a mortgage), he'd book a solo show at a local club.

"In all my years making records, I never made money off selling records," Tweedy says. "I knew about touring, and that's what sustained me and the band."

Yankee Hotel Foxtrot broke the mold, because it did sell. Ironically, the more the band tried to give away the music on *Foxtrot*, the more eager fans were to buy it. There were several reasons for this, not the least of which was the romantic aspect of the band's struggle against the Man and their fans' desire to become a part of it, if only by shelling out for a record they could have easily acquired for free on the Net. There was also the novel idea that widespread exposure to worthwhile music was the best advertisement for buying it.

As Jack Rabid, editor of the estimable fanzine the *Big Takeover*, said, "The only bands who have to worry about the Internet cutting into their sales are the people who make lousy albums.

"Even without the better analog sound and fine art of the vinyl era, the main event, thirty to sixty minutes of an artist's full musical expression sequenced carefully as one total body of work, is not the concept that is dying. What's dying is the idea of only the crappiest crap, made with the crappiest intentions, with the crappiest production, to entice the most airtime on the crappiest giant chains of radio stations, bought and paid for by crappy labels, and dictated by some crappy, contemptuous, lowest-common-denominator-projecting programming exec from his crappy polling printouts in some crappy office somewhere, to ensure we all swallow the same crap all over the country at the same crappy time, and then placing that one slice of crap on a longer disc with a bunch of even crappier crap. That is the concept that is dying. Amen."

Yankee Hotel Foxtrot represented the Rabid-endorsed ideal: fifty-two minutes of an artist's full musical expression carefully sequenced. Here was an album that invited closer scrutiny by yielding new secrets with each listen. Its Internet rollout made headlines, but the news would have faded quickly had the music not held up. In the end, Wilco had figured out a smarter way to sell music that demanded more than a few cursory listens to sink in.

"People at the major-label level are so hot on the big score that it's going to be tough for any band like us to crack that," Margherita says. "Unless you've got blockbuster potential, it's not something to even think about. It's hard to sell smart anything in that environment. Look at movies or books or whatever. With some exceptions, it tends to be at best middlebrow stuff that sells. The entertainment businesses are geared toward mass-marketing lowest-common-denominator stuff. It's about creating a lot of impressions quickly for stuff that can be understood quickly. *Yankee Hotel Foxtrot* wasn't that kind of album. The first few times through it, people might've been thrown off because it didn't sound anything like Wilco had done before. But the longer people sat with it, the more it made sense, the better it sounded. In that sense, putting it out on the Internet and letting people live with it for nine months before the record actually came out did the band a huge service."

For Tweedy, the Grateful Dead were inspiring because they spent a career innovating not just their music, but how it would be presented to their fans. "I don't believe art is going to be worth anything over time if the artists don't stick their neck out the way the Dead did and make aesthetic choices to frame their experiences in a creative and innovative way," he says. "Artists who have been successful on major labels are afraid of being put in a situation where nobody wants to pay for their music. Well, then stop making it. Who said you have to make music and people have to pay for it? At one time, no artist was making money off music that way. Eighty years ago, it was sheet music, and composers were subsidized and given grants and supported by patrons of the arts."

The gray afternoon was giving way to dusk and the sinking sun peered through the smudged windows. A metaphor, perhaps, for an industry with an increasingly uncertain future? Tweedy smirked. What's to be scared of?

"Not many generations live through a time when you see a complete paradigm shift. The corporate world is making decisions based on fear because they perceive a hostile environment and they don't know how to deal with it in any other way except to attack it. There is no doubt in my mind that the industry will change profoundly, or become extinct. But an artist's options are infinite, forever. To do it or not to do it? Do you feel strongly enough to do it? But the question has become, 'Commercially, how can they do it? How are they supported to do it?' It becomes about the sea of voices in the Internet, and how can anyone be heard? But who's to say that being one of those voices in that sea isn't meaningful or important?"

Dear Pitchfork . . .

What does a band need to do to get reviewed by you guys? Yes, yes . . . we all know you are the current fantasy . . . the big bull goose on the block . . . the cheese, if you will, right now and for who knows how long. I'm not convinced a bad review hurts a band but we all know what a good one can do. OK. None of this is what concerns me . . . what irks me is that by refusing to review our three albums so far you are suggesting we play NO PART in the mass tapestry that is modern music. Now . . . if you only reviewed acts like, say, Springsteen, I would shrug my shoulders and eschew my lips and move on . . . but we all know you don't. There are thousands of reviews on yr site but none of The High Strung. Really . . . what does a band need to do?

—High Strung singer Josh Malerman, from an open letter posted on the band's MySpace page

9

Everyone's a Critic

Ryan Schreiber doesn't look much like a multimedia mogul. He is shivering in the Chicago winter chill while painstakingly pulling crumpled bills out of his wallet. He scrapes together $5 in hopes of paying for a ride to a nearby rock club.

"Hey, I can actually afford a cab to the Empty Bottle this year," Schreiber says with a grin. "Life is good!"

It is 2005, and the twenty-nine-year-old Schreiber has just emerged into the winter sun from the basement office of his Internet fanzine, *Pitchfork.* In that dim sanctuary, fueled by a steady stream of Dr Pepper, he spends most of his waking hours listening to the day's mail: stacks of CDs from bands hoping to catch his ear and land a coveted 8.0 review or higher on *Pitchfork*'s ten-point scale.

"I'm obsessed by music to a not healthy level," Schreiber acknowledges while sitting at his desk the next day. Dressed in a brown hoodie, flannel shirt, jeans, and white socks, he looks more like the resident music geek in a college dormitory rather than a big-shot publisher. His passion for music precluded his entering college, and is surpassed only by his distaste for authority.

"I had a bunch of crappy jobs working in places like a used-computer store and a record store," he says. "It convinced me pretty quickly that I do not like working for other people. I barely like working for myself."

Like any budding entrepreneur, he saw an opening for *Pitchfork* on the Internet and dove in, unsure of exactly how to write reviews, let alone how to make money out of publishing them, but certain he'd figure something out once he found himself thrashing around in the deep end.

Schreiber nearly drowned several times, as the money ran out and the rent came due. Ever since he started pitchforkmedia.com in his parents' Minneapolis home in 1995, Schreiber had turned the notion of scraping by into an art form.

Yet by 2003 he was making enough to hire a staff, and two years later had two full-time employees besides himself: ad director Chris Kaskie and managing editor Scott Plagenhoef. Kaskie brought in advertising from major corporations, including record labels, gym-shoe manufacturers, and movie studios, and Plagenhoef weeded out some of the excesses in the writing.

By 2005, *Pitchfork* was drawing 120,000 daily readers who came to inspect the site's comprehensive coverage of all things indie rock: five new record reviews a day, extensive interviews with artists, dozens of breaking-news items ranging from the mundane ("Sleater-Kinney Unveil New Web Site, Tour Dates") to the tragic ("Elliott Smith Dead at 34").

That same year, the e-zine would curate the Intonation Festival. It handpicked forty bands to play Union Park in Chicago, a two-day event that would draw thirty thousand fans from around the world. In subsequent years, the concert would morph into the even bigger Pitchfork Music Festival, and three-day attendance would shoot toward fifty thousand.

By 2007, the magazine would double in size; it commanded 240,000 readers a day, its full-time staff would expand to twelve, and its offices would move into a spacious second-floor loft in a rapidly gentrifying Chicago neighborhood. The Internet was brimming with music sites, but none had the reach or influence of *Pitchfork*.

Not bad for a self-described "starstruck kid" who started *Pitchfork* because "I thought it would be really cool to meet the people in bands I liked and talk to them."

To Schreiber, it beat getting a job or going to college.

"I started small, writing about bands like Low and Jack Logan. Jack Logan was my first-ever interview. I had no previous background at all in journalism. I didn't even write reviews for the school paper. But I had opinions, and I just went for it."

In 1995, the Internet was still in its infancy both as a reliable purveyor of information and as a magnet for young readers. If the music audience read about bands, it overwhelmingly turned for guidance to print media rather than the small pool of digital fanzines. The biggest and best of the early Web zines was *Addicted to Noise*, which debuted in late 1994 when a former *Rolling Stone* writer, Michael Goldberg, invested $5,000. *Addicted to Noise* covered a wide range of music that skewed to an older audience, and it was eventually bought out by MTV.

Goldberg's experience was rare for zine writers, most of whom never made enough from self-publishing to pay the rent, let alone attract an investor. Even at its height, *Addicted to Noise* couldn't compete for readers on the same scale as print publications such as *Rolling Stone,* which boasted a circulation topping 1 million. But Goldberg was just one of thousands who saw the Internet as a remarkably direct and inexpensive means of self-publishing. The Internet made it possible for anyone to become a critic, and theoretically find an audience as readily as any of the pros hired by the big print magazines and daily newspapers.

Before the Net, publishing even a relatively established fanzine was like writing songs for a cult band with a tiny but devoted audience. The money was no good, but the people paying attention were hard-core. Fanzines began sprouting after rock journalism's Johnny Appleseed, Paul Williams, first published his do-it-yourself magazine, *Crawdaddy,* in the midsixties. The rise of punk rock and its anyone-can-do-it aesthetic kicked zine writing into a higher gear in the late seventies. Though not able to command the clout or the advertising dollars of professional rock mags, the zines spoke to small, sophisticated, and active audiences—audiences that would buy records, attend concerts, and argue until dawn about music with anyone.

Most fanzine writers didn't have the money or the staying power to continue publishing more than a few issues. But one that stuck it out and flourished was the *Big Takeover*, published biannually since 1980 out of an apartment a few blocks from now-defunct punk mecca CBGB by Jack Rabid, a punk-rock drummer and scene regular. It began with Rabid running off a hundred copies of his one-page newsletter on a library copy machine and evolved into a thick, slickly produced 225-page publication with a glossy cover and an international circulation of twenty-three thousand. Throughout, Rabid maintained an ardent voice in his endless pursuit of "music with heart." Rabid's gaunt, wiry physique and intense gaze said as much. Music wasn't just for teenage kicks. It was life, and he wrote like his depended on it.

"I wasn't a writer for a long time doing this," Rabid says. "It was more like a newsletter: 'Hear ye, hear ye!' I should have been out on the street corner ringing a bell: 'Great bands are coming, great bands are coming!' It's more fun now because I think I'm needed more. It might sound egotistical, but there were more sources when I started that wrote about a lot of the music I liked. But then a lot of those magazines went bye-bye, like *New York Rocker* and *Slash,* and I stopped finding stuff about bands I liked. I stepped into the vacuum and tried my best."

Rabid's wide-ranging taste in music was unusual in the specialized zine world. He offered thoughtful interviews with artists ranging from Bob Mould to the Cocteau Twins, opinion pieces, and hundreds of album and concert reviews in each issue. Unlike many punk-era do-it-yourselfers, he could write eruditely about sixties bands that predated him: the Zombies, Love, the pre-disco Bee Gees. Just as impressive was his dogged persistence.

"The essence of fanzines is here today, gone tomorrow," he says. "Once people realize how much work it is and how much money they're going to lose, they get out after a very short while. I don't discredit those people or laugh at them—maybe I should have done the same thing. Maybe I'm the idiot. The real problem of fanzine culture is that it requires superhuman dedication that most people will not allow themselves. If they have any ulterior motives, doing it will disabuse them quickly. You don't meet girls putting out a magazine, you don't sell many records for bands, you don't get invited to many parties, you don't become cooler. In fact, you become less cool: 'Oh, there goes that guy who puts out that silly fanzine.' You better really love your subject to do this."

Yet during an era when music journalism gravitated increasingly toward facile celebrity profiles, the fanzine community often outdid its mainstream counterparts in monitoring music trends. In the early nineties, *Jersey Beat*'s Jim Testa interviewed the punk band Green Day and produced one of the first in-depth pieces on the marketing of punk to the mainstream. *Stay Free!*—published by Carrie McLaren out of North Carolina—excelled at media-watch pieces, including a scathing dissection of the co-opting of *Option*, the first mainstream magazine devoted to underground rock. And *Beatlefan*, published six times a year since 1978 by Bill and Leslie King out of the basement of their home in Decatur, Georgia, become one of the best sources of news about the Beatles in the world.

Such journalistic integrity wasn't often associated with fanzines, Rabid acknowledges. "The term 'fanzine' implies second-rate, unprofessional, incompetent, and slipshod to a lot of people," says Rabid, who also writes about rock for a number of mainstream publications. "But almost all of the best writing that I've ever read about rock 'n' roll was in magazines like *Slash* that weren't trying to be like *Rolling Stone* or any commercial magazine of the time. They were putting bands like the Screamers and the Weirdos on their cover, whereas the journalists with a mass audience were often waiting for the great music to come to them, waiting for some publicist to bring it to them."

Fanzines such as *Slash, Flipside, Maximum RocknRoll, Matter,* and *Forced Exposure* helped introduce a generation to music that wasn't heard on commercial radio, seen on MTV, or written about in *Rolling Stone*. They were a crucial link in the underground chain of clubs, record stores, college radio stations, and independent labels that coalesced around bands like the Bad Brains, Black Flag, Big

Black, Naked Raygun, Hüsker Dü, Mission of Burma, the Feelies, and the Minutemen.

What these zines didn't have was reach. At best they could speak to a few thousand people every few months, and only after covering printing and mailing costs. Rabid was spending $60,000 an issue by 2007 to put out a single print issue of the *Big Takeover*. But the Internet instantly gave anyone with a desire to write passionately and persuasively about indie rock a potential audience of millions, at virtually no cost.

"I was at the point where I wanted to quit when the Internet came along," Rabid says. "I was breaking even, but I had been doing it for fourteen years, my band [Springhouse] broke up, and it was time to get a real job. I was pretty dead set on becoming a history teacher. Then the Internet and e-mail changed everything. Suddenly I could effectively market to people who didn't know I existed; the Web page served as a store where people could sample the magazine and instantly order it. People could Google their favorite unsung band and find that I'd written one of three articles on them, and that would lead them to the magazine. I quadrupled my circulation between 1994 and 2004 because of that."

In that same decade, Ryan Schreiber rode the Internet even further by skipping the print side altogether. "I loved reading print fanzines—they were cool to read, cool to look at, and they covered a lot of bands I liked," he says. "But at the same time, their distribution was limited and there was a lot of overhead to cover. I didn't have any money, so it was a case of publish on the Internet or don't publish at all."

He emulated the cheap-shot vigor of the British music press as he championed his favorites while goring mainstream bands and sacred cows. He set up a ten-point scale to rate records, a geekier version of the five-star guide in *Rolling Stone* or the thumbs-up/thumbs-down approach of nationally renowned movie critics Gene Siskel and Roger Ebert. In reviewing Stone Temple Pilots' 1996 release *Tiny Music . . . Songs from the Vatican Gift Shop,* Schreiber let the bile overflow in a 0.8 review, in which he described singer Scott Weiland as "a drug-addled sonofabitch that should have OD'ed a long time ago."

"I gravitated toward pranksterism and snarkiness," Schreiber acknowledges, "because I had no writing ability at all."

But he had persistence, and he kept even his most embarrassing writing and misguided critiques available in an archive that had grown to seven thousand reviews after a decade. *Pitchfork* let it all hang out—the good, the bad, the inexcusable—and fans trolling the Web for information on their favorite indie bands inevitably stumbled upon Schreiber's e-zine.

"Nobody had faith in what I wanted to do, including my parents, and I don't blame them," Schreiber says. "They were pissed at the phone bills I was racking up calling record labels in New York, trying to get promos sent. But I always had an absurd amount of confidence in myself."

Schreiber tried to move his operation from Minneapolis to Chicago in 1999, but failed miserably. "I saved $2,000 to make the move, and it turned into the worst year of my life," he says. Broke, he moved back to Minnesota in 2000, staying rent-free in a summer cabin owned by his parents. There he recharged himself and replenished his bank account. He moved back to Chicago in October, determined to make it work.

That month, Radiohead's *Kid A* was released, and it proved a turning point both for the band and the e-zine. The album represented a significant departure from the band's guitar-oriented sound in favor of eerie, keyboard-soaked atmosphere. It was a bold, controversial move, the three-years-in-the-making follow-up to one of the biggest albums of the nineties, *OK Computer.* Its arrival coincided with the coming of age of Napster and the Internet as a tool for distributing and discussing music.

The *Pitchfork* review, written by one of the site's most audacious and talented contributors, Brent DiCrescenzo, was a 1,200-word rave peppered with overreaching assertions ("completely obliterates how albums . . . will be considered") and mind-numbing similes ("sounds like a clouded brain trying to recall an alien abduction"; "like witnessing the stillborn birth of a child while simultaneously having the opportunity to see her play in the afterlife on Imax"). Even if few people could actually understand the review itself, the 10.0 rating spoke volumes to Radiohead's worldwide fan base.

"It was a watershed moment for us," Schreiber says. "We got linked from all the Radiohead fan sites, which were really big. We got this huge flood of traffic, like five thousand people in a day checking out that one review. We had never seen anything like that. Web boards were talking about our review."

Schreiber had begun to farm out the reviews instead of writing them all himself. He hired fans as obsessive as he was, and he prized attitude. "I felt we were an outlet for really creative writing," he says. "We were radical in how far we let our critics go to say what they wanted to say. My ideas of criticism were very open-ended, and still are. I hadn't read [rock critics] Richard Meltzer, Lester Bangs, Simon Reynolds, Robert Christgau, or anybody. So there were no rules as far as I was concerned."

Johnny Rotten might've said something similar in 1976 about not listening to the Beatles and Rolling Stones and meant it as a darkly humorous provocation. But Schreiber was dead earnest, and his tone was just right for 2000. The disregard for context and the "no rules" pose made the Internet what it was that year, and Radiohead's bold challenge to rock convention made for a perfect, if completely unintended, convergence.

The *Pitchfork* review, timed to the day of the album's release, provided instant satisfaction to Radiohead fans craving info about their band. In contrast, reviews in print fanzines trickled out; some didn't appear until weeks after the album had been released. The bimonthly *Rolling Stone,* with its four-and-a-half-star lead review, might have carried more weight with more readers, but it didn't feel nearly as immediate.

"It was a huge advantage being on the Net, being able to weigh in instantly on an important album to people who grew up on their computers," Schreiber says. "By the time a publishing cycle happens now, the Internet is already done with the story."

The best of the print media could still bring levelheaded professionalism, erudite writing, and historical context to the party. But those values began losing out to timeliness and convenience, factors that were paramount to a generation of music fans who were used to getting what they wanted instantly.

In addition, *Pitchfork* didn't pretend to be comprehensive in its coverage of popular music like the bigger print magazines. It focused primarily in its first decade on left-of-center guitar-based rock: indie, alternative, cutting edge, or a little bit of all three. That niche focused its readership and turned the e-zine into a tastemaker that could influence sales of that style of music, up or down.

"*Pitchfork* has cornered the market as far as being a destination for people looking for a certain kind of music information," said Martin Hall, at the time an executive with North Carolina indie label Merge Records. "Their audience is the college-age consumer, people sitting at their computers most of the day, people eighteen to thirty. That's the demographic you want to get if you're selling records or selling widgets."

A 9.7 review in *Pitchfork* of the Arcade Fire's *Funeral,* released in 2004 on Merge, was the first major demonstration of the e-zine's commercial clout. Arcade Fire was a new band, virtually unknown outside of Montreal, and *Funeral* was its first full-length album. Yet stores across the country sold out of the record within days of the review appearing. It opened the door for the fastest-selling album in Merge's history. The effect was not coincidental.

"I'm not a fan of their writing, which I think is snotty and terrible," said Steve Sowley, the twenty-seven-year-old product manager for the two Reckless Records stores in Chicago when Arcade Fire hit. "But they have an unshakable control over the indie-music scene. If they rate an album an 8.5 or above and you're an indie store, you'd best be ready to stock a lot of those albums.

"Two, three years ago *Pitchfork* did not have this kind of pull, but during this last year, it's 'Boom!' Now they have a lot of say. *Spin* can put people on their cover, but it won't sell the way a *Pitchfork*-endorsed band sells."

Anand Wilder, whose band Yeasayer was endorsed by *Pitchfork* in 2007, says the website's clout is "kind of scary."

"They can make or break bands. I was just in this small record store and I was asking the guy working there why a record I was looking for wasn't in the store. And he said, 'I can't stock records unless they have the trifecta of a good NPR review, a good *New York Times* review, and a good *Pitchfork* review.' Otherwise it's not worth it for him to stock it because no one will buy it."

That formula sounds a little too pat, almost absurd. But Josh Rosenfeld of Barsuk Records sees some truth in it. He says one Texas record store initially refused to stock Travis Morrison's 2004 Barsuk release, *Travistan*, because it received a 0.0 review from *Pitchfork*. Morrison was the singer in a well-respected indie band, the Dismemberment Plan, that had been reviewed favorably by *Pitchfork* in the past.

"The review cast a pall over the record and actually predisposed people to not even listen to it," Rosenfeld says. "There is a tipping-point effect where if consumers are not influenced by *Pitchfork* directly, there are influential people who are themselves influenced by *Pitchfork*, and that has a cumulative effect. In the case of Travis's record, there were a lot of reviews that mentioned the *Pitchfork* review. It had this very meta feeling about it, a review of the record that was really a review of a review about the record. It leads me to believe that *Pitchfork* is at the center of some kind of system of pop-music criticism that has a practical impact on sales. A *Rolling Stone* review doesn't necessarily sell a single record for us. But with *Pitchfork*, you get a review and you can see the impact on sales, for better or worse."

Rabid admired *Pitchfork* for building an audience from the grass roots. But he was more concerned about what *Pitchfork*'s powerful sway over indie-rock commerce said about its readership.

"If people are driven to one place and only that one place, then that place becomes not only the start, but the end," Rabid says. "A friend of mine taught a series of college classes about dramatic litera-ture and he actually despised Frank Rich, who was the theater critic for *The New York Times* at the time. Not because he disagreed with Frank Rich or thought he was particularly wrong about anything, it just pissed him off that one guy could open or close a show. A show could be perfectly fine, but if Frank Rich didn't like it, it failed. And another show, it might be mediocre, but if Frank Rich took a shine to it, it might be on Broadway for a year.

"The whole idea is that you want a diversity of opinion and thought and exposure. So when the eight-hundred-pound gorilla comes in and completely devours everything else, it's not healthy. That's why people don't like megachains. It's kind of funny to think of *Pitchfork* as having the same effect, to think of them as being like Wal-Mart or Home Depot coming to your town at the expense of having a diversity of greengrocers and butchers and hardware stores. But a lot of people are lazy and tend to go to one or two places for their news, and then all the power gets invested in those one or two places and they become trend makers. [Weekly music magazine] *NME* was like that for a while in England—they would open and close band's careers in the eighties and nineties. It was ridiculous. And *Pitchfork* became that in the last few years for a certain kind of rock music."

Yeasayer's Wilder concurs. "They've acquired that kind of Clement Greenberg status," he says, referring to the influential art critic dubbed one of the "kings of cultureburg" by writer Tom Wolfe. "I feel the next step for *Pitchfork* is literally dictating to bands what to do next. 'OK, can you just paint a little more green on that album before you release it? Then we'll give it an 8.5.'"

There's usually not a lot of money to be paid in music criticism, but *Pitchfork*'s revenue leaped 70 percent each year from 2004, to an estimated $5 million annually. This at a time when print publications such as *Punk Planet* and *No Depression* were going out of business, and *Rolling Stone* and *Blender* were experiencing double-digit declines in advertising.

Their kingmaker status was publicly confirmed in the summer of 2007 when *Pitchfork* threw its biggest party yet: a sold-out three-day festival in Union Park on the West Side of Chicago. It drew forty-eight thousand people from fifty states and five continents to see thirty-nine bands. The price was among the bargains of the summer: $50 for a three-day pass.

Sometimes it came off amateurishly; the sound system rented for opening night was so inadequate it had to be removed and replaced by new gear trucked in overnight. But the vibe stood in stark contrast to glitzier summer festivals such as Coachella and Lollapalooza, which were three times as expensive and overrun by corporate signage. While the promoters of those bigger festivals mingled with celebrities backstage and trolled the grounds in golf carts, Ryan Schreiber ran between stages clutching a digital camera, photographing his favorites. The editor in chief may have become one of the more powerful Internet tastemakers, but on this weekend he looked very much like that wide-eyed teen who saw *Pitchfork* as his route to meeting a few bands he admired.

Amid the festival's undeniable success, a serious, grown-up question couldn't be avoided: Can a publication purporting to comment on and critique indie-rock bands maintain its integrity while booking many of those same bands for its annual festival? In April 2008, *Pitchfork* went a step further by launching pitchfork.tv, "the first-ever music video channel dedicated to documenting independent music as it happens." It would air concert footage, video, and movies, again blurring the line between "documenting" bands and exploiting them for profit. Among the first bands featured was Radiohead, with an exclusive live performance from its practice space in England.

Schreiber insists that he's well aware of such ethical trapdoors. "Our integrity is everything," he says. "If we come off as dishonest in a review of a band just because we book them at our festival, it would be immediately apparent. That won't happen."

That remains to be seen. But that *Pitchfork* must now confront such issues affirms the e-zines evolution from bedroom lark to multimedia empire. *Pitchfork* now has a reputation to protect, something that couldn't have been imagined only a few years ago.

———

Pitchfork was certainly the loudest voice on the Net when it came to music journalism, but it certainly wasn't the only one. Hundreds of e-zines and blogs began to shape the dialogue about underground music in the years immediately following the rise of Napster and peer-to-peer file sharing. Audio blogs not only talked up new bands but allowed readers to hear them by posting MP3 files. These sites were instrumental in building an audience for electro-pop producers Junior Boys, Sri Lankan rapper M.I.A., and the Nordic pop singer Annie, among others.

"When I started, we had no competition," Schreiber says. "People would surf the Web for Fugazi, and we'd be one of the few results. Now it seems like everyone has a blog. Starting a website like this is a huge endeavor, and there isn't a lot of quick payoff. If I were starting over, I'd certainly start a blog instead of a Web zine."

By 2007, more than 25 million blogs covering a range of topics were in operation. The Hype Machine, a website devoted to chronicling MP3 blog activity, listed more than eighteen hundred blogs covering music in 2008. No music was too obscure; each genre had its go-to site, from African pop (bennloxo.com) to Polish jazz (polish jazz.com).

This was a boon for indie labels trying to reach a specific audience. "Traditional places for advertising and marketing have shrunk for a label of our size," says Merge cofounder Mac MacCaughan. "In the early nineties, we were getting videos played on MTV specialty programs like *120 Minutes* once or twice and getting some coverage in traditional print media. But the column inches are growing less and less for the type of [underground] music we work with. We're getting priced out and inched out by bigger labels. So blogs, Internet forums, and our own website are having a democratizing effect. It's more niche-driven, but it gives people in our niche a place to go to find out about it."

One of the more respected voices in the morass of Internet bloggers was Matthew Perpetua, an indie-pop fanatic who began running fluxblog.org in 2002 out of his parents' home in Cold Spring, New York, after graduating from the Parsons School of Design. He was among the first bloggers to make MP3 files available on his site so that his readers could hear for themselves the music he championed, an innovation made possible by the wider availability of broadband cable service and faster Internet connections.

"A lot of the stuff I post is in this big gray area legally, but I only post stuff I love and I've never had a cease and desist [order from a record label or artist manager]," Perpetua says. "The overwhelming majority of people are positive about it, because of the ripple effect something like this creates: fans start talking about music, and artists can get record deals because of a song being heard by the right people on the Internet."

By 2007, Perpetua's site was drawing two hundred thousand visitors a month, up from fifteen thousand in 2005. Yet he was still not accepting advertising.

"I'm very paranoid, because I don't clear [licensing for] all the music I make available," he says. "It's totally implied permission. I'm paranoid about being sued by someone who could take ad money from my work. I'd rather make money in ways other than the blog. The safest route for me is not to profit from the blog ever."

Though some bloggers were peppered with cease-and-desist orders for posting unauthorized files, most received a tacit nod of approval from label executives, who saw them as an outlet for building word-of-mouth buzz about unknown bands. In 2004, a Warner Bros. executive sent an e-mail to several bloggers with an MP3 file attached.

"We are very interested in blogs and I was wondering if you could post this mp3," the e-mail read. "It's by one of our new bands—The Secret Machines. They are an indie rock band and we would love for people to hear the band's music from your site. Here it is, listen to it and let me know if you will post it. Thanks!!"

The e-mail was part of an ambitious viral campaign at Warner to break Secret Machines, a space-rock trio from Texas. But most bloggers ignored the request, including Perpetua, fearing even the appearance of looking like they'd been spoon-fed by a big label.

The charm of the audio blogs was their sense of unfettered independence: music fanatics turning on other passionate listeners with their "You have to hear this!" enthusiasm.

The most respected bloggers waded through dozens of mediocre MP3 files before hitting on a track worthy of their enthusiasm. Perpetua says he posts less than 10 percent of the music he evaluates each week.

As Schreiber says, "Everybody loves to listen to great music, but not a lot of people want to listen to a lot of music they don't like to get to the good stuff. That's why there's a place for blogs and e-zines in people's lives."

"The great thing about an MP3 blog is that it not only replaces the friend who tips you to all kinds of cool music, it replaces the friend who actually lends you the music to hear," says Nathan Brackett, a senior editor at *Rolling Stone*. "It's instant gratification: You get a tip on music, and then you have it to hear."

Perpetua and other MP3 bloggers focus on the great song, not the album. "Even a lousy album can have one great song," Perpetua says. "That's what interests me."

In that respect, the bloggers played a key role in bringing the single back to prominence, after three decades of dominance by the full-length album. In 2007, digital tracks were the primary form of Internet commerce, outselling digital albums 581 million to 50 million (though the price of albums was ten times higher and generated nearly as much revenue).

"When you have all these options to listen to music any way you choose, it changes everything," Perpetua says. "I seldom listen to complete albums in their intended order. I listen to custom mixes I make of an artist's catalog. Digital technology is a beautiful thing because you can program a CD any way you want. You don't have to sit through songs you don't like. If the music industry had understood that sooner, they wouldn't be in the trouble they're in now."

———

The avalanche of Internet media raised an unavoidable question for the bands swept along and then sometimes buried by it: too much too soon? Blogs, e-zines, and file sharers weren't just spreading the word about bands, they were competing to be first. For decades, underground bands were able to develop a sound and an aesthetic over several years in relative obscurity. Word was spread by a few sporadically published fanzines, a dash of airplay here and there on college radio stations, and the enthusiasm of dedicated concertgoers who found out about the band's gig from a flyer on a lamppost. Unless a great band had a big-label marketing campaign behind it, it wasn't unusual for it to go three or four albums before anyone above the underground noticed, as Hüsker Dü, the Replacements, and the Minutemen could attest.

The Internet compressed that years-long growth curve to a few months or even weeks. It led to countless bands being championed for a handful of promising songs before they even had an album out. Debut albums were lauded to ridiculous extremes, and follow-ups torpedoed. In some ways, the discourse on indie rock had become as fickle and fad-obsessed as that surrounding the most facile teen pop.

Pitchfork helped launch an Internet feeding frenzy for the East Coast band Clap Your Hands Say Yeah with a 2005 rave review of its self-titled debut. The critique praised the album but reserved its most enthusiastic praise for how the album was released:

> There's something really refreshing about stumbling across a great band that's trembling on the cusp without any sort of press campaign or other built-in mythology—you actually get to hear the music with your own ears. While a lot of bands view the promotional apparatus as a necessary evil, Clap Your Hands Say Yeah prove that it's still possible for a band to get heard, given enough talent and perseverance, without a PR agency or a label. Indie rock has received a much-needed kick in the pants, and we have the rare

chance to decide what a band sounds like of our own accord before any agency cooks up and disseminates an opinion for us. Damn, maybe this is how it's supposed to work!

Certainly, Clap Your Hands' business model held romantic appeal to any journalist looking for a good story. They went into collective hock for $8,000 in studio costs while piecing together their first record. The band did everything itself, from artwork to bicycling packages of CDs to the post office each day to fill orders from its website. The band's self-distributed album ended up selling four hundred thousand copies worldwide within eighteen months. And no, the music wasn't bad. At its best, it delivered a dizzy rush of jingle-jangle guitars and lovesick vocals.

But live, the band was underwhelming. Within a year, Internet-fueled demand had the band easily filling two-thousand-capacity theaters, but the band wasn't ready to make the leap from intimate clubs.

Clap Your Hands's second album, *Some Loud Thunder,* was released in 2007. It too was self-released, but this time the story had lost its novelty and so reviewers were left to deal with the music, which sounded as quirky as that on the first album and even boosted an inviting disco-rock single, "Satan Said Dance." But Internet gate-keepers had already moved on.

"Online opinion is like a magnifying glass in sunlight: Whatever it admires too closely for too long is enlarged, then incinerated," *Pitchfork* pronounced in its lukewarm *Some Loud Thunder* review, without acknowledging that the e-zine was the biggest magnifying glass of them all. "There was truth in the emerging narrative, but it reflected longing more than reality; the band's story became the stuff of myth, and myths beg to be debunked."

The same fate befell countless bands that were overpraised before their first records even came out, then found themselves old news by the time they got around to releasing a follow-up: Tapes 'n Tapes, Franz Ferdinand, the Arctic Monkeys. In 2008, it was Vampire Weekend's turn. Folding African and Caribbean accents inside breezy new-wave arrangements, the Brooklyn quartet became Internet darlings nearly a year before their self-titled debut would be released.

By the time it was, a full-scale backlash was already in motion. In the same month that a *Spin* magazine cover story proclaimed Vampire Weekend "the year's best new band . . . so far" (it was, after all, only the March issue), media pundits were ripping the band for its upbringing (privileged white guys ripping off black culture!), its fashion sense (polo shirts, Dockers, and sweaters tied around their necks!), and its cleverly innocuous lyrics ("Walk to class / In front of ya / Spilled kefir / On your keffiyah"). *Spin*'s article was as much about the surrounding hype, and how the quartet was coping with it, as it was about the music that inspired it. It included a timeline of the band's precareer career: the two years preceding the release of its self-titled debut.

Another 2008 hype, the coed, biracial Florida quintet Black Kids, saw its critical fortunes ascend and collapse within a span of eight months. In October 2007, *Pitchfork* praised the band's four-song *Wizard of Ahhhs* EP, available free on its MySpace site. "They're giving away something we can't buy often enough: a record with not just a distinctive aesthetic, but also one single-worthy track after another," *Pitchfork* gushed.

The e-zine published twenty more articles on the band in subsequent months, tracing its every move ("Black Kids Cover Sophie B. Hawkins on Single," "Black Kids Add Dates," "Black Kids . . . Reveal LP Details"). But when the band's debut album, *Partie Traumatic*, was released in July 2008, the e-zine executed a 180-degree turn. In place of a review, it posted a photograph of two forlorn-looking pugs, a 3.3 ranking, and one word: "Sorry."

The band's music was lightweight and derivative, a tongue-in-cheek rewiring of Brit pop and new wave, but not vapid. It hadn't gotten suddenly worse in eight months; indeed, the key songs on the much-praised EP were rerecorded and buffed up for the album. So what happened? The band's rickety live performances didn't help. If nothing else, *Pitchfork* was reflecting the fickleness and impatience of its own readership.

"The Internet shines a huge spotlight on bands before they're ready for that huge spotlight," says Jordan Kurland, who manages Death Cab for Cutie and Feist. "You make a good record and all of a sudden *Pitchfork* gives you an 8.5 and all these people are coming to your shows before you're ready to play live. Clap Your Hands is indisputably a terrible live band, and it hurt them because they were playing two-thousand-seat rooms very soon after their first record came out. They never had the opportunity to develop the sound onstage.

"Whether you're a manager, or a label, or a journalist, you're always wanting to find the next thing before anybody else. That's the fix. That's my fix, too, being a big music fan. Now you run into this phenomenon with people propping things up that shouldn't be propped up quite so soon. It's the same thing being a promoter. You want to build these relationships with bands and it may be before they're ready. There is that lost art to it. I don't know how that returns. It is a society of instant gratification now, and bands are built up and torn down before they've had a chance to create a body of work that represents who they are or what they can do."

"It's sickening how little I've actually spent on music. I've probably spent $1,000—that's on the high side—on hard drives since I started doing this. And now I have maybe seventy thousand MP3 files on my hard drive. . . . I've bought four CDs since 1998. I would like to spend more money on bands that I like, but if I were to start picking and choosing who I paid money to, I wouldn't know where to start. I feel that I may be doing a band more good by telling every single person I know that 'this band is good' and giving out their music. For growing bands, the general support, the growth, is better than individual album sales."

So you're a musical ambassador? "I'd like to think so. I wear a pompadour sometimes."

—David, Chicago architect, born 1980

10

Arcade Fire: Chocolate Fountains Everywhere

In the first few weeks of 2005, *Pitchfork* editor Ryan Schreiber interviewed Arcade Fire founder Win Butler. It wasn't quite the Jann Wenner–John Lennon summit of 1970, when the *Rolling Stone* publisher interviewed the former Beatle about life, art, and starting over after walking away from the world's biggest rock band. But for a new generation of music fans who read pitchforkmedia.com obsessively, and who had adopted Arcade Fire's debut album, *Funeral,* as its new obsession, it might as well have been.

Butler had founded Arcade Fire a few years earlier, and the band's debut album came out in September 2004 on Merge Records, a North Carolina independent label that had never had a gold-album artist. Less than five months later, Arcade Fire was the most talked-about band in indie rock, and winning mainstream-press accolades. A large reason for that sudden rise was Schreiber's e-zine. By the time *Funeral* was released, the Minnesotan had turned pitchfork media.com into the go-to site for indie-music reviews. *Pitchfork's* over-the-top rave for *Funeral* in September 2004 had helped kick-start the cycle of hype that would include a hundred articles about the band in the e-zine over the next three years.

"Their search for salvation in the midst of real chaos is ours; their eventual catharsis is part of our continual enlightenment," read *Pitchfork's* review, its preacher-on-the-pulpit tone a perfect match for the quivering sincerity of Butler's songs. Here was an album "at last

capable of completely and successfully restoring the tair
'emotional' to its true origin." It scored a 9.7 on *Pitchfork's*
scale, one of the highest-rated albums ever in the e-zine's ...ory. It
was a galvanizing moment not just for the band but for the website.

An avalanche of media—from blogs with dozens of readers to
print publications (*New York Times, Los Angeles Times, Rolling
Stone*) with millions—poured down on Arcade Fire. Many of these
articles name-checked not only the band but the basement e-zine
from Chicago that had primed the pump for its arrival.

Five months after its release, *Funeral* was the fastest-selling album
in the fifteen-year history of Merge Records, already topping one
hundred thousand sales. A prime slot at the Coachella Music Festival
in California was just weeks away when Schreiber and Butler coyly
celebrated their newfound notoriety.

"It's pretty weird that we keep getting tied together in the press,"
Schreiber said as the interview got rolling with Win Butler, the band's
primary vocalist and songwriter. "Like, a lot of the features I've read
on the Arcade Fire mention *Pitchfork* and vice versa."

Butler: "They could be asking you a lot of the same questions
you could be asking me: 'How does it feel?' 'How's the hype?' 'Is it
weird to be mentioned in *The New York Times* and the *L.A. Times*?'
I'm like, 'No, how's that feel?'"

Schreiber: "It's really funny. It's like we can't exist independently
in the press. I mean, are you as sick of that as we are?"

It was a loaded question, one that Butler danced around. But the
singer also knew the band was getting places more quickly than he
ever could have imagined because of all the *Pitchfork*-led Internet
cheerleading.

Less than a year earlier, Arcade Fire was struggling to find an
audience outside Montreal. The band was good enough that, over
time, it likely would have found a sizable audience through steady
touring. But Internet word of mouth compressed the Arcade Fire
growth curve from a few years to a few weeks. The band's rapid rise
stood in sharp contrast to the career trajectory of virtually every
other release in Merge's fifteen-year history.

Before *Funeral,* one of the biggest-selling releases in the Merge catalog was Neutral Milk Hotel's second album, *In the Aeroplane over the Sea,* which came out in 1998. The album ranks with the best of the nineties, a series of rough-hewn but irresistibly melodic songs sung by Jeff Mangum in a delirious warble.

The album eventually topped 150,000 sales, to rank among the label's top sellers—after eight years. Arcade Fire topped that total within a few months. A year after its release, *Funeral* had more than tripled it.

"I don't think Arcade Fire's success could've happened ten years ago, or even five years ago," says Death Cab manager Jordan Kurland. "It's not like people didn't want to hear good music five years ago, they just didn't know it was out there. They were getting spoon-fed music by corporations, and if it wasn't played on commercial radio or MTV or written about in *Rolling Stone,* it took some effort to find it. And now you have a world where people are turning their friends on to music on a mass scale, with the click of a couple of buttons. The Internet media has obviously been a huge part of that. I think that, yeah, I often think Neutral Milk Hotel would have had Arcade Fire–like success had their second record come out now. Or even two years ago."

Death Cab bassist Nick Harmer speculates that it would've been a much different, much slower trajectory for Arcade Fire had the band started playing and recording in the same era Death Cab did, circa 1997.

"In some ways, it might've been even harder for them because they're in Canada," he says. "The international barriers that fell with the Internet are incredible. Just the fact that now I can download a Swedish techno album in my bedroom, whereas a decade ago it might've taken me months to track it down at an independent record store, if at all. Being from Canada in 1997, a band like Arcade Fire would've been able to maybe tour in Canada and do some things, and then it would have splashed down to the States here and there, but it would have never had that all-systems-go push globally, where it happened simultaneously for them in the States and in Canada and in the UK and everywhere. Could they have even licensed their record in all those parts of the world right away in 1997? With the Internet, that question became irrelevant. The music went everywhere to everyone right away, and so did the band."

Win Butler and his younger brother, Will, grew up outside Houston during the eighties, when MTV was just starting to flex its muscle. Music was a part of their lives from an early age; their mother, Liza, played harp and their grandfather Alvino Rey was a pedal-steel pioneer and big-band leader who was something of a minor legend in exotica music circles. He played on countless recordings, served as a sideman for Esquivel and Elvis Presley, and costarred with his wife, Luise King, and daughter Liza on *The King Family Show,* a network variety hour in the sixties.

Win played trumpet, Will clarinet, and the siblings formed bands as teenagers, with Win calling the shots and Will filling in on whatever instrument was available. The Butlers' music was informed by the usual eighties and nineties alternative-rock heroes: the Pixies, Radiohead, the Smiths, the Cure. The six-foot-five-inch Win enrolled in a New Hampshire boarding school, where he played basketball and formed a cover band, and in 2000 moved to Montreal to study religion at McGill University.

There he met his future wife, Régine Chassagne, four years his senior, singing jazz at an art opening with a certain dramatic panache that instantly stamped her as a future soul mate. The Haitian-born Chassagne also played recorder in a pre-Renaissance medieval band and was classically trained on piano. Naturally, she ended up playing drums in the first incarnation of Arcade Fire—an instrument she'd never attempted before but quickly mastered.

The couple's romantic relationship blossomed with their music.

"It was very exciting meeting this really big guy from Texas—he was six feet five inches tall, and he was wearing clogs, which made him appear even taller," says Chassagne with a laugh. "It was also very strange, because we were playing such different kinds of music when we met. He was writing these straightforward songs and I was making medieval music and studying jazz. Our styles clashed, but in an interesting way. We suggested chord progressions and melodies to each other that brought out some things in the music we couldn't have achieved on our own.

"After a while, it became hard to separate the music from the relationship. Music defined who we are as people so much, and when we started collaborating, it's like you want to be with this person all the time. It became one thing socially and musically very quickly."

An early incarnation of the band recorded an EP in 2002 and broke up soon after a disastrous CD-release show in Montreal in March 2003. A new lineup coalesced around Win Butler, Chassagne, and multi-instrumentalists Richard Parry, Tim Kingsbury, and Will Butler, who made contributions in between class obligations at Northwestern University, in Evanston, Illinois, where he was studying poetry and Slavic culture.

The first song the new lineup wrote was "Wake Up," which would open Arcade Fire sets for years to come. A new drummer, Howard Bilerman, was brought in and Chassagne moved out front as a singer, accordion player, keyboardist, and dancer. Her twirling presence and dazzling thrift-shop fashion sense balanced her husband's towering intensity. Remarkably, the rest of the band refused to shrink into the background behind the charismatic duo, and it was this communal playfulness that pushed their concerts well beyond rote recital. Like a precocious child, Will Butler would romp around the stage looking for things to hit with sticks, tambourines, or fists; when he wasn't playing or banging on something, he would act as class clown, wrapping bandmates in duct tape or trying to set fires. Parry was a willing foil, donning a helmet for Will to smash. Whether they had a microphone or not, everyone in the band would shout the choruses. The mix of instruments—violins, horns, mandolins, accordion, even hurdy-gurdy on top of a rock rhythm section—was an amped up, arena-sized version of a gospel tent revival rather than a straight-up rock show. In this context, sex, drugs, and rock 'n' roll just seemed so Mötley Crüe, a relic of a decadent era when MTV dictated its audience's buying habits. They were replaced by a new trinity of themes: community, mortality, transcendence.

"With a good percentage of rock bands, there's a sexual energy onstage," Win Butler says. "But I don't think we're all that sexual. It's more like the ecstasy of Saint Teresa."

Compacting ecstasy into tiny, two-hundred-capacity rock clubs got the band noticed in Montreal and the nearby Canadian provinces in 2003–4. But things didn't really accelerate until the band recorded *Funeral* at Bilerman's studio in Montreal.

As the songs were being written and recorded, Alvino Rey died, as did Chassagne's grandmother and Richard Parry's aunt. Around this time, a fanzine writer asked Win Butler to sum up his life philosophy in eleven words or less. "Death is real," he responded.

Those three words might have served as a working title for *Funeral.* It's the sound of young people confronting their mortality for the first time. But the music doesn't sound dire or morbid; the effect is exactly the opposite. Underlying most of the songs is a palpable urgency: time is short, so let's get going.

The imagery in several songs draws on a 1998 ice storm that crippled Montreal with blackouts. The isolation and darkness were apt symbols for a tumultuous time in North America's history. The fallout from the 2001 terrorist attacks on New York and the Pentagon and the increasingly bloody war in Iraq that had begun in 2003 divided the country in a way that hadn't been experienced for decades. Arcade Fire's music spoke loudly to that state of confusion, without addressing it directly.

"Come on, Alex, don't die or dry up," Will Butler and company shout on "Neighborhood #2 (Laika)," as if they could will even a boy bitten by a vampire back to the living.

Just when things seemed at their worst, Butler's songs still found a way to tunnel out. The music aspired to evoke that exhilaration: it was messy but enthusiastic, dark yet celebratory, mid-fi but grand.

That said, the songs that would make up *Funeral* hardly seemed destined to become a major success. They were boisterous, unwieldy things with dodgy production. But that didn't bother Mac McCaughan, the cofounder of Merge Records. Once he heard Arcade Fire's demo, he became the band's first stateside superfan.

McCaughan turned forty in 2007 but still looks like a freckle-faced kid, probably because he spends most of the time onstage with his band, Superchunk, acting like he's bouncing on an invisible pogo stick. He doesn't really remember when he received Arcade Fire's demo from Bilerman, an old friend. It took him a few weeks to get around to picking the demo out of the mounting stack of CDs on his desk, in part because Bilerman's pitch was so understated.

"He sent the demo, but he really downplayed it," McCaughan says. "He said something like, 'Hey, if you don't like it, don't feel bad. I play drums for them, but it's not my band.' Just protecting himself in case I didn't like it, and I'm thinking, God, this must not be very good. I mean we get tons of music from people who know us. So it sat on the shelf for a few weeks before I checked it out, and when I finally put it on, I couldn't believe how good it was. I passed it around the office, which is something I rarely do, just to make sure I wasn't completely nuts. It was so instantly catchy that I started questioning myself: Am I trying to like it because it's Howard's band? But everyone else, including Laura"—his business partner and Superchunk bassist Laura Ballance—"was like, 'Man, this thing is awesome.'

"So I call the band and tell them we want to put it out, but Win's saying, 'Could you come see us play before you make up your mind?' Win's attitude was, 'I think you'd be even more excited about it if you saw us live.' Both Laura and I had new kids at the time, and getting to Montreal wouldn't have been that convenient for either of us. So I'm saying it's not really necessary, we want to put the record out either way."

McCaughan finally found out what Butler was going on about when Arcade Fire came to Chapel Hill in the spring of 2004 to play a claustrophobic, eighty-capacity basement club called the Cave. *Funeral* was still months away from release. Setting up on the "stage"—little more than an Oriental rug in the corner—Arcade Fire slammed out its new songs to an unsuspecting audience.

"They didn't have a record, so it was basically just us telling people they should come to the show—people who work at my wife's restaurant, our sons-in-law, just random people we knew," McCaughan says. "And it was just completely amazing to see them. They just destroyed this tiny place."

Funeral was a fine record, but the live show raised the stakes considerably, and McCaughan and the entire Merge staff instantly realized it. "We thought, When people see this it's going to be amazing."

Still, Merge's expectations were initially modest. They figured if they could sell eighty-five thousand records, it would be a triumph. They ended up selling that in a few months. *Pitchfork*'s 9.7 rating got the ball rolling, and demand exceeded the label's ability to keep record stores stocked. "We thought it had the potential to be a big-selling record, but based on our previous history, 'big-selling' meant Neutral Milk Hotel," says Martin Hall, Merge's director of media relations. "After the *Pitchfork* review came out, the record was for all intents and purposes out of print for about a week because there were so many orders for it."

The experience of Steve Sowley, product manager of the leading independent record store in Chicago, Reckless Records, was typical. He sold 515 copies of the album in four months, one hundred more than he sold of *A Ghost Is Born,* the new album by hometown favorites Wilco, which came out a few months earlier.

"For a debut album, that's insane," Sowley says. "I hate to give *Pitchfork* credit, but I have to. We got a couple of copies for each store when it first came out, and when that review went up, those sold out right away. We couldn't get it for about a month, and then when we did get more, those sold out. It continued for months afterward."

Part of the problem was the elaborate album art, with intricate foil details woven into the cover image. "It just made *Funeral* physically difficult to reproduce quickly," McCaughan says. "It was such a cool sleeve, and we didn't want to take any shortcuts with it. But at the same time we had distributors ready to wring our necks for not having more CDs available to keep up with the pace they were selling at first."

The artwork also emphasized what made the band so appealing to hard-core music lovers. As much as the band was seen as an Internet-fired phenomenon, its values were rooted in old-school album rock. This was a band that conceived of albums as complete works, designed to be listened to as a whole, complemented by lyric sheets, liner notes, and album art that enhanced and embellished the music. No amount of MP3 file sharing could fully replicate that experience.

"What was so striking to me was that they had the enthusiasm of a new band just starting out, but yet there was this maturity about what they were doing," McCaughan says. "The album felt so complete, a whole piece of art, like they'd been working on it for a long time, down to the last detail."

When Arcade Fire arrived in New York to play the annual CMJ (College Music Journal) Convention in October 2004, the big media battleships circled. For two decades, the annual gathering of college-radio programmers had provided a showcase for up-and-coming bands. Few had risen faster to prominence than Arcade Fire.

"It used to take months of touring and record-shop hype for an underground band to build a cult," Kelefa Sanneh wrote in *The New York Times,* "but now it takes only a few weeks."

"We're the flavor of the month," Butler said by way of introduction to the band's headlining set at the Mercury Lounge. And later, with a wry expression, he mock-solemnly thanked the Internet.

Later the band would dine with Sire Records' Seymour Stein, the man who signed the Talking Heads and Madonna, and pose for a *Spin* photographer.

The band stayed on the road, without the help of managers or roadies. Inside their bubble, they were multitasking—they had to do everything from driving to gigs to collecting cash at the merchandise booth—and stayed relatively sane.

"We weren't surrounded by yes-men telling us what to do or how great we were," Will Butler says. "We were surrounded by ourselves. It never became 'unreal.'"

Butler pauses and chuckles to himself. "Well, it became unreal, but not unmanageable. We were still loading our own equipment on and off stage. It's hard to feel like you're such a big deal when you're still doing everything yourself."

Backstage at a show in New York during a 2007 winter storm not unlike the one that inspired many of the songs on *Funeral*, violinist Sarah Neufeld and bassist Tim Kingsbury sat next to each other on a couch and laughed about war stories from the road.

Kingsbury: "The Internet made everything happen faster. Going into releasing *Funeral* we were optimistic, we felt it was a good record . . ."

Neufeld: "But the scale was surprising. When the first pressing sold out, it was really weird. It set us up for the next surprise, and each surprise prepared us for the next: the shows sold out, they got bigger and sold out some more, the record sold a hundred thousand, then a hundred and fifty thousand. It kept leading from one to the next."

Kingsbury: "It wasn't like we couldn't cope. It was weird, but it didn't flip everything upside down."

Neufeld: "We were still doing everything ourselves. We were still driving ourselves around in a van. We weren't all of a sudden propelled into stardom and this easy rock-star life and there were chocolate fountains everywhere."

Those would come later.

In 2005, Arcade Fire made a habit of stealing festivals from bigger, better-known bands. In April at the Coachella Festival in southern California, the band took its biggest step yet onto a national stage. Neither the band nor its loyalists could have safely predicted whether Arcade Fire's set would translate in the vastness of the California desert, or transcend the predusk heat. It was one thing to play a lights-out show in a club in front of a few hundred rabid fans, quite a different and more difficult task to make a major impression before an audience of fifty thousand overheated people, many of whom had only heard of the band and had strolled over with arms folded to one of five Coachella stages wondering what all the fuss was about. One duff moment from the newbies onstage and it would be off to the nearest palm tree or beer tent to chill in preparation for the night's bigger attractions, New Order and Nine Inch Nails.

But Arcade Fire not only held the crowd's attention, it galvanized it. They banged away on their instruments and every available hard surface, the exuberance amplified by the band's physical presence: These young people just looked damned good standing next to one another in their black suits and dresses, their gloves, white shirts, and suspenders. They swept into "Wake Up" with the giddy grandeur of drunk opera singers, and the nine people onstage turned the tens of thousands on the vast polo field into an impromptu backing choir.

> *Children, wake up!*
> *Hold your mistake up,*
> *before they turn the summer into dust*

Onlookers were now participants: smiling, singing, hopping up and down, pressing closer to the stage, swept up in a delirious wave.

"Seeing them in front of that many people outdoors, it really reminded me of the first time I saw U2, when I was fifteen and it was the first date of the *War* tour at a football stadium in Chapel Hill," McCaughan says.

U2? Not quite. But bubbling beneath the surface of McCaughan's comment was the notion that Arcade Fire had already outrun *Pitchfork*'s influence and audience and had graduated to another level of notoriety altogether.

Pitchfork would soon find out the hard way. Soon after it published its Arcade Fire review, the e-zine was invited by a Chicago promotion company to curate the first Intonation Festival and was given a budget to invite two dozen bands to play Union Park, on Chicago's West Side, on the weekend of July 16–17, 2005. Topping their wish list, of course, was Arcade Fire.

But the Montreal band turned them down. Instead, they showed up in Chicago a weekend later, at Intonation's competitor Lollapalooza, the corporate rock festival revived by a handful of hotshot

Texas promoters whose previous claim to fame had been managing bicyclist Lance Armstrong. Lollapalooza wasn't as indie-cool as Intonation, but it was an opportunity to play in front of a bigger audience (thirty-three thousand, versus Intonation's fifteen thousand) for a bigger payday. The band's brain trust clearly saw it as a way to reach some new fans, not just the indie kids who read *Pitchfork* every day.

For public consumption, the Arcade Fire and *Pitchfork* camps kept things civil about their little parting of the ways. David Viecelli, the band's booking agent, denied that Arcade Fire was trying to distance itself from its Internet champion. He explained that the band had intended to take the month off from touring, then decided to play another festival for a friend in Guelph, Ontario, the same weekend as Lollapalooza. "There was no particular attachment to Lollapalooza," Viecelli said. "But it made sense to play Lollapalooza and make a weekend out of it when the other offer came in."

Schreiber tried to remain stoic but had a more difficult time masking his disappointment. "It's a really good question," he said about why he lost his new favorite band to Lollapalooza. "It's one of the bands we would've wanted. I love that band. But we can't make crazy demands on them."

Schreiber's diplomacy was admirable, his exasperation understandable. Deep down, he knew that he'd started a cycle that had turned Arcade Fire into the year's most talked about band. But his was just one more crazy demand in a year full of them: prime slots at the Coachella and Lollapalooza festivals, elbow rubbing and onstage collaborating with celebrity fans David Bowie and David Byrne, and the hearty endorsement of U2, which blasted the *Funeral* song "Wake Up" to open concerts on its 2005 tour.

On a scorching Sunday afternoon with temperatures hovering near a hundred degrees at Lollapalooza, Arcade Fire took the stage dressed like undertakers and played with astonishing fury, heat exhaustion be damned. The dis of *Pitchfork* had paid off. Win Butler came off stage looking like a man who had just spent the last hour sealed in an oven, his face the shade of a ripe tomato, the sweat dripping from his black suit coat. But he was grinning. "That audience," he said, "was unbelievable."

Lollapalooza's headliners included the Pixies, Weezer, and the latest project engineered by Lollapalooza founder Perry Farrell, Satellite Party, which immediately preceded Arcade Fire on stage. But by the end of the weekend, no one had made a bigger impression than Win Butler's band in black.

By fall of 2005, the nine-piece juggernaut was taking a victory lap: a sold-out theater tour of North America. Win Butler told twenty-two hundred fans at the Riviera in Chicago that the band was going away for a while and wouldn't return until he had "written a million songs." But the band still played as if it had something to prove, only now the arrangements had all solidified into anthems, the band shouting every word and the audience shouting every word right back. It was a celebration, one of those we've-done-it! moments for both the band members and the fans. It refused to end. For the encore, Win Butler led the band into the cramped theater lobby, where they set up like street buskers with acoustic guitars and a parade drum. As the fans engulfed them, the band members sang without amplification, as if they wanted to prolong the moment and their improbable year as long as possible.

The year capped off with a Grammy Awards nomination for best alternative album. The band traveled to Los Angeles for the ceremony in February 2006. They lost out to the White Stripes' *Get Behind Me, Satan,* but it didn't much matter. The whole event was surreal, right down to the chocolate fountains at the after-party. "You don't see many of those in Montreal," Neufeld recalls with a laugh. "We didn't feel part of that world. Like, there are all these rock stars, and then there's this group of people from Montreal staring at everything with their mouths open."

To record the follow-up album, the band once again cocooned at home, this time in a rustic nineteenth-century church an hour's drive south of Montreal that the band converted into a recording studio and clubhouse, with beds in the basement and recording equipment beneath the vaulted ceiling and stained glass.

The band had rebuffed a few major-label offers, instead opting for self-sufficiency. Rather than borrowing money from its label to record, the band covered its recording costs with tour revenue and *Funeral* royalties. They even had enough to splurge a bit by venturing to Budapest to record with an orchestra and choir on a couple of tracks.

Just as the band had proven expert at taking its music out into the world with a multifaceted stage show brimming with distinctive personalities, it was equally strong at insulating itself from the outside pressures that can weigh on a band trying to follow up a successful album.

"They invested in their own future, which isn't the way the [mainstream] music industry typically runs," McCaughan says. "The industry tells a band that it needs to take a big advance, which allows the label to put in its two cents of advice about how the band should make the record. Then the band ends up owing the label money until it sells a certain number of records. Arcade Fire doesn't want any of that. It gives them a lot of freedom. It's their money and they decide how to spend it and how their record is going to sound."

That do-it-yourself approach stemmed in large measure from Win Butler's deep skepticism about the music industry. He loved music. He did not love the industry that had been built on its back. "Ninety percent of all labels, managers, and lawyers involved with music do more harm than good," he once said with typical earnestness. "The only thing you can control is music you make in your bedroom."

The second Arcade Fire album reflected a year spent on the road, traveling the world. Whereas *Funeral* was personal, *Neon Bible* veered more overtly into the political. Its songs addressed the marriage of religion and war. Central to the album, Win Butler succinctly says, "is this idea that Christianity and consumerism are completely compatible, which is the great insanity of our times."

The arrangements reflect that cultural dissonance, as East European strings and heavy church pipe organs coat the melodies in dread and drone. Paranoia is a running theme: "Mirror, mirror on the wall, show me where them bombs will fall." "There's a great black wave in the middle of the sea." "I can taste the fear, lift me up and take me out of here."

The album begins and ends with two ink-black songs, "Black Mirror" and "My Body Is a Cage." They are slow, ominous, forbidding—everything that *Funeral* is not. *Funeral* confronted mortality and strived for transcendence. *Neon Bible* wrestles with a loss of faith in God, country, and self.

"I don't wanna fight in a holy war," Win Butler sings on "Windowsill." "I don't want the salesman knocking at the door / I don't want to live in America no more."

Those lines brought a loud cheer from an audience in Greenwich Village the first time they were performed in America, on a snowy winter night in February 2007, weeks before the album was released.

The band all noticed the reaction. "I was like, 'Whoa!'" Chassagne said the next day. "Win has lived in Canada for five, six years now, and traveled around the world, and he has a perspective on what people outside America think and how America is perceived."

Her husband was fighting a bronchial infection, his neck wrapped in a scarf after the show, but he spoke with conviction. "I wrote that song after our headlining tour in the States," he says. "It was the first time in my life that I felt like I was visiting my own country as some sort of outsider. I had lived in Montreal for a few years, but I didn't realize that I had really made it my home until that trip. In theology there is this idea that it is easier to say what God isn't than what God is, and in a way that song is my trying to say everything about my country that is not great or beautiful. In a way, it makes more clear what is great and beautiful and worth fighting to preserve."

It was a dense, forbidding premise for a highly anticipated album. But the band leaked a couple of songs from its website months before its official release and previewed the songs in a series of winter shows at undersized, nontraditional venues: an Ottawa high school, a church basement in Montreal, a small nondenominational church in New York's Greenwich Village. Tickets for the last of these were selling for as much as $2,000 on eBay.

Neon Bible leaked on the Internet weeks before its official release date and still debuted at number two on the *Billboard* album chart, with ninety-two thousand sales—the best single week figure in Merge Records history. *Pitchfork* chimed in with another laudatory review, but this time it was part of a multitude, all generally singing the band's praises but with somewhat more restraint than greeted *Funeral.*

No matter. The *Neon Bible* tour attracted bigger crowds than ever. Three sold-out concerts at the Chicago Theatre drew eleven thousand fans, with the $31 tickets being hawked by ticket brokers for hundreds of dollars. At those shows, the band struggled to balance the surging momentum of the *Funeral* tracks with the brooding intensity of *Neon Bible.*

This was not music of transcendence, but of moral reckoning. Will Butler smiled when that idea was suggested to him. For him, the idea of performing *Neon Bible* in concert conjured up an evangelical sermon he once heard.

"This preacher was saying, 'It's Friday and Jesus is on the cross and blood is streaming from his forehead and the heavens are ripping with thunder, but Sunday's comin'!'" he said, waving his arms as if delivering the sermon himself. "'It's Friday and the Romans are laughing and they've got blood on their hands, but Sunday's comin'!' And at the end, he's just yelling, 'Sunday's comin'! Sunday's comin'!' There was anger there, but there was also rejoicing. It's like that with this album. We're gonna dance again, but first we gotta get something off our chest."

We have a little community, mostly college kids, who work in Web design and coding. Someone can come to my server and say, "I never heard the Rolling Stones," and grab their entire catalog, plus sixteen albums' worth of outtakes, and ten live shows. You're either disgusted, or curious, about how I justify this. Well, I'm not sure I do justify it. But I've bought a zillion records. I've taken entire paychecks to the Jazz Record Mart in Chicago and bought thirty CDs. But record stores can't give me the selection of music on the Internet. My CD buying habits the last two years have dropped to ten percent of what they were.

—Thomas, Web designer in Detroit, born 1967

II

Innovation Out of Necessity

Hip-hop was much like the Internet in its infancy: a free zone of chaos and creativity in which anything goes, mainly because so few of the entitled and powerful were paying attention. The first hip-hop deejays played old funk records at house parties in the South Bronx, a destitute section of New York City, during the midseventies. Soon they were rapping over break beats; the deejay would isolate and then repeat small but particularly exciting portions of those dusty old records to get the crowd dancing. It was only a matter of time before those break beats began to appear on records as unauthorized "samples," and an underground sound once confined to the inner city started to seep out into the suburbs.

At first these samples consisted of little more than a drumbeat or a bass line, but as sampling technology advanced, hip-hop production grew in ambition and sophistication. Whereas in the early days of rap, a deejay might drop rhymes over a looped four-bar beat, producers in the late eighties were merging dozens of beats and textures from many different sources with microscopic precision. The Bomb Squad production on Public Enemy's late-eighties albums was so dense that it was often difficult to discern the source material. "We'd take a vocal loop from a reggae song and put it over some Slayer guitars and a James Brown bass line and some crazy drums and it would sound like something completely different than any one of those sounds individually," recalls Bomb Squad producer Hank Shocklee.

"We were working with fragments to create something new, instead of just laying a vocal over the top of something really obvious."

The Dust Brothers, the Los Angeles production team of Mike Simpson and John King, took a similarly ambitious approach on the Beastie Boys' 1989 album, *Paul's Boutique*. The Beastie Boys were coming off a hugely successful 1986 debut album, *Licensed to Ill*, that had made them stars by combining their guttersnipe wordplay with heavy beats. *Paul's Boutique* was a far more adventurous effort, with the Dust Brothers carving up and layering samples into elaborate collages. The apex of their efforts was the nine-part track "B-Boy Bouillabaisse," which crammed together more than thirty samples, ranging from a Joni Mitchell drumbeat to snippets of a Bob Marley interview.

"It was just an extreme amount of freedom—lots of time, being able to do what we wanted to do, and having the money to do it, and hooking up with some really talented people," the Beastie Boys' Mike D says. "The Dust Brothers taught us a lot about sampling. On *Licensed to Ill*, it was more beats and tape loops. It was really raw and basic. On *Paul's Boutique,* the sampling technology had improved, and it made sampling really accessible. We just completely went wild with it. The combination of technology and freedom made that record what it was."

Among studio creations of the eighties, the album was in a class by itself. The Beastie Boys didn't even bother to tour behind it; this was a record so dense and detailed that it demanded to be heard on headphones. A year or two later it probably could not even have been made—none of its samples was cleared for use, in part because the relationship between sampling and copyright law had yet to be clearly defined in a court of law.

But all that changed in December 1991 when a federal court ruling turned rapper Biz Markie and his record label, Warner Bros., into scapegoats for a decade's worth of sample-based hip-hop outlaws. Markie paid dearly for lifting three words and a snippet of music from Gilbert O'Sullivan's 1972 hit "Alone Again (Naturally)." The New York rapper, born Marcel Hall in 1964, had sampled the song for his third album, *I Need a Haircut*, without authorization from the artist or his publisher, and the court determined that Markie in effect stole copyrighted material from O'Sullivan. Markie was a clownish rhymesmith with a number of hits to his credit; his use of the O'Sullivan sample was in keeping with an approach that was irreverent, offbeat, and disarming in its comedic charm. But Judge Kevin Thomas Duffy essentially ruled the song's artistic merit was irrelevant to the issue at hand: theft of intellectual property. He ordered Warner Bros. to pull from circulation all copies of the album with the unauthorized sample, a ruling that had three effects: it derailed the rapper's career, required record companies to clear all samples with publishers before releasing any sampled-based music, and raised the price for such samples to a level that most rap producers couldn't afford.

It was a business boon for unsung blues and soul men such as Syl Johnson, whose sixties and seventies recordings became prime fodder for rap acts that could afford him. He says he licensed seven samples at $50,000 each to the Wu-Tang Clan for the group's 1997 album *Wu-Tang Forever.* He'd also licensed samples to TLC, En Vogue, Raekwon, Hammer, and the Geto Boyz, among others. "I got my retirement all set," said the singer in 1997.

At those kinds of prices, sampling became prohibitive for most hip-hop artists. Record labels and sampling artists decided it was better to pay copyright holders or not sample at all rather than risk a potentially crippling lawsuit. In 2001, Bridgeport Music Inc. filed more than five hundred copyright infringement suits against eight hundred artists using samples from George Clinton's catalog.

The idea that every piece of copyrighted music, no matter how small or how artfully recontextualized, needed to be licensed before it could be sampled changed the way most hip-hop was made for the next decade. Major producers such as Dr. Dre, the architect of the NWA albums and later the debuts of Snoop Doggy Dogg and Eminem, gravitated away from sampling and toward live instrumentation. But an aspiring hip-hop producer working in his basement couldn't afford to hire musicians. The Biz Markie ruling effectively pushed the most innovative hip-hop producers deeper underground, in search of break beats so obscure they couldn't possibly be sued for them.

Among the most innovative of these producers was Josh Davis, aka DJ Shadow, a Californian whose 1996 full-length debut, *Endtroducing,* was constructed entirely out of samples, most from the kind of records found only at flea markets and garage sales.

Using two turntables, a sampling machine, a four-track tape recorder, and a formidable collection of records—everything from college-band cover versions of "Spinning Wheel" to seventies saxophone instrumentals—Shadow orchestrated disparate, often unrelated sounds into expansive pieces that shifted mood and meter with organic grace.

"Samples convey personality," Shadow says. "When I'm working with a particular rhythm, I try to answer the question 'What kind of mood does a seven-eighths beat convey?' I know it must sound pretentious, but it's fun for me to see how deep I can take that idea without relying on clichés. I like using voices, but I hate words. Words are so specific they limit you because they tell the listener what to think. Certain people I work for [in the record company] would love me to slap some soul-singer vocal on my music because it would be easier to get a hit, but that's not the point."

Endtroducing wasn't a hit in the traditional sense, but its impact was broad. Ten years after its creation, it remains one of the landmark works of the nineties, in any genre. If anything else, it forcefully countered the argument that underlined the Biz Markie ruling, which turned the rapper into a poster child for hip-hop's perceived artistic shortcomings. The court in effect said that "sampling" another artist's work was equivalent to stealing it. In this view, rap producers were seen as little more than thieves, button pushers, and opportunists, riding a get-rich-quick fad rather than contributing to an art form.

Shadow was appalled. One of the driving forces behind *Endtroducing* was his determination to demonstrate that sample-based music could be as creative as any music made with more traditional instruments, that turntables and samplers could be as expressive as guitars and drums. "What I was trying to champion was the craft of it, the craft and the discipline of it," he says. "I heard those Public Enemy records and 'B-Boy Bouillabaisse' as a teenager growing up in northern California, and I wanted to do something on that level. That meant going through a ton of records, finding little moments or happy accidents of brilliance in otherwise mediocre records, and trying to make something good out of them."

Yet the deejay was wary after the Markie ruling. "I put out records with hundreds of uncleared samples to this day, but I try to clear the ones that I think are most likely to cause a problem. I live in fear of getting a call five minutes from now with some lawyer saying, 'We want your house,'" he says with a laugh. "I try to be conscious of who could be litigious, who could make a fuss over even a four-bar sample of a bass line. Which publishing companies are dangerous, which labels are watching. I've also learned the hard way that avant-garde jazz musicians listen. It doesn't matter if they pressed two hundred copies of a record you sampled, they are out there and they will catch you."

It was an odd state of affairs, given that music history is one of creative "borrowing." Or as songwriter Steve Earle once put it, "Good songwriters borrow, great ones steal." Would there even be a blues tradition without musicians passing songs down from one generation to the next, each singer making a song his own by changing a few words or embellishing a melody line? Why is that sort of oral "sampling" any more legitimate than the electronic variety?

Lawrence Lessig, a professor at Stanford Law School and one of the country's leading thinkers about cyberspace legal and cultural issues, says that the court rulings against sampling technology are tied in with myriad social and generational issues.

"The courts look at this form of music and they don't really see it as music," he says. "The thing to recognize is that every generation looks at the next generation's form of music and says, 'That's not music,' because we're all stuck in the conservative view of our present culture. Free culture has been about the right of the next generation to make its mark by either demonstrating how they are really artistically creative and worthy of attention, or at least having the chance to fail at that showing. We've never used the law to block the next generation's form of creativity, but that's what we're doing in this case in particular.

"I interviewed Jeff Tweedy about this issue in particular, a specific case where a court blocked the ability of people to engage in this type of sampling, and he had an instantaneous response. He said it was 'racism.' That's a very strong charge to make. It's not racism in the overt sense, where you're saying I'm going to try and hold back a particular group, but it is a product of the kind of segregated cultural life that we live in. So this one form of music develops that white people have no direct connection with most of the time, and they don't even recognize it as art or recognize it as creativity. But African-Americans have deep experience with this type of culture, which not only happens to be art but happens to be a way for them to express themselves."

Or as Tweedy himself said during a 2005 presentation with Lessig in New York: "What the music and movie companies are asking of artists—to create in a vacuum—is impossible. Not being able to sample, use a piece as a jumping-off point for another piece, borrow tunes from other songs, or otherwise be influenced by an artist or poet or writer, it's not possible, because that's what art is. . . . There's a reason you can't copyright a chord progression."

Perhaps because of the shadow world in which they worked, the best of the sample-based producers came up with the most innovative-sounding pop records of the last twenty years. Most rock records sounded staid and complacent next to the work of deejay/producer/mixers such as Dan the Automator, Prince Paul, DJ Premier, the Wu Tang Clan's RZA, Timbaland, the Neptunes, Cypress Hill's DJ Muggs, and El-P, aka Jamie Meline.

"Hip-hop is innovation out of necessity, the necessity of being broke," El-P says. "I started out at age twelve using my friend's beat-up drum machine and a cheap sampler. At first I was the only one my age who was serious about it. I was on a mission. Some people call what I do 'progressive' hip-hop, but it comes humbly from my love of hip-hop music. I am not better than hip-hop. If anything, I'm just trying to remind people what hip-hop meant, and what it still means."

These producers worked in an area where the avant-garde touched on pop. The sounds they were making weren't always considered "musical" and their instruments (turntables, samplers, drum machines) weren't traditional. Their art was postmodern in the extreme; like a kid with a channel changer, they would flick on fragments of electronic data, from the esoteric to the familiar, and stitch them together to create strange new soundscapes.

The idea of mixing and matching unrelated bits of electronic information spun off into mash-ups, a trend that gripped club culture for several years beginning in 2001. That year, the Belgian duo of David and Stephen Dewaele, calling themselves 2 Many DJ's, released an album of mash-ups in which they overlapped the a cappella track of a famous song and the instrumental track of a different, completely unrelated song to create a Frankenstein hybrid. The results were enchanting and sometimes hilarious: the vocals of Destiny's Child's "Independent Women Part 1" riding over the reggae riddims of 10cc's "Dreadlock Holiday," and the garage punk of the Stooges' "No Fun" swinging beneath the vocals from Salt-N-Pepa's "Push It." That same year, Christina Aguilera's vocals on "Genie in a Bottle" were mixed over the guitars from the Strokes' "Hard to Explain" by the Freelance Hellraiser, and began circulating in clubs and on the Internet as "A Stroke of Genie-us." Yes, it was.

Then, just as the novelty aspect of mash-ups began to fade, the most ambitious and fully realized mash-up yet came along: *The Grey Album*, by DJ Danger Mouse, aka Brian Burton.

When it first surfaced in the winter of 2004, it showed up in only a handful of retail stores and it never stood a prayer of denting the *Billboard* charts. Commercial radio stations either never heard of it or had to ignore it, for fear of inviting a lawsuit. Its maker never saw a dime of profit. Yet *The Grey Album* inspired media attention that rivaled well-financed major-label projects. By conflating two revered albums—the Beatles' self-titled 1968 double album, better known as *The White Album,* and Jay-Z's 2003 release, *The Black Album*— Danger Mouse ensured himself an audience far beyond his small fan base and demonstrated his savvy as a self-promoter. The album spread on the Internet and became one of the year's most talked about releases, finishing tenth in the *Village Voice*'s annual national critics poll. The notoriety was well deserved. *The Grey Album* was a dazzling example of mix-and-mash creativity.

Burton acquired an a cappella version of *The Black Album,* released by Jay-Z and his Roc-A-Fella label expressly to encourage club remixes. He then spent two nearly sleepless weeks in the bedroom studio of his home in the Los Angeles suburbs synching up the rapper's vocals with musical bars and beats that he meticulously isolated off the Beatles album. He altered tones and pitches, and then layered the samples on his computer with a $400 software program called ACID Pro. The result was, if not greater than the sum of the two parts, certainly an ear-expanding reinterpretation, a recontextualization so spirited that even a devoted fan of either album could go back to the original work with fresh perspective.

Danger Mouse circulated three thousand copies of *The Grey Album* in the first weeks of 2004, giving most of them away. Some turned up in record stores, others were sold on eBay, and MP3 files of the twelve-track album began circulating on peer-to-peer filesharing sites. That's when EMI, which owned the publishing rights to *The White Album,* jumped in and sent cease-and-desist letters to Danger Mouse, websites, and stores demanding that the record be destroyed. In response, more than 150 websites staged "a day of coordinated civil disobedience" on February 24, 2004, and offered the album for download. "We are certain that *The Grey Album* was the number one album in the country," the greytuesday.org website announced. "Danger Mouse moved more 'units' than Norah Jones and Kanye West . . . with well over 100,000 copies downloaded. That's more than 1 million digital tracks."

Lawyers and record industry executives saw the "Grey Tuesday" protest as copyright infringement run amok, a low blow directed against one of the central pillars of the recording industry. The websites and Danger Mouse supporters, arguing that they weren't profiting from the downloads, viewed the cease-and-desist orders as an affront to creativity and new technology.

For Burton, the project was in keeping with what he'd tried to do all along: blend musical worlds. He grew up outside New York City listening to the hair-metal bands that dominated eighties pop radio, while his older sister banged hip-hop by EPMD and Eric B. & Rakim nonstop: a subliminal mash-up if there ever was one. While attending the University of Georgia in Athens, beginning in 1995, he fell in with the psychedelic pop collective Elephant 6. He did a hip-hop remix of a Neutral Milk Hotel track, "The Fool," and began putting together mix tapes that blended old-school rap and rock.

"I would take Hall and Oates and mix it with the Wu-Tang Clan, and people would react to it, and immediately want to play it for their friends to get their reaction," he says. "That's when I knew there was something worthwhile about it, that it had its own language. I'd have the football players, the indie kids, and the frat boys all at the same show, and they were hearing this music in a different context and in a new way. When I was growing up, hearing different kinds of music—even hearing my sister's hip-hop records through the bedroom door—did something positive for me. It showed me that I'd been ignoring a lot of things because of how we've been trained: you hang out with certain people, you eat certain foods, you listen to a certain kind of music. Music knocked me over the head and said, 'Hey, if you continue down that path you're gonna miss a lot of stuff.' This [the mash-ups] became my way of shaking people up, the way music did to me."

But the concept's novelty quickly wore thin as underground mix CDs by a bevy of bedroom deejays proliferated around the world.

"More than ninety percent of the mash-ups I've heard are bad," Burton says. "They match up in beats per minute, but they don't work structurally."

The Grey Album was Burton's attempt to up the artistic ante. He wasn't thinking about breaking down copyright-infringement barriers, nor did he seek EMI's permission to sample the Beatles. He saw the album as a fun experiment and declined to make money off it. Danger Mouse also undoubtedly knew that sampling two of the biggest artists of the last fifty years would bring him plenty of attention and that he would profit in other ways from creating such a fuss.

Indeed, he would use the notoriety from *The Grey Album* as a springboard to a successful career as a producer, with hit records for Gorillaz, Gnarls Barkley, and the Good, the Bad & the Queen in subsequent years.

But even a cursory listen to *The Grey Album* affirms that this was a work that didn't just capitalize on its source material but cast it in an entirely new light. Danger Mouse makes the Beatles sound funky, turning even the stately piano chords of "While My Guitar Gently Weeps" and the harpsichord in "Piggies" into break beats on "What More Can I Say" and "Change Clothes," respectively. The intensity of Jay-Z's angry riposte to his critics, "99 Problems," is ratcheted up considerably by the roller-coaster guitar riffs from the Beatles' "Helter Skelter," punctuated by Paul McCartney's exultant scream. Danger Mouse's juxtapositions create a dialogue between the imperious hip-hop kingpin and the Summer of Love dandies that spans generations and cultures, as when the reminiscences of Jay-Z's mother on "December 4th" are underpinned by the lilting acoustic guitar in McCartney's bucolic folk ballad "Mother Nature's Son."

Jay-Z didn't say a word to discourage *The Grey Album*, his silence a form of tacit approval. But the Beatles' label, EMI, was determined to squash it. Imagine what might have happened had they licensed the rights to the tracks and shared any future royalties, or better yet signed Danger Mouse to a deal and built a full-fledged marketing campaign around the album. In this scenario, everyone might have won: the sales of Jay-Z's and the Beatles' catalogs might have been boosted by renewed interest in their work; the record labels and Danger Mouse would have been financially rewarded for their efforts; and consumers would not have had to scrounge to find an instant-classic remix album that remains more heard about than actually heard.

"EMI's response was discouraging but not unexpected, a twentieth-century response to a twenty-first-century art form," Stanford's Lessig says. "That kind of digital remixing, mash-up culture is being encouraged by new technologies, but it is not allowed given the architecture of copyright law. What we have to decide is if we want this kind of creativity stifled by the law or whether we want to rewrite the law to protect the kind of creativity that needs to be protected in this era and allow this kind of creativity on top of it. I'm a believer in copyright, but it needs to be adjusted to make sense in the twenty-first century so that it nurtures the kind of creativity the twenty-first century makes possible."

For Burton, the threat of a lawsuit left a sour taste. "What happened with *The Grey Album* is still kind of surreal, and I can't predict how it will affect music," he says. "I feel like it made its own statement, and now it's time to move on."

Move on he did, to a lucrative career jump-started by an "illegal" work of art.

We use our computer as an artistic multimedia device. It's a great way of discovering new music and it brought back my interest in collecting music. My older brother got involved in Napster, and started buying CDs again. I'm a high school teacher and ninety-five percent of my kids will make mix CDs. Very seldom do they want to buy a whole CD of one artist. A lot of them can't afford a $20 CD. The same thing happened with cassette tapes when I was growing up. Ten people might want an album; one buys it and nine tape it. But music is still popular, I think.

—Sarah, teacher in Ontario, born circa 1970

12

Girl Talk's Illegal Art

Emo's has a history. It's a punk club at the nexus of the vibrant live music scene in Austin, Texas, at the corner of Sixth Street and Red River. Legends have performed there; the bar stool where Johnny Cash once planted himself onstage still dangles from the rafters.

In the spring of 2007, a twenty-five-year-old biochemist from Pittsburgh named Gregg Gillis—stage name: Girl Talk—came to rock this hallowed dive armed with only a gray hoodie, a handful of electrical cords, and a laptop.

Tucked inside a parade of more tradition-based rock bands at the twenty-first annual South by Southwest music conference, Gillis incited a riot of dancing by mouse-clicking through the sounds stored on his computer hard drive, then mixing and mashing those digital samples to create an explosive collage of contraband music. He turned a chaotic blend of samples—from hit songs by Young Jeezy, Fleetwood Mac, Justin Timberlake, Elton John, Clipse, Biggie Smalls, Boston, the Verve, and dozens of other mismatched bands from the worlds of rock, hip-hop, R&B, and pop—and ordered them into a killer party mix. It's one thing to sample particularly inviting snippets of well-known songs, quite another to mix them together into something coherent, audacious, and danceable on the fly. While doing everything from handstands on his rig to leading conga lines of dancers through the audience, Gillis laid to rest any doubts about a self-described computer nerd's ability to entertain.

By Girl Talk standards, it was a fairly tame show. Gillis has a false front tooth necessitated by a stage-diving accident on Thanksgiving weekend, 2006. His family had come to see him perform at a Pittsburgh club, and at the height of the dance frenzy Gillis launched himself over his father's head in front of the stage and crashed into the shoulder of his sister's best friend. His tooth dislodged, blood poured from his mouth, and his mother screamed, "Stop the show!"

"I never wanted to be the laptop guy onstage who looked like he was busy checking his e-mail," Gillis says. "From the start, I always aspired to make this the equivalent of the Who, the greatest rock show you ever saw."

Who-isms aside, what made the performance resonate was the way it furiously compressed the mash-up strategy employed on Girl Talk's 2006 album, *Night Ripper*. The sixteen-track, forty-two-minute album was constructed entirely out of electronic samples brazenly lifted from hundreds of mostly well-known songs, including hits by major acts such as Madonna, LL Cool J, Elton John, Nirvana, Nelly, Lady Sovereign, and Fleetwood Mac. It was released on the Illinois-based Illegal Art label, which specializes in experimental sample-based recordings.

Since the early nineties, electronic sampling had become increasingly expensive; the Biz Markie court ruling ended hip-hop's Wild West era, forcing labels to compensate copyright holders even for the smallest samples. The Beastie Boys' brilliant *Paul's Boutique* was literally the last of a breed, a sample-based hip-hop album that took the familiar, the famous, and the faded and turned them into something new. Danger Mouse's *The Grey Album* reinvigorated that venturous spirit for a brief time, before sinking back underground under legal pressure. Danger Mouse clearly had no appetite for a fight. But *Night Ripper* was something else: it made the case that *Paul's Boutique* was not the end of an era but actually the start of a new, more brazen one. It was a burst of outlaw creativity that would only be enhanced by more sophisticated technology in subsequent years.

"You can't overestimate the role *Paul's Boutique* played," says Mark Kates, who ran the Beastie Boys' Grand Royal label for a few years beginning in the late nineties. "There weren't rules there, and it helped create a new art in the way it manipulated preexisting recordings. Nobody had really done it on that level before. You can draw a straight line from *Paul's Boutique* to Girl Talk."

Illegal Art wasn't exactly spoiling for a costly court fight to reverse the Biz Markie ruling, but its business premise was essentially a legal dare: some sampling of copyrighted material, especially when manipulated and recontextualized into something new, is legit and qualifies as art. Illegal Art debuted in 1998 with *Deconstructing Beck,* an album consisting of unauthorized samples from Beck's catalog in collagelike compositions by a variety of mixers with fanciful names (Mr. Miridies, Corporal Blossom, the Evolution Control Committee). The album was widely distributed and swapped on the Internet, and established Illegal Art's modus operandi: every release would consist entirely of sample-based music, all of it testing the boundary between copyright theft and fair use, the legal principle based on the belief that the public is entitled to freely use portions of copyrighted materials for purposes of commentary and criticism.

Illegal Art was founded by Philo T. Farnsworth, a pseudonymous university professor in Illinois with a master's degree in electronic music from Dartmouth College. He refuses to allow himself to be photographed or be interviewed face-to-face, to preserve his anonymity at his day job. He started the label in 1998, naming himself after the man whose vital role in the invention of television was buried beneath corporate machinations in the thirties and forties. "It all ties into the concept of appropriation," he says. "I'm appropriating his identity because I have a lot of respect for his history."

Farnsworth is an artist himself who uses sampling in his own work. "I'm somewhat biased, but I listen to a lot of rock and other genres where people play instruments, and I see them as much more derivative than sample-based music," he says. "I grew up in the eighties and listened to a lot of 'normal' music. I loved it. But I came to the opinion that some of the most original and unique music is being made from recontextualizing and editing things: Negativland,

John Oswald, a lot of academic things going back to the sixties. What appealed to me about it is that so many people from different backgrounds were experimenting with it. It really isn't a genre. It exists on the fringes of multiple genres. Negativland came from punk, and Oswald is a saxophonist. There are the experimenters in the academic and avant-garde worlds, and there are rock bands working with samples. It's all over the map. That's why I wanted to work in this area."

Oswald's 1985 essay "Plunderphonics, or Audio Piracy as a Compositional Prerogative" provided an aesthetic framework for the label. "Plunderphonics" soon became an umbrella term for any music made completely out of existing audio recordings, including copyrighted material, and then altered in some way to create a new composition.

"A plunderphone is a recognizable sonic quote, using the actual sound of something familiar which has already been recorded," Oswald said in the liner notes to his *69 Plunderphonics 96* retrospective. "Taking Madonna singing 'Like a Virgin' and recording it backwards or slower is plunderphonics. But the plundering has to be blatant. There's a lot of samplepocketing, parroting, plagiarism, and tune thievery going on these days which is not what we're doing."

Deconstructing Beck was very much in that tradition. It was intended as an experimental one-off, a tongue-in-cheek tribute to Beck designed to reward creativity, not reap financial profit, much less start a label. Farnsworth solicited remixes on Internet message boards, and soon got way more than he could use.

Once the disc surfaced, cease-and-desist letters arrived at Farnsworth's P.O. box from Beck's record label, publisher, and personal lawyer. Farnsworth ignored them all, without consequence, perhaps because the sales figures for *Deconstructing Beck* weren't worth the legal time, effort, and expenditure. But the media notoriety helped win the project a small audience, and the album ended up selling more than seven thousand copies—barely a blip at a major label but enough to encourage Farnsworth to keep going. "We got way more media attention than a lot of start-up labels get," Farnsworth acknowledges. Similar legally dicey compilations followed, including one sampling movie music and another advertising music.

Then Girl Talk took the label's notoriety to a new level.

Gregg Gillis grew up in Pittsburgh and studied saxophone in grade school, but set it aside soon after discovering Nirvana while he was in fourth grade. "Seeing Kurt Cobain and grunge, it made a lot of kids feel anyone can do this," he says. "Alongside that was Dr. Dre. Growing up, we always saw rock and rap side by side, so it was almost inevitable to see that mash-up scene start up a few years later."

Gillis was playing in bands during high school as a keyboardist and vocalist. He specialized in mucking up top 40 songs with electronic noise in his band, then honed the vision while attending Case Western Reserve University, in Cleveland, where he formed Girl Talk.

"The key moment for me was hearing [electronic artist] Kid 606 remix NWA's 'Straight Outta Compton' in the late nineties," Gillis says. "It was the first time I heard someone take a computer and digitally massacre a well-known song and rearrange it. It seemed so punk rock and so exciting that you could do that. I didn't have a computer yet, but then I got a laptop before going to college in 2000. And I thought, Why not start a new band where all it is, is me cutting up pop music?"

Gillis aimed "to make experimental music using all pop source material, taking familiar elements and twisting them into new things that are pretty weird." He began sending out Girl Talk demos to underground labels, and got an enthusiastic response from Illegal Art.

The first Girl Talk album (*Secret Diary*, 2002) was more experimental, the second (*Unstoppable*, 2004) more beat heavy, the samples more blatant. *Night Ripper* was bolder still in sampling readily identifiable source material, and yet also more meticulous and refined in how it layered and juxtaposed those bits of electronic data.

"A lot of mash-ups are made with dance clubs in mind, and there is an art to that and a purpose for that," Gillis says. "But there are not too many guys making mash-ups who want it to sound more like Squarepusher, with tight editing and really crazy rhythmic patterns. Cutting up things electronically and making a cool track out of it— that's my world. So I think I bridge the gap between traditional dance music and experimental dance music. It's weird and challenging, but it also changes so quickly that the listener can still party to it."

Rave reviews started to pour in.

The sheer density of *Night Ripper* puts it several cuts above most mash-up projects. Gillis spent a year concocting different sample combinations, editing them into tight compositions. The album's sixteen tracks are sequenced like a deejay set, with the beats per minute gradually ascending from 90 to 125. And though Gillis designed it as a dance album, it rewards closer scrutiny on headphones. The opening track, "Once Again," crams sixteen samples into 180 seconds, some so fleeting they barely register on the consciousness before new sonic treats drift within earshot.

A piano line from Elton John's "Tiny Dancer" slips beneath a Notorious B.I.G. rap from "Juicy," while the organ on Boston's "Foreplay/Long Time" ripples beneath a vocal loop from Ciara's "Goodies" and Ludacris's saucy rhyming on "Pimpin' All Over the World." Oasis's "Wonderwall" crumbles into Arrested Development's "Tennessee," and the Boredom's frantic "Acid Police" collides with the soothing harmonies of the Five Stairsteps' "O-o-h Child." One track alone ("Friday Night") blends at least twenty-one samples in three minutes, spanning four decades and artists as disparate as the Black Crowes, Salt-N-Pepa, the Waitresses, and Daft Punk.

"I built *Night Ripper* as a whole piece," Gillis says. "About seventy-five percent of the work I put in on it at home, no one heard. I'm always sampling loops and hooks, and cataloging them and quantizing them, and then I try out different combinations all day long of those samples. I sample a guitar line and see how it goes with this vocal line. I have a live set that is a big puzzle of material, that I can pull pieces in and out. With the live set I've roughly been working with the same template for the last seven years, but I'm always working in new parts. For each show, I have about three hundred loops lined up, and I can isolate different sounds—a kick drum, vocals, high-hat, hand claps—and bring them in and out, layer them, or peel it back and keep it really minimal. Only a small fraction of what I mess around with at home makes it into the live set, and then only a small fraction of what I perform live ends up on the finished album. It's nerve-racking to come up with the best forty minutes."

Night Ripper was like a Girl Talk greatest hits, each bit honed in live sets and refined for maximum impact on the dance floor. If a combination of sounds wasn't cutting it in the live setting, it didn't make the album. Gillis honed the collages in his home studio, which doubled as his bedroom. "A great idea, and not a great idea," Gillis says. "It meant I was dreaming combinations of sounds. I'd wake up in the middle of the night with an idea swimming around in my head and get back to work."

He'd work through headphones on two computers, valued at about $1,000 each, and a mixer-monitor laptop worth about $3,000.

"I work on music minimally eight hours a day, and on weekends I usually play shows," he says. "That forty hours of work results in about two minutes of new music in my set. I can work for eight hours and get a five-second transition out of it. It's a process of trial and error, mix and match, and it requires a certain amount of patience until you get just the right combination of elements."

That rigorous work ethic translated to a giddy, danceable listen, and one of the best party mixes ever made. *Night Ripper* ended up on countless top 10 lists at year's end, hailed by critics as a brilliant piece of postmodern art, a reconfiguring of the past into something fresh, fun, and startling. It could also just as easily have been interpreted as a criminal act, a brazen affront to copyright law, a deliberate attempt to steal from other artists' work and then resell it as one's own.

"I feel all music does what I do," he says. "You take your influences and manipulate them into something your own. It's like the Beatles 'stealing' a Chuck Berry riff."

Gillis says he never gave a thought to trying to clear any of the samples. "It would've taken ten years to work out all the clearances, and I didn't think anything I was doing was going to hurt anyone's sales," he says. "And I didn't have any ethical or moral concerns, because I feel what I was doing wasn't hurting anyone. No one was not going to buy a Smashing Pumpkins album because I used a five-second snippet of one of their songs. But I also realized that I was taking it over the edge of what I had done before, but Illegal Art never flinched. It's an extreme example of what they do, but not unusual."

"It was a watershed album for us in that it was the catchiest album we'd ever released to that point," Farnsworth says. "And we were definitely trying to test the waters with it, with more of a marketing push. It was a conscious decision on our part not to be this micro-indie label forever."

Yet because of the broader notoriety, Illegal Art had difficulty finding partners to manufacture and distribute the CD.

"We haven't received any sort of legal threats from the artists sampled," Farnsworth said about a year after the record's release. "But we have had trouble manufacturing and distributing it. We could've sold a lot more if there weren't distribution problems. The popularity makes people nervous, even though there's been no legal reaction whatsoever."

Many of the manufacturers had signed antipiracy agreements with the record labels in exchange for their business. "This left no middle ground for many of them," Farnsworth said. "Either the samples were cleared or they weren't allowed to manufacture."

Farnsworth realized that as Girl Talk gained traction in the media, he could be setting himself up for a legal battle he couldn't afford. But the success of *Night Ripper* also made him realize that a legal face-off on copyright law is more necessary than ever to take into account the type of artistry his label promotes.

"You'd have to be an idiot to want to go to court," Farnsworth says. "It's a lengthy, time-consuming process that can be very costly. Yet eventually I would like to see the issue resolved in court. A lot of people automatically assume what these artists are doing is illegal simply because some copyright holder sends out a cease-and-desist letter. Most normal people would comply because they don't want to risk a lawsuit. It creates a perception that all of this type of sampling has no defense and is definitely illegal, when in fact a lot of it exists in a very gray area that is wide open to interpretation."

Farnsworth says that he's not against artists being compensated for having their work sampled. "But the way compensation for sampling is set up now, it's an impossible situation," he says. "People can ask whatever they want for every sample, and that has turned sampling into a prohibitive art that even the biggest artists can't afford."

The entrepreneur envisions a sliding scale, where artists who sample only a four-bar beat would pay much less than those who lift a chorus. "A type of hip-hop has suffered. You can't make a *Paul's Boutique* or *It Takes a Nation of Millions to Hold Us Back* anymore," he says. "There has been a positive effect from the prohibition on sampling, which is that a lot of hip-hop producers are hiring musicians and creating a different kind of hip-hop. But it's wrong that the other kind can't exist."

He was disappointed that Danger Mouse's *Grey Album* didn't wind up deciding the matter. "It was a conceptually brilliant album that I like quite a bit," he says. "But he didn't take it far enough. By caving in to [EMI's] cease-and-desist right away, he furthered the perception that what he was doing was illegal. I don't blame him for not wanting to get into a court fight, but he was a little bit too worried about hurting his relationship with the industry to say anything inflammatory. Yet he was able to capitalize on the publicity."

Like Danger Mouse, Gillis also didn't want to be cast as a fair-use freedom fighter. "It's more about fun for me," he says. "I've done this music for a long time, and even if it wasn't being put out on CD, I would still be making it and giving it to my friends. The laptop has always been my instrument. I never considered myself a deejay technically. I make sample-based laptop music, and I like to make fun music. That's my main purpose. I hold my own views on sampling, which align with [Illegal Art's] school of thought. But I'm not trying to push an issue. It's opening up a lot of minds, and making people question a lot of our copyright issues, which is cool, but that is not my direct intention."

Indeed, like Danger Mouse, Gillis has turned his rebel persona into a lucrative career. A year after *Night Ripper* was released, Gillis was able to quit his day job as a biomedical engineer and concentrate full-time on music. He was being approached by major-label executives for remix work, and even Illegal Art nemesis Beck invited Gillis to open a major concert in London. Unlike *The Grey Album*, *Night Ripper* was allowed to float along in a lawsuit-free zone, a tacit endorsement of sorts from the major labels.

As one major-label executive said when asked point-blank about the possibility of suing Gillis and Illegal Art, "It would've been extremely bad publicity for anyone to sue a little label over a record that has sold barely ten thousand copies. Besides, everyone I know loves the album. We may be worried about what the copyright implications mean for our business, but no one can deny that the album is a cool piece of work."

Gillis and Farnsworth were in no hurry to broker a truce with the majors. Indeed, Gillis released a similar album, *Feed the Animals*, through Illegal Art in 2008.

"*Night Ripper* has gotten bigger than I ever expected or even wanted," Gillis says. "My dream wasn't to make this album so the majors would scout me out and then I'd make the next Gnarls Barkley record. I'd be interested to work with the majors; it would force me to expand my musical palette. But I wouldn't be able to use samples that they could get sued for, and one of my goals is to continue making sample-based music that I like."

Farnsworth understands the dynamic that made *The Grey Album* and *Night Ripper* work: their status as musical contraband turned them into underground hits. And there's nothing the musical-file-sharing community likes better than something illicit.

"Getting the major labels involved would legitimize sampling as an art form," he says. "It would save us all a lot of legal bills. But there is a subversive edge to sampling that gives it more essence, more meaning. Any sort of collaboration with any sort of larger music industry would lose that edginess. And that's a big problem. The more we can push artists like Girl Talk into the market, the more we're legitimizing what they're doing. At the same time, I don't think Gregg's project has been successful because it's illegal. I think people just like it for what it is—an incredibly catchy piece of experimental pop music."

Technology has made hip-hop more accessible. Anyone can have Pro Tools in their house, burn a CD, and put it up on the Internet. But to have lasting effect, [rappers] have to go out and do open mikes, and pay their dues, and prove themselves. They can put out a record from their house, but not at the expense of working on your craft.

—Jean Grae, hip-hop artist, born 1976

13

Future Shock from Wham City

In the summer of 2007, Girl Talk's Gregg Gillis toured regularly with another rising laptop producer, Dan Deacon. Together, they nearly ended up shutting down one of the year's biggest summer festivals. They had become viral pop stars, and not even the bookers of the Pitchfork Music Festival in Chicago knew it until it was nearly too late.

As dusk loomed on July 14, the festival's second day, Deacon walked on a stage containing his usual setup: keyboards salvaged from garbage Dumpsters, modulators, delay pedals, pitch shifters, and a glowing green plastic skull.

With his oversized, red-framed glasses and pudgy frame packed into an ill-fitting T-shirt, Deacon did not radiate star power. Yet on a weekend packed with indie-music royalty, from the New Pornographers to Sonic Youth, none could match what happened next. Deacon set up in the middle of the crowd and injected his cerebral, classically structured compositions with frantic beats and orchestrated ecstatic crescendos. The audience collectively flipped out.

Many of the fans in attendance had already downloaded his 2007 album, *Spiderman of the Rings,* and heard the single "Wham City," which had been made available as a free download from the pitchforkmedia.com website. When Deacon joined the party on the asphalt in front of the stage, the audience engulfed him. A fence bordering a major road next to the stage nearly buckled as fans pressed against it while surging closer. On the city street outside, about five hundred additional revelers dodged cars while dancing to the music. Party out of bounds. Police and fire officials moved in and pulled the plug.

"There were too many people in a confined space," Deacon said later. "It was chaos, just total chaos."

Gillis was up next. He was under strict orders from the promoter not to venture into the audience, but the fans were just as pumped up for his set, packing into a narrow passageway between two fences to dance. The festival was designed to hold nineteen thousand people in a thirteen-acre park. But Deacon and Gillis were booked on a side stage, which could accommodate a club-sized audience of a few thousand. Twice that many people tried to squeeze into the space when Deacon began to perform.

The side-stage booking reflected the relatively low profiles of Deacon and Gillis at retail stores and on commercial radio—the traditional metrics for gauging a performer's popularity. "Their music doesn't get played on radio, except for college stations," says Tom Windish, their booking agent. "They don't show up on SoundScan"—the service that collects weekly music-store retail figures, which are the basis for the *Billboard* chart rankings. "People don't realize how big their audience is until they see them perform and then it's like, 'Where did all these people come from?'"

Deacon had a ready answer.

"If my album didn't leak [on the Internet] as far in advance as it did, not as many people would have heard it and the shows I did over the summer wouldn't have been as well attended. All these markets that the music industry has ignored are now being exploited by people you would not think of as pop stars. No label would look at me and ever say, 'This is the guy the kids are gonna be dancing to. This guy, the creepy weirdo with the blotchy hair and the gut sticking out, he's the next star.'"

Deacon grew up in New York but moved to Baltimore in 2003 while completing his master's degree in electro-acoustic composition at Purchase College, north of New York City.

"I went on tour for the first time after I finished school in May 2004, six days on the East Coast, and it changed my life," he says. "It was more fun than I expected it to be, and I made money, which I didn't expect. Suddenly I had a way to pay rent without going to a job. My days of being hunched over a desk writing sheet music didn't exist anymore."

He assembled his electronic gear from a variety of dubious sources, including Dumpsters at the college and at a nearby cell phone company, and moved in with a commune of artists at a former bottle cap factory dubbed Wham City in a run-down section of Baltimore. Rent was $180. Dumpster runs from some of the city's finer restaurants produced regular meals. Wham City parties, advertised only by word of mouth, became the place to be on weekends.

"New York got huge in the seventies with the Talking Heads and Ramones and early hip-hop because it was a wasteland, a cheap place to live where it was easy for people to do creative stuff," Deacon says. "Now it's expensive and everyone has something going on and it's tough to make a living. People laughed at me when I went to Baltimore, because in comparison nothing was going on there. But you do the one cool thing on a night when nothing's going on, it becomes easy to get known. And when you become the most known thing in a city, it's a lot easier to get known on a national level."

Within a few blocks of a train station, an interstate highway, and an art college, Wham City was ideally located. It drew crowds of curious kids looking for affordable thrills and kept them coming back with unforgettable shows. Deacon developed a reputation as a must-see performer by setting up on the floor amid the audience, the gambit that got him in so much trouble at the Pitchfork Festival.

"It came up by default," he says. "When I first started I mainly played warehouses, houses, art galleries, a few small bars or clubs, and a lot of those didn't have stages. The best shows were the ones without the stage, because the audience would be right up against you. Early Wham City shows never had a stage, and hundreds of kids would pack into this warehouse space, and you couldn't really tell where the music was coming from, except for the mound of speakers. You could never see the performer. But it wasn't about seeing the show as much as it was about being part of this large visceral beast in the audience. There would be this feedback loop of energy."

Demand grew from his live audience for recordings. So Deacon applied his first-rate composing skills on his second- and third-hand gear and cranked out a half dozen CD-Rs of original material, which he sold at shows: $7 each, or two for $10.

A freak live performance on an NBC morning show in Savannah, Georgia, in March 2005 further raised his profile. Bobbing and weaving over a nest of mad-professor electronics while filtering his voice through a variety of processors so that he sounded like a deranged chipmunk, Deacon gave one of the more surreal performances ever hosted by a network news program.

"I had a friend who convinced the local affiliate that it would make sense to have me on the morning news," Deacon says, still laughing at the memory. "I put the performance on my website and it got downloaded a half-million times in a day, and crashed my server. That changed things quite a bit. It was a joke that I never thought anyone would see. The context was all wrong. One of the tags for one of the sites that hosted the video was 'Actual Retard Plays Music on News.' Ever since, I've been the zany, goofy guy who makes people dance."

Actually, much of Deacon's early music couldn't be described as danceable. The music veered over a range of styles, but was steeped in avant-garde experimentation and the sound-installation recordings he studied in college. Two discs consisted of little more than droning sine waves. Sampling, some as daring as that of Girl Talk, also figured into his aesthetic. One track featured every song from Aerosmith's 1987 album, *Permanent Vacation*, layered on top of one another; another stretched and manipulated two Beatles tracks on separate channels.

Despite his strange encounter with a network news show, Deacon was still enough of an underground artist that he didn't have to fear a legal ruckus with Beatles attorneys. But he says he doesn't consider anything he did illegal, and he's got the musical precedents to prove it.

"Using prerecorded music as an instrument I don't believe is controversial in any way," he says. "Even in the classical era, so much of music was just expanding on the past. So many pieces take a motif from a previous era, and then build a new framework for it. That's what samples are. The fact that it has been transferred into the business world to serve a business context rather than a creative context is just disgusting.

"John Cage used tons and tons of samples from radio in a lot of his work, but as soon as you put it into a pop setting, it's against the law. Why? In the art world, it's interpreted as advancement for our culture; in the pop world it's interpreted as someone trying to make money off someone else's work. It's insane how context defines what's right and wrong."

For *Spiderman of the Rings,* Deacon relied on entirely original compositions, save for one sample (of the cartoon character Woody Woodpecker), to create his version of "loud, danceable but still complex party music." It was a sound that enabled him to play to thousands of people in cities across the country without radio, MTV, or SoundScan acknowledging his existence. Yet even though the sound was shaped and distributed by new technology, what allowed the artist behind that sound to have a life beyond Internet faddishness was a centuries-old discipline.

"Gregg Gillis and I are future-shock composers," Deacon says "We're writing music at a time where the technology and the way music is being heard are leapfrogging over the past, and the industry cannot keep up with that. The music industry does not know how to deal with the technology and the culture that it lives in, and it's panicking.

"A hundred years ago you could only hear music if you were sitting in the same room where people were playing it, and now a song can be completely recorded on a computer, and then instantaneously put on the Web, and a week later it could be the most popular song in the world. But conversely it can be just as quickly forgotten. It's created an in-one-ear, out-the-other culture. And that's why these Internet fads, these bands who get hot on MySpace or certain Web pages, are fly-by-night one-hit wonders. And that's why it's important for bands to build up a scene through touring. So many bands will have a hit single through iTunes or on blogs, and they play live, and people think, 'This is a fucking joke. These guys suck.' People like me and Gregg have been touring the DIY scene for a while, we have put in our dues. We had a fan base, and it grew faster because of the Internet. But we weren't just sitting at home making music."

Future shock or not, Deacon and Gillis were much like the old troubadours traveling from town to town with little more than guitars on their backs. "Yeah, put your keyboard or your laptop on your back and walk across the land playing music," Deacon says with a laugh. "That's why it's lasted all these years. Touring is still important. People can believe something that they hear through their headphones and see on their computer screen, but if they see it happen in front of them, it's going to last a lot longer and they're going to want to see it again."

The corporations that own radio have a vested interest in not rocking the boat. Thank God for the Internet, because we're fighting against a corporate culture that makes it practically impossible to get a protest song on the air.

—Mike Mills, R.E.M. bassist, born 1958

14

"George Bush Doesn't Like Black People"

In the late summer of 2005, Kanye West had the top-selling album in the country, *Late Registration,* a grandly ambitious statement that bridged hipster acclaim and huge sales figures. Nominally a hip-hop artist, West was making music that defied categorization. *Late Registration* blended refined orchestrations, grimy beats, avant-classical strings, and syrupy low-rider bass into banging pop music.

Yet West was selling records almost in spite of himself. He had quickly developed a reputation for outspokenness, liable to say anything to anyone at any moment, no matter what the damage might be. His outbursts at awards shows when denied prizes he thought he deserved had already earned him a reputation as a petulant brat. His inability to censor himself obscured the foundation of his success: that he approached everything he did with a workaholic's attention to detail, and palpable sincerity. West at times resembled the restless kid flipping cartwheels and reciting nursery rhymes backward to win the attention of the adults at a family picnic, simultaneously exasperating and charming.

So what happened at a nationally televised benefit concert on September 2 that year, a few days after Hurricane Katrina devastated New Orleans, shouldn't have come as a complete surprise. In the hurricane's aftermath, local and national institutions were pilloried for relief efforts that were beyond inadequate as the poorest residents of New Orleans suffered for days without food, water, and shelter.

West was now a household name, a musical powerhouse whose every word carried weight and ignited media firestorms. He was among the entertainers enlisted to host the Katrina telethon, and once again he spoke from the heart. As he and cohost Mike Myers watched video of the homeless wading through the devastation in search of food, West deviated from the script prepared by the telethon organizers. His voice quivered with emotion as he spoke.

"I hate the way they portray us in the media," he said. "If you see a black family, it says they're looting. See a white family, it says they're looking for food. . . . It's been five days because most of the people are black."

West was not done. "It's too hard to watch . . . those are my people down there . . . the way America is set up to help the poor, the black people, the less well off, [is] as slow as possible."

Myers returned to the scripted text, then looked again to West, who blurted out: "George Bush doesn't care about black people," and the telecast cut away.

NBC, which telecast the event, and the American Red Cross both immediately issued statements distancing themselves from West's remarks, which were edited out of the broadcast on the West Coast later that night. The White House and other commentators disparaged West's statement as ill-considered and unnecessarily divisive.

"I think all of those remarks are disgusting, to be perfectly frank, because, of course, President Bush cares about everyone in our country," First Lady Laura Bush said.

"The storm didn't discriminate and neither will the recovery effort," the president said a few days later.

But West's commentary did more than ratchet up the volume in a national debate about the Katrina relief effort. It reflected how many Americans felt, and struck a chord with social activists who shared his view that the federal government dragged its feet in aiding a city in which one-third of the residents lived in poverty.

It also sparked one of the best political protest songs of all time: "George Bush Doesn't Care About Black People," by the Houston rap group the Legendary K.O. The song surfaced on the Internet a mere four days after West's remark and was downloaded more than 1 million times over the next month.

It's a brilliant piece of homemade art. The Legendary K.O.—rappers Micah Nickerson and Damien Randle—built the song by sampling West's televised sound bite and a portion of his then current hit song "Gold Digger." Those elements forged a musical backdrop for a series of densely detailed rhymes by Nickerson and Randle. They present a chilling narrative, culled from televised news reports and their own experiences as volunteers in Houston tending to Katrina victims:

Five days in this motherfucking attic
I can't use a cellphone I keep getting static
Dying 'cause they lying instead of telling us the truth . . .
Screwed 'cause they say they're coming back for us, too
But that was three days ago and I don't see no rescue . . .

Their song reflected not just West's outrage but also his sense of heartbreak and helplessness. "George Bush Doesn't Care About Black People" is less a diatribe about how government doesn't work than a moving series of vignettes that personalizes the struggles and frustrations of the hurricane's victims.

Swam to the store, tryin' to look for food
Corner store's kinda flooded so I broke my way through
Got what I could but before I was through
News say the police shot a black man trying to loot

Randle said he was shocked by the bluntness of West's comments, but not their substance. Nickerson lived near the Astrodome and Randle near a convention center in Houston, both of which were used to house New Orleans refugees. "Not till you see these people face-to-face and talk to them can you appreciate the level of hopelessness," said Randle, a financial adviser at a Houston bank. "The one common feeling was that they felt abandoned, on their own little island."

Four days after West's comments, the rappers put together the song in their home studios. "I finished my verse at six fifteen [P.M.] and we had it on the Internet by six thirty and circulating to our friends and people we know in the music industry," Randle said. The group said the song was downloaded for free ten thousand times the first day it was made available on its website, www .kotix.com.

"What's surprising to me is not the level of the response but the demographics of the people responding," he said. "It's not just a hip-hop audience. I got an e-mail from one guy in Austin who described himself as a 'typical middle-class conservative white male' who didn't necessarily agree with the politics but liked the fact that we were speaking out."

No commercial radio station would dare play "George Bush Doesn't Care About Black People." But it became a hit anyway. Within a month it had been downloaded more than a million times. At year's end, it finished in the top 20 of the *Village Voice*'s annual Pazz & Jop poll of the nation's critics, the first piece of music released exclusively as an MP3 file to ever rank so high in the poll's three-decade history.

A few years earlier, the song might have been released as a CD or a twelve-inch single. But it would've taken weeks to record and manufacture, and its circulation would've been severely limited. The Legendary K.O. had been making records in Houston since 1992, but none of their releases had found much of an audience outside the Southwest and a few pockets around the world where the duo had toured previously. "It's the nature of being an independent artist with no real budget for promotion and distribution," Randle said.

But on the Internet, the song found a huge audience almost instantly. "People would google Kanye West and Katrina, and the song would pop up," Randle said. "It was a spur-of-the-moment decision to record it. We weren't interested in profiting from the song, just doing something because everyone had a reaction to what Kanye said. Within ten minutes of the broadcast, we were getting calls and e-mails from friends, 'Did you see that?' We felt the song almost instantly, and we wanted others to hear it too. It was a big domino effect. We were amazed at how extensive the whole blog community is, because we were getting feedback on the song almost instantly from as far away as Europe, Japan."

For decades, popular music had been the art form most attuned and best equipped to offer instant feedback on the world outside the concert hall and the recording studio. In any given year, music offered more than just escapist release. It presented a running commentary on who we are and where we are as a society.

"Music comes and goes in cycles, and it gets good only when the people making it can feel the wall against their shoulder," says Mike Watt, bassist for the postpunk band the Minutemen, whose early-eighties recordings were dominated by Reagan-era protest songs. "When young people feel that wall, they push back in their music, their art, their self-expression."

Indeed some of popular music's most fertile eras coincided with hard times: the Vietnam era saw the rise of rock 'n' roll commentators like Bob Dylan and the MC5; the stumbling English economy led to the rise of punk (Sex Pistols, Clash) in the seventies; escalating Cold War tensions and repressive social policies provided a backdrop for everything from the indie punk of Minor Threat and the Minutemen to Springsteen's *Nebraska* and Prince's *1999* in the early eighties; and a militant strain of hip-hop (Public Enemy, NWA, Ice-T) emerged in the late eighties, describing the destruction of the poor inner-city black community.

"The Black CNN," Chuck D once said of hip-hop. "It is the way black people communicate with one another about who we are. It's a music about the things you won't see on the nightly news."

Anyone who spent even a few hours listening to gangsta rap records out of Los Angeles in the late eighties could have foreseen the Rodney King beating in 1991, and the rioting that tore apart Los Angeles in 1992 after the four officers accused of assaulting King were acquitted.

"Like throwing a match in a pool of gasoline," is how Chuck D described the King verdict.

NWA's "Fuck the Police," LL Cool J's "Illegal Search," Cypress Hill's "Pigs," Boogie Down Production's "Who Protects Us from You?," Public Enemy's "Anti-Nigger Machine," and Body Count's "Cop Killer" were among the countless rap records that had detailed how police dealt with young blacks in America's ghettos. They described with chilling accuracy the anger and resentment that had been building in these communities and that bubbled over after the King trial ended.

Most of these records sold hundreds of thousands of copies, some even millions, even though they were virtually banned from airplay on commercial radio and video outlets. The mainstream wouldn't touch the most politically intense hip-hop, but the music found a way to thrive anyway.

The relative prosperity of the late nineties coincided with music that largely pandered to the most heavily marketed group of young people in history: the 71 million born between 1977 and 1994. But the September 11, 2001, terrorist attacks on the World Trade Center in New York and the Pentagon again shifted the political and musical climate. Suddenly Americans found themselves in the middle of a war zone, instead of being distant observers of overseas conflicts. There was also a growing sense that Americans weren't getting the whole story from media outlets. For two years after 9/11, the Bush administration vowed to go anywhere in the world to wipe out terrorism, and it targeted Iraq in particular as a nuclear threat.

"The original function of songwriting is to tell a story that might otherwise die," Texas songwriter Steve Earle said at the time. His 2002 album, *Jerusalem,* was devoted to telling those stories.

Earle had been writing politically tinged songs most of his adult life, focusing on issues ranging from the death penalty to racism. In making *Jerusalem,* he said in the album's liner notes, he felt "like the loneliest man in America." Recalling the Vietnam era, he wrote, "Back then, as now, it was suggested by some that second-guessing our leaders in a time of crisis was unpatriotic, if not downright treasonous." But Earle didn't so much second-guess America's policy makers as dare to see the world through the eyes of their enemy.

His "John Walker's Blues" told the story of John Walker Lindh, the northern California teenager–turned–Taliban fighter. It didn't judge Walker's actions. It looked at him as a human being instead of a demon: "I'm just an American boy, raised on MTV / And I've seen all those kids in the soda pop ads / But none of 'em looked like me."

It stood in startling contrast to the initial batch of post–September 11 songs, which focused on socially sanctioned themes (the heroism of fire and law enforcement, flag-waving patriotism, God-is-on-our-side butt kicking) without exploring the more complex issues raised by the disaster.

Weeks before Earle's album was officially released, the song was already making the rounds on the Internet and was the subject of numerous news stories. The *New York Post* declared that the song "glorified" Lindh, in a story headlined "Twisted Ballad Honors Tali-Rat," and a Nashville talk-radio host claimed Earle had written the song to inflame the public and bring attention to a sagging career. But Earle says the sight of the emaciated twenty-year-old Lindh being paraded before TV cameras with his head in a sack prompted thoughts closer to home.

"I don't agree with what John Walker Lindh did, but this is also a human being who the powers-that-be don't want us to know or have access to," Earle said. "My son, Justin, is only four months younger than Lindh, and I realize that someone that age is still a work in progress. I could see myself in that position very easily."

He didn't discount the idea that the song would stir up debate and controversy. To him that has always been the point of a career devoted to protest singing.

"I started out playing music in coffeehouses and folk clubs in Texas in the seventies," he said. "I never separated songwriting and politics. I don't think Woody Guthrie was necessarily a political songwriter. He just happened to be a songwriter in politically charged times. He wrote about what was in the air, what was around him. The idea for writing a song about John Walker Lindh just fell in my lap. A few months ago, after the plea bargain deal, we're still talking about John Walker Lindh, although the people who arrested him and put him in prison wanted us to forget about him. But I couldn't. That's the kind of role music can play."

That role took on a new urgency the next year when the United States invaded Iraq. The tentative trickle of musical responses to 9/11 escalated instantly. The vast majority was not heard through mainstream outlets, as big commercial radio stations dropped controversy-stirring artists and songs from playlists.

But in the days leading up to the March 19, 2003, invasion, dozens of songs protesting Bush's threats to invade Iraq began popping up on websites across the world. The Beastie Boys surfaced with "In a World Gone Mad," R.E.M. posted "Last Straw," Chuck D's Fine Arts Militia laid down "A Twisted Sense of God" parts 1 and 2, Mexico's Molotov hammered out "Ferocious," John Mellencamp wrote "To Washington," Billy Bragg ranted about "The Price of Oil," Luka Bloom declared "I Am Not at War with Anyone," Pakistan's Junoon simply demanded "No More," Nanci Griffith damned the "Big Blue Ball of War," and Spearhead spat out "Bomb the World." These instant musical commentaries spanned several generations of songwriters—symbolized by a collaboration between Peter Paul and Mary's Peter Yarrow and his daughter Bethany Yarrow on a haunted version of the folk ballad "The Cruel War"—and mushroomed at such a rapid rate that Sonic Youth's Thurston Moore built a website, protest-music.com, to document them all.

The Internet became more than just a conduit for songs; it also served as a community bulletin board for artists to express themselves about the war without filtering from record companies or radio stations. Sheryl Crow posted a long commentary on her website denouncing the war, and hip-hop impresario Russell Simmons issued an open letter to President Bush urging, "War on Iraq now is not the solution." System of a Down posted a video—"Boom!"— that included footage shot by filmmaker Michael Moore at a protest march. At times, the line between protest and self-promotion was perilously thin. Madonna played clips on her website from her forthcoming single "American Life," a song about materialism inexplicably accompanied by a graphic antiwar video.

But other artists took stands that cost them financially. Senegalese superstar Youssou N'Dour, for example, canceled what would have been his most ambitious U.S. tour, a thirty-eight-city trek, because "coming to America at this time would be perceived in many parts of the world—rightly or wrongly—as support" for the war on Iraq.

"It's an exhilarating feeling to see so many people" rising up in opposition, said John Sinclair, former White Panther Party leader who served as the manager of agit-punks the MC5 at the height of the Vietnam era. Tens of thousands were killed in Vietnam before a significant protest movement developed in America, he said. "We're ahead of where we were as a society in the sixties in terms of building awareness about and opposition to the war."

Artists also paid more quickly for their outspokenness. Dozens of stations pulled Dixie Chicks' songs from their playlists because one of the bestselling country band's members, Natalie Maines, criticized Bush from the stage at a London concert.

The Chicks had just sold $49 million worth of concert tickets for their 2003 North American tour. But Maines's remark—"We're ashamed the president of the United States is from Texas"—caused the band's stock to plummet. The band's website was flooded with posts from irate fans.

"I have been a big fan of the Chicks as I love country music and the sound that you bring, although I cannot and will not be a part of anything that supports the ideals of anyone who makes remarks such as that," one fan posted on the Chicks' message board. "Personally, I will not support the Chicks in any way, shape, or form in the future."

A Louisiana country station rented a thirty-three-thousand-pound tractor to crush Dixie Chicks' CDs and merchandise; a Missouri station held a "chicken toss" party where irate listeners were encouraged to dump the group's recordings into garbage bins; and programmers from San Antonio to Nashville pulled the band's songs off their playlists.

In contrast, those same programmers were playing the hell out of Darryl Worley's "Have You Forgotten?," which essentially read like a Bush position paper for entering Iraq with guns blazing ("We vowed to get the ones behind Bin Laden / Have you forgotten?"). Another country star, Clint Black, posted a prowar song, "I Raq and Roll," on his website.

Though Worley's song was a number one hit on commercial stations and Black's got enough airplay to rise to number forty-two on the country charts, most of the antiwar songs never got past programmers' desks.

"You take them, pro or con, on a case by case basis," said John Ivey, vice president of programming at Clear Channel, "but I don't think anybody is looking to fill up the airwaves with songs about the war."

Rather than playing protest songs, stations owned by the Clear Channel conglomerate in Atlanta, Cleveland, San Antonio, Cincinnati, and other cities sponsored rallies endorsing Bush's strategy for ousting Iraqi leader Saddam Hussein. It was hardly coincidental that the owners of the San Antonio–based Clear Channel had close personal and financial ties to the Bush administration.

Artists continued to speak out. "September 11 cast a long shadow, made artists hesitant to put pen to paper for fear of being deemed antipatriotic or not being fully respectful of the dead," said Billy Bragg, one of the most forceful political songwriters of recent decades. "But that hesitation is quickly dissipating, and it will be gone completely when young American men and women start coming home in body bags."

Bragg was proven correct. Five years later the war raged on. The protest songs kept coming and public opinion had turned strongly against the war. Even the Dixie Chicks were vindicated. At the 2007 Grammy Awards, a music industry that tried to distance itself from the outspoken trio in the first few days of the Iraq war embraced them. The Chicks swept five awards, including song and record of the year for "Not Ready to Make Nice," a pointed rebuttal to the band's critics.

The trio was primed for a big night by awards presenter Joan Baez, who linked them to the protest tradition of Woody Guthrie. The relatively mild-mannered "Not Ready to Make Nice" isn't exactly "This Land Is Your Land," but the Chicks' nationally televised performance that night brimmed with conviction and drew a boisterous response from the music-industry crowd at the Staples Center in Los Angeles.

"I think people are using their freedom of speech tonight with these awards," Natalie Maines said. "People were using their voice the same way this loudmouth did."

Kanye West could relate.

Artists are taking it into their own hands again, and it's really showing the record companies that it's time they get their act together. It's not the end of the world for EMI. They are like family to me. But the funny thing was, they understood. I'd told people I'd known for years at the label, "Hey, guys, I've gotta make this move." And some of them said quietly, off the record, "I really don't blame you, man."

—Paul McCartney, ex-Beatle, born 1942

15

A New Boss, Same as the Old Boss

By the end of the nineties, the major labels had become a high-priced specialty business addicted to blockbusters. It was a fatally flawed system, but with profits still rolling in, no one saw a reason to change. The majors had stopped developing new artists and had little interest in sustaining middle-tier careers (veteran artists who sold one to two hundred thousand albums). But they knew how to exploit a hit, how to turn a million seller into a 3 or 4 million seller. The nineties saw a bevy of artists with releases that sold more than 10 million copies: Garth Brooks, Shania Twain, Alanis Morissette, Hammer, the Backstreet Boys, Santana, Whitney Houston, Boyz II Men, Jewel, Pearl Jam, Nirvana, Matchbox 20, TLC, Kid Rock, Céline Dion, Green Day, Mariah Carey, No Doubt, the Notorious B.I.G., among others. Those megasellers paid for the label's underperformers: the remaining 90 percent of the roster who didn't recoup their advance or barely broke even.

So when the system started to buckle in the post-Napster era, upper-crust artists were reluctant to pull a Prince and go into business for themselves. Some, including Metallica and Dr. Dre, spoke out against the onrushing tide of digital file sharing. But most bit their tongues and waited for the storm to pass, reluctant to abandon the system that had given them a lucrative living for decades. Musicians loved to complain about their record companies almost as much as they loved to complain about music critics, but few were

192

eager to assume the responsibilities of distributing and marketing their music.

"My band was saying, 'We want to have our own record label,'" says Bert Holman, manager of the Allman Brothers. "And my response is, 'Yeah, great, but there's more to it than you guys think. We need distribution. We need professional distribution, accounting, licensing, all that stuff. It needs to be handled by people who know what they're doing.' It's like asking you as a writer to start publishing a Web magazine. Maybe you can write it, but do you know how to construct the site and attract subscribers? And what about the financial component? There are so many pieces. You can do it all, but could you do it as well as somebody who has been working their whole life at it?"

John Mellencamp, notoriously cranky about record company politics for decades, nonetheless found himself signing another deal with another major, Columbia, in the late nineties. After years of discontent at his previous label, Mercury, he briefly considered following Prince's lead and going it alone, but in the end he opted for the security of a system that was familiar, if ill-equipped, to sell the music of an artist who was no longer getting airplay on commercial radio or MTV.

"People had suggested to me that I follow what Prince is doing, but it just wasn't an option for me," he said at the time. "I think someday it will be an option for everybody. But now's not the time. I wouldn't be surprised if you see his situation changing because I think it's more work than he wants it to be. It has to be. You gotta do it yourself. Who wants that?"

But less than a decade later, the major labels' decline could no longer be written off as a hiccup. The industry was sick, and some name artists weren't about to stick around for the wake. Among them was Paul McCartney.

No artist was more entrenched in the major-label system than McCartney and his seemingly ageless band-turned-franchise, the Beatles. The twentieth-century music business had been built on the bestselling careers of artists like the Beatles, and it would sustain itself for decades by repackaging and reselling its classic artists to generation after generation, first on vinyl records, then on cassettes, and finally on compact discs. McCartney had been signed to Capitol/EMI Records since the sixties, first with the Beatles, then as a solo artist and later with the band Wings (his Capitol tenure was briefly interrupted during the eighties by a short stint at another major, Columbia Records). McCartney's career had made EMI a lot of money, and helped turn the Capitol Tower in Hollywood into a powerful symbol, the music-industry equivalent of Disneyland's Magic Castle.

"With the Beatles you have a franchise like Disney has with Mickey Mouse," said Bruce Kirkland, a vice president with Capitol in the midnineties. "Just like every generation has a bunch of new seven-year-olds that love Mickey, the Beatles are becoming the same kind of phenomenon."

In 1995–96, Capitol kicked off a new wave of Beatlemania by releasing three double-CD *Anthology* sets consisting of studio outtakes, rarities, and live performances. The campaign was launched by some dubious "new" music: a couple of marginal singles in which the surviving band members (McCartney, George Harrison, Ringo Starr) doctored recordings left behind by the late John Lennon. The rest consisted of outtakes that the band members and producer George Martin had for decades declared "inferior" and unworthy of release. Yet these leftovers enabled the Beatles to outsell every single artist in America in 1996. The record industry was proving more adept at selling also-rans from a band that had been extinct for three decades than it was music from new artists.

About 40 percent of the *Anthology* sales were to teens and young adults in their twenties who weren't even alive when the Beatles stopped recording. In addition to nearly 5 million *Anthology* sales in the first year of the Beatles' midnineties comeback, the band's back catalog sold 6 million copies.

The notion of finding new ways to sell the same music (or in the case of *Anthology,* a lesser version of it) to consumers was the bedrock of the compact-disc boom years of the late eighties and the nineties. The back catalog of major artists such as the Beach Boys, Rolling Stones, David Bowie, Elvis Costello, and Pink Floyd was repackaged and resold on CD countless times. In addition, careers were sustained and record-company earnings swollen by selling CDs containing the musical dregs of Elvis Presley, Jimi Hendrix, the Mexican pop singer Selena, Jim Morrison, Tupac Shakur, and Biggie Smalls.

The constant repackaging of his past made McCartney one of the world's wealthiest pop stars. Yet in 2007, McCartney walked away from the major-label system that he helped sustain over five decades. The record industry knew how to sell McCartney's legacy, but they had few fresh ideas on how to market his current music—or just about anybody else's, for that matter. Sales for McCartney's new albums had flattened out at about half a million, and Capitol was losing revenue and laying off employees. In 2006, the Capitol Tower—for fifty years a symbol of major-label dominance at 1730 Vine Street—was sold. Major-label Disneyland was effectively closed.

Not just labels were shrinking. So were record stores. No North American record store was more revered than Tower, which opened in 1960 in California and later spread internationally. It soon defined the record-shopping experience for generations of music lovers. Its deep and eclectic stock of music in all genres made it a must stop for connoisseurs, while still serving casual fans who only wanted the latest number one hit.

But in 2006, mauled by rising Internet activity, the bankrupt chain was $210 million in debt. It closed its stores for good and laid off twenty-seven hundred employees. The demise of the biggest of the so-called privately run mom-and-pop stores was a convenient way to mark the end of an era not just for retail, but for a particular kind of community experience. Tower and stores like it were gathering places for like-minded people to shop, chat, and exchange information about cool music. For a new generation, those activities had shifted online. For those who still wanted a CD of a big hit, there was still Wal-Mart or Best Buy, but good luck trying to find anything more adventurous than a top seller there. Those retail behemoths stocked no more than five thousand titles, whereas a typical Tower store would have twelve times as many.

That shifting landscape had a major impact on McCartney. The business was changing. Why weren't the major labels keeping up?

Rather than jump to another major after departing Capitol, McCartney signed with Hear Music, an independent label run by coffee-making giant Starbucks and the Concord Music Group, a venerable jazz company.

Starbucks had already had success with the Hear Music imprint, working with Concord on the 2004 Ray Charles release, *Genius Loves Company,* which sold more than 5 million copies and won eight Grammy Awards. More than a quarter of those sales came at Starbucks, which was no longer just in the business of selling $3 lattes, but promoting an ambiance, a lifestyle, with its own java-friendly soundtrack.

McCartney was the first artist to sign directly to the label. Part of McCartney's frustration with Capitol stemmed from the lack of commercial radio airplay he was getting for his new music. With Hear Music, he saw a new opportunity: airplay in fourteen thousand Starbucks stores that attracted 44 million customers a week.

"One of the issues the industry has is that artists like Ray and Paul McCartney no longer get the radio airplay they used to get, which was a main way of communicating with their potential fan base," said Glen Barros, Concord president and CEO. "Now a large part of their fan base is walking through Starbucks stores, so when they discover that music, and talk about it with friends and family, it creates a buzz and awareness that has a positive effect in all channels."

At sixty-five, McCartney had a new album, *Memory Almost Full,* of which he was particularly proud. It was his most personal work in years; he had invested himself in unusually revealing lyrics that looked back to his childhood and forward to his death. It was an album that McCartney was more than justified in wanting people to hear. That he didn't see the major-label system as the best vehicle for achieving that was a stunning affirmation that things had changed, perhaps irreversibly.

"They were floundering," McCartney says of EMI, which changed ownership soon after he left. "Like a lot of these record companies, they were in the old world, and they needed to enter the new world. . . .

"People had been telling me the last couple years that I was selling most of my records in Best Buys and Wal-Marts. You're getting most of your sales in supermarkets anyway. So it was more logical to me to do it in Starbucks, because it has a music connection. It's the same thing: it's still a distribution machine. Particularly with the world changing so much that you've got tragedies like Tower Records closing, I said, 'The time's right.'"

He also agreed to release his music through digital retail for the first time, cutting a deal with Apple to make all the post-Beatles McCartney music available at Apple's iTunes store. In another first, the iconic singer allowed himself to be featured in a television ad for Apple's portable music player, the iPod, playing a song from *Memory Almost Full.*

"That was more like a music deal than a commercial for me," McCartney says. "I didn't have to say, 'And I believe in iTunes and Apple, and the iPod is the greatest invention ever.'"

The deal paid immediate dividends. *Memory Almost Full* debuted at number three on the *Billboard* 200 with 161,000 sales, nearly double the first-week numbers of his 2005 Capitol swan song, *Chaos and Creation in the Backyard.* Nearly half the sales for *Memory* were at Starbucks stores, which played the album continually on the first day of availability. Veteran artists such as Joni Mitchell and James Taylor followed suit and released albums of their own on the Hear Music imprint.

A few months after McCartney's Starbucks deal, Madonna announced she was leaving Warner Bros. after twenty-five years to sign with Artist Nation, a new full-service label launched by North America's largest concert promoter, Live Nation.

It was a deal for and about celebrities, allowing Live Nation to share in every aspect of Madonna's career: not just touring, but merchandising, fan clubs, record and DVD sales, music-related television and film projects, and sponsorship deals. It was reportedly worth $120 million over ten years, an astonishing deal for a pop artist who turned fifty in 2008.

This was a new type of music corporation, tailored for multimedia stars for whom music is just one aspect of what they do, and how they sell. By signing Madonna, the nation's dominant concert promoter had set itself up as a new breed of music company, gunning to sign the same big-name artists that have been the majors' meal ticket for a half century and offering them one-stop-shopping benefits. For Madonna, it represented an opportunity to partner with a huge marketing machine that could help her cash in on all the business opportunities that her music made possible. Within a year, two more artists with long, lucrative major-label careers—U2 and Jay-Z—had signed similar deals with Artist Nation. As part of a twelve-year deal, U2 received an estimated $19 million in Live Nation stock.

One of the biggest-selling releases of 2007 was by another former major-label staple, the Eagles. The California country-rockers had sold 100 million albums for the majors over thirty-five years, but in 2003 formed their own label and then partnered with Wal-Mart to release *Long Road Out of Eden,* their first new studio album in twenty-seven years. *Eden* sold 2.6 million copies, with the band keeping a higher percentage of each sale thanks to a more generous royalty rate.

A year later, the architect of the Eagles' Wal-Mart deal, manager Irving Azoff, partnered his Front Line management company with Ticketmaster, the nation's biggest ticketing agency, to create Ticketmaster Entertainment in a $123 million deal. The company aimed to reinvent how artists distribute music by marketing directly to concert ticket buyers.

This was hardly a Prince-like palace revolt, however. This was power speaking to power. With the rise of file sharing as the new distribution system, the Internet as the new radio, and YouTube as the new MTV, the major labels had lost their clout. Now a new corporate elite was emerging to replace them: Live Nation, Starbucks,

Wal-Mart, Apple. The names had changed, but the system remained much the same.

"The money has gotten ever more ridiculous," said the longtime Beatles press officer Derek Taylor during the band's midnineties resurgence. "And, of course, no matter how much money you have, everyone wants a bit more."

McCartney tried to put a folksy spin on his move to Starbucks and his deal with iTunes. For him, he said, it was a matter of being able to pick up the phone and talk to Starbucks CEO Howard Schultz or Apple founder Steve Jobs and "talk like a couple of guys."

"Strangely enough they're two guys running companies that I can get through to direct. You'd think I could get through to everyone, but it's not the case. I'd often meet layers of secretaries before I can talk to the guy in charge [at EMI]. 'Hey, it's Paul McCartney, can I speak to the boss?' 'He's in a meeting.' If I get Steve Jobs's number, I get Steve. And I like that."

But in reality, it was little more than a trade of one corporate system for another. McCartney didn't disagree.

"There were a few people saying, 'Are you kidding? Starbucks?' and I'm saying, 'But are you kidding, Best Buy?' What's the difference?"

By April 2008, Starbucks had already reconsidered its position as a record label and handed over management control of Hear Music to Concord. The move to expand into a more ambitious boutique label had flopped. CD sales had increased 20 percent, to 4.4 million in 2007, at Starbucks, but the number of sales per store had actually declined.

Instead of CDs, Starbucks announced it would focus on—what else?—selling music online through a deal struck with—who else?—Apple's iTunes store. Eventually, it seemed, if you wanted to sell music in the post-Napster era, you had to deal with Steve Jobs.

I used to download songs quite a bit in college, but iPods and iTunes changed everything. Having a little more income helps too. You knew with file sharing there was always a chance you were going to get in trouble. You knew that it was wrong. You still did it, but in the back of your mind you knew you were wrong. With iTunes, you could get the music easily, and not have to worry about that stuff.

—Maggie, Chicago hotel executive, born 1984

16

Steve Jobs and the iPod "Burglary Kit"

In 2004, U2 made a deal in Steve Jobs's kitchen in Palo Alto, California. There, singer Bono, manager Paul McGuinness, and Interscope record-company chairman Jimmy Iovine met with the Apple CEO. McGuinness wrote down the details in the back of the diary he carried: for the first time, U2 would allow its music to be used in a television advertisement in return for a royalty on a custom U2 iPod.

The occasion was the release of U2's eleventh studio album, *How to Dismantle an Atomic Bomb*. Instead of releasing the album's first single, "Vertigo," as a video, U2 launched the album with a commercial that showed the band belting out the song interspersed with images of silhouetted iPod-clutching dancers.

The convergence of the world's biggest stadium-rock band and the world's savviest computer company ensured *How to Dismantle an Atomic Bomb* would be a hit: it ended up selling more than 3 million copies in the United States, while "Vertigo" moved 2 million copies (mostly downloads), the Irish quartet's biggest-selling single yet.

At the time, in an interview with this writer for the *Chicago Tribune*, U2 singer Bono acknowledged that associating the band's music with a product was "alarming." But "you've got to deal with the devil."

"The devil here is a bunch of creative minds, more creative than a lot of people in rock bands. The lead singer is Steve Jobs. In the band on lead guitar, [Apple senior vice president] Jonny Ive. A beautiful spirit. A man who has helped design the most beautiful art object in music culture since the electric guitar. That's the iPod. . . .

"We looked at the iPod commercial as a rock video. We chose the director. We thought, How are we going to get our single off in the days when rock music is niche? When it's unlikely to get a three-minute punk-rock song on top of the radio? So we piggybacked this phenomenon to get ourselves to a new, younger audience, and we succeeded. And it's exciting. I'm proud of the commercial, I'm proud of the association. We have turned down enormous sums of money to put our songs in a commercial, where we felt, to your point, where it might change the way people appreciated the song. We were offered [and turned down] $23 million for just the music to 'Where the Streets Have No Name.' . . . But we have to start thinking about new ways of getting our songs across, of communicating in this new world, with so many channels, with rock music becoming a niche."

Iovine said the deal represented the best way to expose U2's music, because his label could no longer count on support from commercial radio or MTV. "We're fighting radio, all these ancient things that have stopped putting people like U2 on the air," he said. "We gotta cut through that. TV can cut through that, the Internet can cut through that. You've got to feed that if you want to stay in the game. The iPod commercial didn't hurt with young kids. The iPod is the new electric guitar."

But three years later, the U2 camp was no longer singing Apple's praises. The U2-iPod deal was done back in "the days when iTunes was being talked about as penicillin for the recorded music industry," Paul McGuinness said at his 2008 keynote speech at the MIDEM music conference in Cannes, France.

The penicillin never took. The music industry continued to decline. But as the iPod's status took hold as the ultimate music accessory, the cigarette-sized portal to thousands of songs, Jobs's business thrived.

At the time of the U2 ad, the iPod and the iTunes music store were still in their relative infancy. When the iPod was first introduced in the fall of 2002, it was a cult item, selling 376,000 copies in its first twelve months on the market. Sales crept up to 1.6 million in the first half of 2004. But in the last half of the year, thanks in part to the massive U2 marketing campaign, sales skyrocketed to 6.5 million.

In the last quarter of 2007, Apple reported record revenue of $9.6 billion, 42 percent from iPod sales of 22 million, pushing the six-year total for the portable music players to 141 million.

Meanwhile, the iTunes store, which opened in 2003, reported similar increases. Downloads jumped from 70 million in April 2004 to 300 million a year later. In January 2008, the store marked 4 billion downloads. Three months later, it became the nation's leading music retailer, for the first time surpassing music sales at the world's largest retailer, Wal-Mart Stores Inc.

A number of artists followed U2's lead with iPod commercials, including Bob Dylan, Paul McCartney, Wynton Marsalis, and myriad lesser-knowns. Some of these ads proved effective sales tools not just for the iPod but for the music itself. In the fall of 2007, wispy Canadian singer-songwriter Feist saw sales of her album *The Reminder* jump to twenty thousand a week from six thousand when her video for the song "1234" started airing as an iPod ad. But there was little doubt who was steering the ship.

As Bob Lefsetz, a former record industry executive–turned–commentator, wrote in his Internet-based Lefsetz Letter: "What kind of screwed-up world do we live in where the iPod is cooler than the music it plays?"

In a few short years, Steve Jobs had gone from a tech-head cult figure to the maverick visionary the music industry could no longer ignore. "At first, they kicked us out," he said of major-label CEOs in a 2003 interview with *Rolling Stone*. But as one industry strategy after another failed to stem the tide of Internet file sharing, "we started to gain some credibility with these folks. And they started to say: 'You know, you're right on these things—tell us more.'"

By 2007, Jobs was playing a role in shaping major-label strategy; as the biggest player in selling digital music, he had begun to function much like a fifth CEO among the Big Four labels. In February, he called on his business partners in the music industry to drop all antipiracy software limitations from online music sales.

His prescription was radical medicine by industry standards. Ever since the emergence of Napster, the multinational conglomerates had sought to limit the ways that consumers could copy and share digital music files. Their efforts reached ridiculous proportion in 2005, when Sony BMG imbedded copy-prevention software on CDs of fifty-two releases that unintentionally exposed consumers' computers to debilitating viruses.

The company was pilloried in the media and targeted in several lawsuits, including one filed by the attorney general of Texas. It eventually pulled all the CDs off the market. In 2007, the U.S. Federal Trade Commission commanded Sony BMG to reimburse consumers for damage caused by the "root-kit" software.

Jobs's timing was impeccable. He released his digital-rights manifesto only a few weeks after the trade commission ruling, which capped one of the more embarrassing chapters in the record industry's file-sharing saga. So when Jobs argued that copy-protection efforts by the industry had not worked, and had served only to alienate consumers, he met little public resistance from the labels. He advocated an end to digital rights management systems, which would create a world in which "any [digital] player can play music purchased from any store, and any store can sell music which is playable on all players."

"This is clearly the best alternative for consumers," he wrote, "and Apple would embrace it in a heartbeat."

Two months later at a news conference in London, EMI responded to Jobs's plea by announcing that it would make its digital repertoire available free of digital rights management restrictions. In addition, these digital tracks would be of significantly higher sound quality (256 kilobits per second versus 128 kilobits per second). Jobs appeared alongside the chief executive officer of EMI Music, Eric Nicoli, to answer questions about the new policy.

Jobs was the only executive from the digital domain at EMI's announcement. In addition, he and Nicoli answered questions from the media together, as if they were partners. It was a clear indication that EMI saw Jobs and his iTunes store as its future, the one area of growth in an industry otherwise besieged by bad news.

"We remain optimistic that digital growth will outstrip physical decline" in CD sales, Nicoli said. But it didn't happen soon enough. Nicoli quit five months later as EMI was about to be taken over by the private equity group Terra Firma.

Jobs's publicity coup was couched in corporate double-speak. Tucked inside the announcement was that the price per premium track would increase a dizzying 30 percent at iTunes (to $1.29 from ninety-nine cents).

When asked about the price increase, Jobs responded, "It's not a price increase. . . . It's a second product that you get to choose to buy or not."

Technically, he was correct. The iTunes store would now offer consumers two options: copy-protected digital music files of lower sound quality at the old ninety-nine-cents-per-track price, and the new, higher-priced "premium" files, which would be of better sound quality and free of copy-protection software. But even Jobs acknowledged that this latest step merely brought digital files in line with CDs.

What's more, Apple's profit margin on each iTunes sale was enormous. Benn Jordan, an Illinois-based electronic artist who has recorded under ten pseudonyms for a decade, says a contract his independent label signed broke down iTunes revenue for his music this way: 36 percent to the store, 30 percent for the digital distributor, 17 percent to the label, and 17 percent to the artist.

"This should be insulting to artists because iTunes does not promote or manufacture your product," Jordan says. "They simply host bandwidth, which many places will do for much less."

David Byrne, who has recorded for both major and indie labels, says that artists essentially make the same royalty amount from an iTunes sale as they do from a traditional CD sale. "There's no manufacturing or distribution costs" for a download, he says, "but somehow the artist ended up with the exact same amount."

Yet there was little resisting iTunes when it controlled the digital-sales market. Despite the rise of other online music stores, most formidably amazon.com, Apple still represented about 70 percent of digital music business in 2007.

Whereas CD sales had declined to 500 million units in 2007, from 942 million in 2000, digital music sales were booming and overall individual music purchases hit a record 1.4 billion. Yet most of that growth was attributable to ninety-nine-cent tracks on iTunes, while sales of $15 CDs plunged 15 percent.

Clearly the route to rejuvenating revenue, presumably not just for record labels but for artists, ran through the Internet. Suing consumers had not stemmed the tide of peer-to-peer file sharing, which outdistanced legit downloads twenty to one. Even Steve Jobs acknowledged that only 3 percent of the music on the average iPod was bought from iTunes. Some of the remaining music came from legitimately purchased CDs that had been ripped onto the MP3 players. But the majority of it was, in the industry's eyes, contraband.

McGuinness did not spare his old business partner Jobs in his 2008 MIDEM keynote: "I wish he would bring his remarkable set of skills to bear on the problems of recorded music. He's a technologist, a financial genius, a marketer, and a music lover. He probably doesn't realize it but the collapse of the old financial model for recorded music will also mean the end of the songwriter. We've been used to bands who wrote their own material since the Beatles, but the mechanical royalties that sustain songwriters are drying up. Labels and artists, songwriters and publishers, producers and musicians—everyone's a victim."

The veteran manager's words reflected the grave doubts sweeping through the industry about Jobs and his true motives. No other major quickly followed EMI to offer unrestricted files to iTunes. Universal, U2's label, pointedly announced that it would seek deals with other digital stores to sell its unprotected files. In 2008 it followed through on its threat, joining Warner Bros. and Sony BMG in striking a digital music distribution deal with iTunes's top competitor, Amazon. The labels grumbled that iTunes pricing wasn't flexible enough. They were also vexed by Apple's refusal to license its software so that other music stores could sell music that could be played on the iPod, and so that other digital devices could play songs bought from iTunes. "Hardware makers should share with the content owners whose assets are exploited by the buyers of their machines," McGuinness demanded.

In 2009, Apple finally reached a compromise with the majors and introduced a three-tiered pricing structure for its 10 million-song iTunes store (sixty-nine cents, ninety-nine cents, and $1.29). In exchange, the labels agreed to remove all copy-protection restrictions. It was a positive step in untangling the web of distrust that had settled over the relationship between the music industry and Apple.

But by then the big labels were looking for other business partners to bully, most notably Internet service providers (ISPs).

"I've met a lot of today's heroes of Silicon Valley," McGuinness railed. "Most of them don't really think of themselves as makers of burglary kits. They say: 'You can use this stuff to e-mail your friends and store and share your photos.' But we all know that there's more to it than that, don't we? Kids don't pay $25 a month for broadband just to share their photos, do their homework, and e-mail their pals."

He called on Internet service providers to share their revenue, or else: "We must shame them. Their snouts have been at our trough for too long."

At about the same time, the Songwriters Association of Canada proposed a $5-a-month licensing fee on every wireless and Internet account in the country, in exchange for unlimited access to all recorded music.

The deal aimed to put $1 billion annually in the pockets of artists, publishers, and record labels. The money would be distributed to artists based on how frequently their music is swapped online; the more downloads, the more money the people responsible for the music would accrue.

For sixteen cents a day, the plan proposed to give computer users access to every song that could possibly be made available online.

But a lot of questions needed to be answered before the plan could be set in motion, including who would collect and distribute the money—a job that wireless carriers and Internet service providers weren't equipped to do, and would likely fight to avoid.

The proposal also opened the door to government involvement in the music industry, hardly a happy prospect. A few months earlier, the French government stuck its nose into the downloading fray by creating an antipiracy agency charged with shutting down customers' Internet access if they engage in illegal file sharing.

If the Canadian songwriters' plan was deeply flawed, it at least had the advantage of appearing far less punitive than any previous industry proposal dealing with file sharing.

A more refined version of that approach was put on the table at the South by Southwest music conference in Austin, Texas, in March 2008. There, music consultant Jim Griffin proposed that broadband users pay for any music they download through a fee bundled into their monthly Internet access bill. His plan would allow consumers to download, upload, and share music without restriction, and create a pool of money collected from Internet service providers to compensate music copyright holders, but do it without government involvement.

"Government involvement in the arts is abhorrent to me, and I do not favor a tax," Griffin said. Instead he proposed a fee on broadband users. The fee would not apply to users who do not download music. Still, Griffin expected that "seventy to eighty percent of users would pay" to gain access to all the music their hard drives could hold.

"Our industry now functions on a tip jar," he said. "We have to make it roughly involuntary to pay" in the same way that "sports has made it roughly involuntary to pay with cable TV deals."

A week later he was hired by Warner Bros. to put his plan in motion. It envisioned a live-and-let-live world in which peer-to-peer file sharing would coexist with iTunes and other legitimate MP3 music stores. With an estimated 750 million people expected to be hooked into wireless broadband networks in Western Europe and the United States alone in the next decade, the potential revenue from licensing fees on Internet service providers could be substantial.

Yet such a forward-thinking plan might already be too little too late for the industry, said Sandy Pearlman, a McGill University professor and former producer for Blue Oyster Cult and the Clash. A portable database containing all the music ever recorded is imminent, he said. "Once this paradise of infinite storage is entered," he said, "it will represent the end of all intellectual property rights."

Ya'll don't want to go cop our CD, you'd rather download our shit. Which is cool, whatever. But c'mon man, we do this, spend a lot of time in the studio, and put this work in, to come out with no results when we drop our album. So I got 115,000 friends on MySpace, and then to get 30,000 [sales] in the first week, that's not good. I know a lot of you got my shit, but you just download it. I'm asking you to go to the store and buy that, man. I'm using all these samples tryin' to put all this shit together for you, and you . . . are on that bullshit. Snap out of it. This is real talk. I think it's gonna make me leave the game. . . . I will take a personal meeting with all you . . . when I'm in your town. Just show me the CD. We can all have a powwow . . . But don't front on me like that.

—Ghostface Killah in a YouTube video soon after the release of his album *Big Doe Rehab,* in 2007

Dear Ghostface,

Being a MySpace "friend" does not actually mean we are "friends" in the deeper, bff [best friend forever] sense of the word. While I greatly admire your music, I sincerely doubt you would come over for brunch, help me move, or lend me money just because we share a tenuous "online relationship." MySpace friendship doesn't obligate me to purchase your album.
Also, people don't really buy records anymore, just fyi.

—A big fan, The Playlist

17

"The Feedback Loop of Creativity"

Lily Allen was bored. After dropping out of school at age fifteen in London, she had made ends meet by working at a record store, studying horticulture, and recording a little music. In the fall of 2005 she signed a modest $50,000 deal with Regal, a division of Parlophone, and the U.K. label was doing what a major-label usually does: finding a suitable producer for an inexperienced artist they hoped to turn into a pop star. The execs were in no particular hurry because they had bigger priorities: the promotion of Coldplay, Gorillaz, and Kylie Minogue, among other big acts. But the twenty-year-old singer was in no mood to wait her turn.

She ran into Louise Harmon—nineteen-year-old U.K. rapper Lady Sovereign—at a London bar, and the two young artists traded notes. Harmon tipped Allen about MySpace.com, a twenty-two-month-old social networking site that at that point had attracted 36 million users. Sov had used her MySpace page to introduce her songs and eventually scored a major-label deal.

In November 2005, Allen opened a MySpace account and uploaded a few demos that her record company considered a long way from album-ready.

"I wasn't one of those people looking around for music all the time online," she says. "But I saw that everybody else was doing it, and I just thought I'd follow suit. It wasn't about getting paid or anything. It was about a social scene, and a way for me to get my

211

music out. I didn't think it was going to turn into this . . . craziness."

Allen's songs cut through the Internet traffic with their engaging, deceptively sunny Caribbean-flavored melodies. Her clever putdowns of the unfortunate boys who had done her wrong and the hapless ones who tried to pick her up resonated with her club-trolling, instant-message-happy peers.

It didn't hurt that she could also dish like nobody's business on her MySpace blog. She posted personal photos and videos, and chattily described her boozy escapades. Fans started to download her music, and flooded her with e-mail. Allen made a point of writing back.

"I started getting huge amounts of messages and fan requests, and at first I didn't realize it was anything special," she says. "I just assumed the same thing was happening for everyone else."

Her record company started getting requests for interviews from major media, which baffled the company's press officer, who hadn't heard of Allen and saw no Lily Allen album on the company's release schedule.

Within a few months, the songs she posted on her site had been streamed millions of times. One of them, "Smile," became a number one hit in the summer after U.K. radio stations caught up with the song and Regal got around to releasing it. Her debut album, *Alright, Still*, was rush-released in July 2006 and sold more than three hundred thousand copies in the U.K. within a few months.

Yet it wasn't until 2007 that the album was finally released by Capitol Records in the United States. By that time, Allen had already played a sold-out tour of North American clubs.

"A few years ago, something like this couldn't have happened," says Dave Rockland of Jam Productions, who booked her sold-out Chicago show in the fall of 2006. "But the generation that Lily Allen is speaking to is who we're trying to sell concert tickets to. Her show sold out weeks in advance with no radio and no major-label release. This is completely a MySpace buzz-driven thing. It's a perfect delivery system for music: you click on a page, and a song starts playing.

More and more with these kinds of artists, the hype is being generated online. Radio and MTV aren't driving the business the way they
used to."

MySpace debuted in January 2004 and took the concept of social
networking to unprecedented levels of popularity by adopting and
refining the more user-friendly characteristics of previous sites, such
as Friendster. Musicians who signed up to MySpace were allowed to
upload songs, enabling them to reach an audience that was adding 4
million users a month by 2006.

A competitor, Facebook, soon emerged. Initially available only
to college students, it had expanded to allow anyone to use it by
2007, and by 2008 was attracting more than 115 million visitors a
month worldwide. But MySpace retained a three-to-one lead in
monthly visitors over Facebook in America, in part because of its
more refined music strategy. By creating a separate music page and
allowing artists to stream their music, MySpace gave bands several
advantages over Facebook, which did little to differentiate bands
from other users.

By 2008, more than 5 million bands had opened MySpace pages in
an effort to draw attention from the site's 72 million unique monthly
visitors. Even defunct bands had MySpace accounts; English postpunk band Joy Division, which fell apart in 1980 when singer Ian
Curtis hanged himself, had posthumously accumulated more than
fifty thousand MySpace friends, ranging from U2 to a woman calling
herself Tinkerbell.

The site, bought by Rupert Murdoch's News Corp. for $580
million in 2005, was every bit as formidable a player as Steve Jobs's
iTunes and iPod franchises in shaping major-label strategy. MySpace
had been selling digital music by indie artists since 2006, but by 2008
had struck a deal with three of the majors (Universal Music Group,
Sony BMG, and Warner Music Group) to sell everything from music
merchandise to ring tones.

In the same year that Lily Allen tunneled out from obscurity
through her portal on MySpace.com, another little-known Capitol

Records act, OK Go, danced its way into the hard drives of a huge audience when its homemade videos became the talk of YouTube .com.

The video site, created in February 2005 by three former PayPal employees, was attracting 100 million video views a day by the time OK Go started to take advantage of it. YouTube had started as an outlet for homemade novelties and comedy skits, but soon evolved into a treasure chest of music videos, in which fans posted everything from grainy footage of the Velvet Underground in all their menacing sixties glory to a Bright Eyes concert snippet captured on a cell phone.

OK Go, a four-piece Chicago power-pop band, hadn't made much of a commercial impression with its first two studio albums for Capitol, then decided to take matters into their own hands. They taped themselves parodying 'N Sync dance moves in singer Damian Kulash's backyard to their song "A Million Ways." Total budget: $20, including a coffee run. Without their record company's knowledge or permission, they distributed copies of the video to their fans, who uploaded it on YouTube. It was downloaded 9 million times. Capitol was impressed; rather than file an infringement suit against its own band for essentially giving away one of its songs, it encouraged a follow-up.

Kulash brainstormed with his sister, professional dancer Trish Sie. She invited the band to her home in Orlando, where she set up eight rented treadmills in a spare bedroom. She choreographed the foursome through a series of synchronized leaps, spins, duckwalks, and moonwalks on the moving exercise machines to the song "Here It Goes Again." It took the quartet more than fifty takes and a series of bumps and bruises to nail the finished, unedited take on a borrowed video camera.

The video debuted July 31, 2006, on VH1, and fans quickly posted copies on YouTube. As geeky video goofs go, it embodied the essence of YouTube's anyone-can-do-it enterprise and inspired hundreds of parodies, including a spoof on *The Simpsons*. Two years later, the video had been viewed more than 42 million times, and had led to appearances by the band on the MTV Music Awards, *The Colbert Report,* and *The Tonight Show with Jay Leno.* It also won an improbable 2007 Grammy for best short-form video. The treadmill dance not only turned OK Go into YouTube's poster child, it saved the band's career. Sales for its albums jumped, and the quartet began selling out club concerts around the country.

Faring even better were YouTube founders, Chad Hurley and Steve Chen, who sold YouTube to Google Inc. for $1.65 billion in Google stock less than three months after "Here It Goes Again" first aired. By 2008, the site was hosting 83 million videos and had effectively usurped MTV as the go-to site for music videos.

OK Go's viral success turned Kulash into an outspoken advocate for network neutrality, the principle that the Internet should not discriminate against any data carried over it. The net neutrality campaign arose amid growing fears that service providers would create tiers of access based on users' ability to pay. It paralleled OK Go's own struggles with the record business, where access to commercial radio and MTV was often determined not by content but payola.

In March 2008, Kulash testified before the House Judiciary Antitrust Task Force on the subject. His presentation was an eloquent overview of where the music industry had been and where it was going, thanks to the opportunities afforded by the Internet. Exhibit A was Kulash's own band, which he said wouldn't have had a prayer had the old record-industry hierarchy been in place. But in the democratic marketplace created by the Internet, OK Go had a career, and was actually making money from playing music.

Kulash outlined the mechanics of making and distributing music in the pre-Internet era: expensive recording studios, costly manufacturing and distribution, and a handful of gatekeepers at commercial radio and MTV determining what records would be heard, and at what price.

"Some songs succeeded primarily on the merits of the drugs and Super Bowl tickets that were delivered to radio stations with them," the singer wryly noted in his written testimony. But unfettered access to the Internet had turned that system "on its head."

For artists, this transition ushered in a new "golden age" where "anyone with access to a decent computer now has recording tools that the professionals of my parents' generation couldn't have dreamed of—making high quality recordings is now nearly as easy as word processing."

Kulash described how fans from around the world created their own versions of OK Go's videos in "a feedback loop of creativity."

"Our success couldn't have happened in the pay-to-play music industry of ten years ago, or in a world without an open, unbiased, and unfettered Internet," he said. "Of course, like most bands, we use the Internet for everything today; it's not just a medium for our videos. We connect with fans through our website, our online forums, and through social networking sites like MySpace and Face-book. We alert our online fans to concerts and television and radio appearances, and we promote those appearances to new fans. We sell our merchandise and CDs, and book our tours online. We broadcast some concerts online, and have done many performances solely for an online audience. Today, as I speak to you, some dedicated portion of our fans is listening to this testimony, online. (Hi, guys.) Basically, the Internet stops just short of writing our music for us. But it takes care of just about everything else."

For Jenny Toomey, the former president of the Future of Music Coalition, which had led the fight for net neutrality, OK Go rep-resented just one of countless bands benefiting from a new digital marketplace.

"Artists used to have to be on a label that had a relationship with a distributor who had a relationship with a store and then the con-sumer," she said at the 2007 Future of Music Coalition Policy Sum-mit in Washington, D.C. "Otherwise you were selling CDs out of the back of your truck."

Toomey knew what that felt like. She had been playing in rock bands for twenty years and had once run an independent label.

"There was always a line between indie and major: we could be in a mom-and-pop store, they could be in major chains; we could be on cable access, they could be on MTV; we got played on college stations, they got on commercial radio," she said.

The Internet made many of those relationships irrelevant. "OK Go won a Grammy without having all the 'necessary' relationships," she said. "The only relationship that matters now is between the artist and the fan."

There are two reasons for getting this music and sharing it. There's the "Hey, you've gotta check this out because this is great and you probably haven't heard it." That's the biggest factor. And then there is the feel big and important factor, because you got something cool ahead of time. Me and the other guys have contests going on to see who can get certain albums first, and then we spread it around to everyone else.

—Adam, college student in Iowa, born 1988

18

"I Love Picking Fights"

And now we're back where this book started, with Radiohead and *Kid A* in the year 2000. A strange brew of future-world paranoia and lost-in-space atmospherics, delivered not with broadstroke guitars but creeping keyboards, *Kid A* was the album no one expected from the band that had made *OK Computer.*

The album leaked on the Internet weeks in advance, yet when it finally arrived in stores on October 3, it was an instant hit—the number one album in America, with more than 210,000 first-week sales, beating out such heavy hitters as Nelly and Green Day. It instantly qualified as the strangest rock album ever to debut atop the U.S. pop charts.

Radiohead singer Thom Yorke had been wringing his hands about the premature leak, fretting that it would dilute the album's impact. It was as if the band were living out the information-age paranoia outlined in *OK Computer,* the fear that the digital bits of media we consume so voraciously will eventually become our undoing.

But in this case, those fears were not realized. The potential Internet sabotage of *Kid A* had turned into a watershed moment for not only the band but for the fans.

"We were paranoid, actually," Yorke says. "In fact, there was too much paranoia about *Kid A* being out before we wanted. That was a mistake that made us look awfully precious."

After the first-week numbers were confirmed, fear turned to relief, and vindication. Number one! Really? "When we found out, we went out to celebrate in New York and sat around a table in an overpriced restaurant in Manhattan not able to say anything because of the shock," the singer said. "We couldn't understand it. I mean, we all thought there must have been some sort of clerical error."

As the band toasted its success, Yorke says, "I remember just being exceptionally proud that we'd just let off this little stink bomb that was actually going to have some sort of effect."

Yorke wasn't exaggerating. The leak played the role that radio and MTV once might have in trumpeting the album's arrival. In the past, Radiohead had enjoyed modest success on commercial radio. *Creep* even crept into the top 40 in 1993. But nothing on *Kid A* sounded very much like a radio single. Indeed, individual tracks sounded orphaned once removed from the broader context of the album. Little wonder *Kid A* barely registered on commercial radio; but the album was in heavy rotation on the Net months before its release, thanks to Napster. The result was an extraordinary confluence of underground taste and mass popularity: an affirmation that avid music fans trading information on laptops, not programmers at radio stations or video channels, were shaping the tastes of a new generation of listeners.

The album was the subject of feverish weeks-long discussion on Radiohead message boards after it leaked. It demanded one. *Kid A* required time and patience to hear it for what it is: a stream-of-consciousness tone poem infinitely spookier and stranger than the guitar anthems on *OK Computer*.

Adriaan Pels, a Dutch fan who in 1996 founded At Ease, a website devoted to all things Radiohead, had seen some of the new songs performed live in the summer of 2000, only to be taken aback when he heard the *Kid A* leak.

"'Everything in Its Right Place' sounded worse than what I'd heard live in Berlin that summer," he says. "A lot of the tracks had been changed around, and at first it sounded like a very difficult album, very different from anything they'd done before. But as a fan you listened to it more often than you might something else that you weren't sure about, and you give it more time. Now it's one of my favorite albums of all time."

Capitol Records executives watched it all go down with a mixture of excitement and frustration: excitement because the file-sharing community had actually done their job for them and built feverish anticipation for the album; frustration because they saw firsthand how the new Internet reality could be worked to their advantage, even as their industry expended untold energy and dollars to knock Napster out of business.

A few weeks after *Kid A* hit number one, Capitol Records executive Steve Nice told a roomful of college radio programmers and record-industry executives at the CMJ Music Conference in New York that Radiohead "is pro-Internet and pro-Napster."

"The more Internet stuff we did, the better," he said. But mostly, the Internet campaign that made *Kid A* a hit had nothing to do with the label or the band.

The Internet served as a de facto radio station for Radiohead fans. On first listen, it may have seemed that Radiohead was trying too hard to escape its not inconsiderable past, to bury the very things that made it great on *OK Computer* (the tension between Yorke's melancholy vocals and the surging guitar-driven melodies). The shift toward the esoteric got the album panned by *New Yorker* critic Nick Hornby, previously a Radiohead fan, and British weekly *NME*, which dismissed it as a "lengthy and over-analyzed mistake."

For all the outrage it stirred up, *Kid A* was perhaps the only logical follow-up to a masterpiece. Rather than try to top *OK Computer*, the band decided to try something completely different. It took the experimental colorations that served as window dressing on *OK Computer* and turned them into focal points on *Kid A*.

"After the *OK Computer* tour we felt we had to change everything," says bassist Colin Greenwood. "There were other guitar bands out there trying to do similar things. We had to move on."

The climax of the aptly titled *Kid A* track "How to Disappear Completely" says as much. With queasy strings and a ghostly choir playing like the lost soundtrack to Alfred Hitchcock's *Vertigo*, Yorke free-falls in slow motion. "I'm not here," he croons, and he sounds totally unafraid to, as Elvis Presley once said, get real, real gone.

For Radiohead acolytes excited about what *Kid A* represented, it was the moment where suddenly anything seemed possible. How could a record this oblique debut as the bestselling album in America? The band had become a new generation's version of commercialized cool: a big seller that didn't act or necessarily even sound like a big seller. Radiohead embodied contradictory impulses: a self-conscious "art project" that went multiplatinum; a band capable of holding the gaze of fickle MTV addicts and underground-music aficionados alike. Just as R.E.M., Nirvana, the Clash, and Talking Heads had been before them, Radiohead had become the mainstream band that fans of nonmainstream music loved.

Or to paraphrase R.E.M.'s Peter Buck, Radiohead had become the acceptable fringe of the unacceptable. With *Kid A*, Radiohead set in motion a new career phase that found them operating like an underground band rather than a major-label cornerstone like U2. It was a status that ensured that their career, both as artists and businessmen, would become something of a measuring stick for every other band that tried to make music in the first decade of the twenty-first century.

The quintet's life as a reluctant juggernaut is glimpsed in the 1998 film *Meeting People Is Easy*, one of the more deflating tour documentaries ever released. It made Radiohead look less like the most vital major rock band of recent years than the survivors of a plane crash.

"It was a snapshot in time, and it was a pretty depressing snapshot," Colin Greenwood acknowledges. The larger story was a band sick of hopping gerbil-like on the industry exercise wheel, even as the sales of *OK Computer* soared. The inner tension nearly shattered the band. "We were all terrified at the prospect of making another album, which is then preserved in aspic or amber as a promotional device for the already-booked two-year world tour, with merchandise deals and the TV rights sold to the relevant syndicate companies."

Rather than break up (a prospect contemplated each time the

group struggled through the making of an album), the band members began to let go of expectations about how a Radiohead album should sound. "The first thing people ask is, 'Where are the guitars on the new record?'" the bassist says. "Well, we recorded guitars on all the songs, but they just didn't get there in the mix stage. *Kid A* is an acoustic-based record that has been digitally manipulated afterward. There isn't an overarching aesthetic criterion. It was more a case of a bunch of guys with microphones and tube gear going to interesting spaces, recording it, and seeing what happens. You use what works. It was a case of someone like [guitarist Ed O'Brien] playing a keyboard instead of a guitar, or Jonny recording strings with an orchestra at a twelfth-century abbey."

The band blended these bits of sonic information with producer Nigel Godrich into a seductive whole, experimenting with more than twenty different running orders for the album. Several more "tradition-based" songs, as Colin Greenwood calls them, were left off and saved for the follow-up, *Amnesiac*, released eight months later.

"We had so many people expecting us to do the big guitar stadium record, but none of us felt comfortable in that territory," O'Brien says.

Ideas borrowed from the worlds of U.K. trip-hop band Massive Attack, *Remain in Light*–era Talking Heads, German art-rockers Can and Faust, and Teo Macero's postproduction on early seventies Miles Davis albums informed the work. With *Kid A*, Radiohead began to see record making more as a process in which no song was ever "finished."

"We had to come to grips with starting a song from scratch in the studio and making it into something, rather than playing it live, rehearsing it, and then getting a good take of a live performance," O'Brien says. "None of us played that much guitar on these records. Suddenly we were presented with the opportunity and the freedom to approach the music the way Massive Attack does: as a collective, working on sounds, rather than with each person in the band playing a prescribed role. It was quite hard work for us to adjust to the fact that some of us might not necessarily be playing our usual instrument on a track, or even playing any instrument at all. Once you get over your insecurities, then it's great."

Yorke acknowledges he was the one pushing the hardest to get his bandmates out of their comfort zones. "There is a restriction about people defending their own musical patch, which just gets a bit daft after a while," he says.

Contrary to his image, the singer is not without a sense of a humor, and he's self-deprecating when he talks about how the recording sessions differed from the band's nineties albums. "I have these friends in my band who grew up with guitars in their hands, and suddenly they're staring at laptops all day. It was a bit boring at points, I suppose. But it was also liberating to see this music on a screen, and to see how we could move it around, manipulate it. With that kind of tool at your disposal, it's difficult to still justify just being a rock band, and that's it. Laptops are the new electric guitar, I reckon, but I still love electric guitars and drums and singing.

"I don't disown our old stuff at all. But A&R departments all around the world went on a feeding frenzy, circa 1998–99, and perhaps now we are witnessing the results."

Where a lot of bands want to sound like *OK Computer*–era Radiohead?

"This question makes me feel ill. Yes, we've heard that sort of thing is going around. We, however, have moved on."

At the same time, the band clung to a traditional ideal: the idea of presenting a group of songs, designed to be listened to in a particular sequence. In that sense, Radiohead might as well have been Pink Floyd, circa 1975.

"Yeah, you're right," O'Brien says with a laugh. *Amnesiac* and *Kid A* drew from the same pool of songs, recorded in 1999–2000, but came off as two distinct works. "It was very liberating to be doing two records, because we didn't get so desperate about certain tracks not working within the context of *Kid A*. It helped us realize that a song wasn't working not because it was a bad song, but because it wasn't right for the album."

And the album is everything.

"Yes. They each have their own character. *Kid A* is emotionally numb. *Amnesiac* has a bit more spark. A person in my family said *Kid A* 'is like making a phone call and nobody is home, so you leave a message. *Amnesiac* is making that same phone call, only this time there's somebody home, and you have a conversation.' It's engaging in that way. It's got a bit more of the old humanity to it."

But *Amnesiac* doesn't hold together as seamlessly as *Kid A*. It's not quite a collection of leftovers, but nor is it as cohesive as its predecessor. Too many songs overlap the experiments introduced on *Kid A* and one track ("Morning Bell") appears on both albums, albeit in different versions. What sounded bold on *Kid A* now flirts with self-indulgence, particularly the closing "Life in a Glasshouse." In what could pass for a desultory New Orleans funeral march, Yorke is reduced to a whimper: "Is someone listening?"

The difficulty of the transition from a relatively traditional guitar-bass-drums band into something less easily defined can be inferred by comparing the live versions of the *Kid A* and *Amnesiac* songs to the recorded ones. Song structures became more like blueprints ripe for reinterpretation rather than fixed forms demanding to be duplicated. In the studio, "Everything in Its Right Place" was essentially created on Yorke's keyboard and then edited on computer into its finished form on the album. But live it became something else entirely with O'Brien and Greenwood cutting up the keyboards and vocals on foot pedals.

The *Kid A* songs in particular took on new dimension on the road, and *Amnesiac* tracks such as "Knives Out" and "Pyramid Song" achieved a towering authority.

On a crushingly hot midsummer night on Chicago's lakefront in 2001, Radiohead played one of their finest concerts ever in front of twenty-five thousand fans. With the city's gleaming skyline as a backdrop, and the geysers from Buckingham Fountain shooting off behind the stage like some unintended special effect, the setting was magical, and Radiohead rose to the occasion. If there were doubts about how the more atmospheric songs from *Kid A* and *Amnesiac* would fare in a large outdoor setting, they were instantly answered when Colin Greenwood's booming bass line introduced the opening, "The National Anthem."

This was guitar-based rock with avant-garde trimmings, not a gathering of precious art students donning white lab coats in their studio—though at times Jonny Greenwood resembled a mad scientist as he conjured an array of instrumental sound effects from behind an armada of keyboards and guitars.

If anything, the insular studio version of Radiohead circa 2000–2001 highlighted the boldness of the band in concert. On "Idioteque," the diminutive Yorke shook with the violence of a roller-coaster passenger enduring a bumpy ride, while "Everything in Its Right Place" mutated from a devastated soliloquy into a majestic symphony of distorted electronics underpinned by Phil Selway's massive drumming.

For Radiohead, the summer tour of 2001 was a triumphant affirmation of their prowess as a live rock band after a difficult couple years of studio tinkering. "The live performances of the record have validated the recording process," Colin Greenwood insists. "The songs are brought into a different state. I think if any of us had doubts about what we were doing in the studio they were put to rest when we played those shows."

Nothing ever came easy for Radiohead. It was part of the personality of the band; the constant questioning and self-doubt, the refusal to stand pat, was as crucial to the band's makeup as Yorke's distinctively high, fragile voice, the multi-instrumental abilities of O'Brien and the Greenwood brothers, and the protean drumming of Selway.

The band's sixth and final studio album for Capitol Records, *Hail to the Thief,* was released in 2003, and it made *Kid A* seem positively lighthearted. It was the year's bleakest and most disturbing mainstream record, a fifty-six-minute soundtrack for political betrayal, paranoia, and psychosis.

Hail to the Thief confirmed that Radiohead had become masters of anxiety, tension that hovers rather than stabs. When the tension breaks, it does not resolve in an anthemic chorus but in a rush, a fit, the sound of someone suddenly awakening from a cold-sweat nightmare.

Yorke laughs when that description is conveyed to him. "Actually, that's funny you should write something like that because I wake up in the middle of the night a lot and think about stuff that isn't healthy to think about at that hour," he says. "In England, we've been going through this heat wave, and I wake up every night at four in the morning having panic attacks about stuff like global warming."

Hail to the Thief plays like a soundtrack for one of those panic attacks. It was informed by the birth of Yorke's first child, Noah, who was two years old when the album was released. The perspective on many of the songs is that of a worried parent fretting over what kind of mess he's leaving for his child.

Its oddball centerpiece is "The Gloaming," in which Yorke murmurs, "Murderers, you're murderers, we're not the same as you," over twitchy electro beats. For Radiohead, never particularly cheery on record, this truly was the deep end of a murky pond.

By album's end, "A wolf is at the door," and Yorke is scrambling to protect his family: "Calls me on the phone, tells me all the ways he's gonna mess me up, steal all my children if I don't pay the ransom." It's a verse that echoes a line from the mournful "I Will" a few songs earlier, which finds the characters huddled in an underground bunker, vowing, "I won't let this happen to my children." It's a chilling conclusion to a claustrophobic album, a series of allusions to a world where "The Gloaming" is about to thicken into darkness.

Yorke acknowledges he's prone to depression, and the U.S. invasion of Iraq in March 2003 and the burgeoning global-warming debate hadn't helped his mental equilibrium. "While we were making the record, I used to sit around thinking, It can't carry on like this. It just can't."

Yorke laughs as if to reassure himself. "This isn't something that is with me all the time. It's when I sit down to think about stuff that this comes up. I think about this as most parents do, I suppose. I choose to put it in the music because I don't want to get locked up."

Radiohead had succeeded in making its third straight "difficult" album. The wait for *OK Computer II* would go on. Yet the band again found its audience primed for its dense, prickly new music. Like its predecessors, *Hail to the Thief* leaked on the Internet months before its release, and like *Kid A* and *Amnesiac,* it debuted in the top three of the U.S. album chart.

By this point, Yorke was no longer guardedly neutral about the impact of the unauthorized leaks on his band.

"I hate to say it, but it sort of helped, because people are able to hear bits of the music beforehand," he said soon after *Hail to the Thief* was released. "It's not ideal. I want people to hear the album as a whole. But access to radio for us has been quite limited. So [the leaks] were a nice way of spreading the word. It may affect how many people buy CDs. But I want to chuckle when I hear the record company heads are moaning about this. It makes me want to throw up when that's the excuse that's always given for why the revenues are slipping in the music business. The reason that revenue is slipping in the music business is because most of the stuff they're trying to sell you is shite. And they're surprised when people listen to shite, then don't want to buy it.

"The idea that they are the victims of an immoral act is incredible to me. They claim to have the best interests of the artists at heart. Oh, really? They haven't had the best interests of the artists in mind for fifty years."

Yorke is an animated man when he gets worked up, and his pale complexion was flushed red. He had seen firsthand how the major labels dealt with massive technological change, and he was neither impressed nor sympathetic.

"The best was, when the record industry wasn't working that good, they invented the CD, and got everyone to buy their record collection again on CD. So what happens when you haven't invested in any new artists? You're stuck basically. They've already sold the back catalog twice, at inflated prices, and developed no new artists in the meantime. And now people have discovered they can copy music on the Internet for free. Oh dear, now what?"

In 2003, it was as if Yorke were priming himself for a future that didn't involve a major label. Radiohead were now effectively free agents, and the world of music distribution was changing rapidly. What Radiohead would do next was the subject of constant speculation on Internet message boards and panel discussions at South by Southwest in Austin and the Future of Music Coalition in Washington, D.C. The band, unwittingly or not, had found itself in the forefront of the debate on Internet downloading, and now it had the opportunity to deal with the downloaders more directly than ever.

University-educated lads that they were, the members of Radiohead could always see both sides of every argument. Flipping through the seemingly infinite options opening up for music distribution, there were no easy answers. They were still touchy about this Internet stuff. When the lyrics to Yorke's 2006 solo album, *The Eraser*, showed up weeks before its release on atease.com, website founder Pels heard from Yorke's record label.

"I got my hands on *Eraser* a month before the release," Pels says. "I didn't post the record. But I was up all night listening to it and I typed up all the lyrics, and posted it the next day. That same day, the album leaked. Everyone thought I leaked it because the next day I had the label [XL] calling and e-mailing me. There were links on my message boards to the leak, which I couldn't control. I try to control the posts, but I can't control the leaks. The Radiohead management people said it was OK, that they didn't blame me, but then they told me they had all this nice stuff planned; they claimed they were going to offer previews of the album on the fan sites. And they ended up not doing any promotional stuff on the fan sites. It was their way of saying [in a scolding voice], 'See what you've done?'"

That summer, Radiohead was test-driving a bunch of new songs on a tour of North America. How those songs would be released and by whom was still a matter of almost daily discussion in the Radiohead camp. Why did a band of Radiohead's stature even need a record label at this point in their career?

"It's tough, because there's an element of retreat in all this, isn't there?" Jonny Greenwood confided from behind a veil of black bangs one summer afternoon in Chicago between concerts. "You can worry so much about these things that you don't bother to leave Oxford. You don't go on tour, you don't put records out. You have to confront the business at some point just to carry on. And we want to carry on. So I'm sure there will be a deal eventually, or a label, or a record company doing something with a recording of ours."

Yorke, sitting across from his bandmate, grimaced.

"Well, not necessarily."

"We're not going to do it in our back shed," Greenwood responded, in mock consternation.

"Well, this is an ongoing discussion, because we don't have to if we don't want to," Yorke sighed. "To be perfectly honest, it's about effort. Effort and energy. And whether we really can be asked to start a 'revolution' at this particular moment, when actually the first priority is all the other stuff. And it should always remain that way. . . . I think it's great to pick fights. I love picking fights. However, there has to be a natural reason to do it."

I buy ninety-nine percent of the albums I have, about four CDs a month. I'm pretty much the only one out here that I know of out of my group of friends who buys albums from stores on a regular basis. Most people I know rarely pay for albums. A lot of them get music online. MP3 blogs. They download albums for free. Rip it onto a CD. One of my friends was trying to defend the idea that everyone downloading was OK as long as you go to a show. And I'm uncomfortable with that notion.

I feel like true music fans, if they're downloading and still going out and seeing the shows and maybe spending money on merchandise and things like that—that's the argument that people that download use. I can see that argument somewhat, but at the end of the day they are still getting the album for free without supporting the artist. I don't care as much for a band like Metallica, because they're already filthy rich, but the thing that bothers me is when it's done for smaller artists that are struggling and have day jobs and are trying to make music pay. When people aren't buying those records it does bother me. People feel like music is public domain, so they download whatever they want.

—Paul, health-care risk analyst in San Francisco,
   born 1979

19

"It's Up to You"

In 2003, Pearl Jam fulfilled its contractual obligation to Epic Records and became free agents. Anything seemed possible. Pearl Jam had all the tools it needed to go into business for itself: long-running success, a loyal audience, and a strong Internet presence thanks to its tenclub.com fan site.

Though its record sales had declined since its grunge-era heyday, the Seattle quintet still regularly sold out its tours. The notion that the band would form its own label seemed like a real possibility, one that singer Eddie Vedder hinted at soon after Pearl Jam released its final Epic studio album, *Riot Act.*

"I think the goal ultimately would be to go completely independent, and look into the future of music distribution," Vedder said. "I think we'd like to be able to control as much of it as we can, just because we have a different way of doing and saying things. There are some cool, independent approaches we'd like to take in the future. We'd love to structure something that way."

The alternative sounded far less palatable.

"Once you sign on to a major corporation," Vedder said, "it renders your opinion impotent, in regards to anticorporate globalization."

Such words would've been empty rhetoric coming from most rock stars, but Pearl Jam had walked the walk. The band had a long and contentious history with the big businesses that run the music

232

industry: boycotting Ticketmaster, refusing to license its songs to advertisers, and declining for years to make videos to promote its albums. In addition, the band had becoming increasingly outspoken in its lyrics, and headlined the Vote for Change tour in 2004 in support of Democratic presidential candidate John Kerry.

After departing Epic, Pearl Jam released a single, "Man of the Hour," in partnership with amazon.com. So it came as a surprise when Clive Davis announced in 2006 that he had signed the band to a deal with his J Records label, a subsidiary of Sony BMG and the home of Alicia Keys, Barry Manilow, and Rod Stewart. In May, the band released its eighth studio album, *Pearl Jam,* on Davis's imprint.

In the end, Pearl Jam preferred the marketing and distribution muscle of a major record company rather than the independence—and business hassles—of a do-it-yourself operation.

Vedder said he and the band had decided that going the indie route would be too distracting. "I think the conversation is boring to someone who is interested in music," he said. "We like to be creative with the business side, but we're not good at using both sides of our brain at once. I might work on a bridge part of a song for three weeks, but I can't imagine listening to anything about the business ideas of what we do for more than an hour without taking a hammer to my head."

Jonny Greenwood, Radiohead's guitarist, could relate. He had talked to the members of Pearl Jam about how Ticketmaster had become the unintended focal point of its life in the midnineties, and how the battle took its toll on the band's career and music.

Whenever he considered the possibility of Radiohead going into business for itself, Greenwood got a little queasy. "It makes me think we're gonna be sitting in endless business meetings talking about how to do it off our own backs, rather than sitting in studios recording music."

But Radiohead was genuinely unsettled by what it saw as the majors' inability to adapt to the marketplace. The long lag time imposed by the majors between finishing an album and actually releasing it to set up a proper big-budget marketing campaign was particularly irritating. The band appreciated that its fans were almost ridiculously vigilant. As soon as word would get out that Radiohead had finished working on an album, the Internet began to buzz with anticipation. A leak of the new music would inevitably follow, and Radiohead fans were soon sharing the music and debating its merits. Inevitably, websites would jump in with their critiques of the still-unreleased work. It was flattering and yet frustrating for the band; increasingly, they sensed the problem was not with the fans, but with their label's inability to keep up with how fans were consuming music.

By the fall of 2007, Radiohead had a new album ready to go, but still hadn't pulled the trigger on any kind of record deal. It decided to release the album anyway, through its website. On October 1, Jonny Greenwood posted a terse announcement on radiohead.com: "Well, the new album is finished, and it's coming out in 10 days. We've called it *In Rainbows.*"

So much for the big marketing plan. In the land of the major labels, Greenwood would've been drummed out of the public-relations academy for his utter offhandedness. For an artist of Radiohead's stature, it was customary for a big label to plot out the details of an album release months in advance, to line up shelf space at retail stores, programming at commercial radio, and full-page ads and interviews in *Billboard, Rolling Stone,* and the usual print-media suspects. But for the first time in its existence, Radiohead had no such constraints. It could now effectively function as its own record company, record store, and distribution service rolled into one—at least temporarily. So Radiohead instructed its fans that on October 10, it would provide an access code to a digital download of the new album to any customer willing to part with an e-mail address.

The price was left to the customer's discretion, the virtual equivalent of a giant tip jar.

"It's up to you," the checkout screen read for preordering the ten-song disc.

Also available to order was an expanded, physical version of the album, to ship two months later. Priced at £40 (about $81), it would include an eighteen-track double album packaged in both CD and vinyl versions, with lyrics, artwork, and photographs in a hardback book and slipcase.

Radiohead's distribution strategy for *In Rainbows* reduced the decade-long debate over Internet downloading to a single, deceptively simple question: "What's this piece of music really worth to you?" It was a question that respected the intelligence of the potential buyer, a question that bristled with moral, ethical, economic, and aesthetic considerations. And yet it was a question that could be answered with a simple mouse click, in prices ranging from $0.00 to $99.99 (the order form didn't accommodate three-digit dollar figures).

It was a brilliant move made even more potent by its timing. Only a week before, a federal jury in Minnesota had awarded the record industry a $220,000 judgment against Jammie Thomas for the crime of downloading twenty-four copyrighted songs and making them available for file sharing. Thomas was hardly alone. At the very moment her verdict was being read, more than 9 million consumers were sharing music files around America, according to media management company BigChampagne.

As one of the more marketable names in the business, Radiohead was in a position where it didn't have to give away anything. It had the cachet to charge $10 or more for its music, and rest assured that most of its fans would gladly pay. But it clearly wanted no part of a music industry that labels its own customers as thieves. By declaring, "It's up to you," Radiohead made it clear whose side it was on.

Even nonfans were intrigued. "I don't really like Radiohead all that much, but I like this idea, so I think I will give them two of my American dollars," commented one poster on the I Love Music website (ilxor.com).

The Internet exploded with Radiohead-related chatter. In the three days after the announcement, blogpulse.com, a search engine that reports on daily blog activity, showed more than a 1,300 percent increase in the number of posts mentioning the band.

For the next few weeks, the heaviest hitters in the music industry could seemingly talk of nothing else.

"That's all I heard about for days afterward and in general everyone's reaction was the same: 'My goodness, this is incredible,'" says R.E.M. manager Bertis Downs. "It's the public-radio model applied to music distribution: 'If you feel like it, make a contribution. We wish more of you would. But if you want us to quit doing these campaigns, please call up and give us some money.' It's the patronage model. It's Mozart all over again. It wasn't like he was making money on a per sale basis."

Bert Holman, the Allman Brothers Band manager, was impressed by the confluence of street buzz and sound business strategy engineered by the Radiohead brain trust.

"They bought themselves a zillion dollars' worth of publicity," he says. "And they're also capturing the e-mail addresses of all the people who want the record. They'll go on tour and spend little if any money on advertising because they already know where their audience is."

The behind-the-scenes mechanics of the deal were intriguing, all the more so because Radiohead really wasn't interested in talking about them—perhaps because it might've appeared unseemly to gloat. The band stood to profit handsomely from any paid download. What's more, they didn't have to share the money with any middlemen. Reports circulated that the Radiohead website had been inundated by more than 1 million downloads of *In Rainbows,* and that 40 percent of those fans had paid an average of $6, representing about $3 million in revenue.

The band brushed aside such speculation, but in an interview with David Byrne for *Wired* magazine, Thom Yorke said, "In terms of digital income, we've made more money out of this record than out of all the other Radiohead albums put together, forever—in terms of anything on the Net."

Ken Waagner, the tech guru for Wilco, saw a similar but far less sophisticated strategy work for his band in 2001 when it was between labels. Radiohead's audience was ten times the size of Wilco's, and Waagner was awed by the possibilities. "It's such an attractive model to the detriment of an industry that swallows eighty percent of the money that is out there," he said. "If the transaction is the artist to the fan, and the cost of distribution is so low—there is no physical cost, no manufacturing cost, no shipping cost, no fuel cost—then it basically becomes pure profit for the band outside of costs for the server space."

Waagner estimated the band spent $5,000 to $10,000 to process the flood of orders and downloads on its website.

Those distribution costs are minimal compared with what pioneers such as Prince faced a decade ago when fans ordered CDs from his website. Rather than e-mailing a code to customers leading them to a download page, Prince had to manufacture, package, and ship CDs, and struggled to keep up with demand.

Prince, like Radiohead, was able to pull it off because he had a large fan base for his music built up over years of promotion and marketing by a major label before he went into business for himself. This factor often was overlooked in media coverage of Radiohead's new business model, but it was critical to its success.

"Radiohead's developed a pretty good brand name over the years," Holman says. "There's artistic merit, but they also had a major label doing a lot of marketing for them. They're in a position where, of course, they can do something like this. And so could a few others—U2, Pearl Jam, Dave Matthews. These are bands that benefited from the old system. But it's not really applicable to reinventing the music business."

Radiohead didn't want to lead a revolution. Its goal was far more modest: to leak its own album, give fans a taste of the new music, and invite them to buy the sonically superior physical product once it became available in a few months.

If the band screwed up, it was in offering *In Rainbows* in the form of relatively low-fidelity 160 kilobits per second MP3s.

"There is no excuse for this," wrote Tom Johnson on the *Blogcritics Magazine* website. "These should have been 192kbps at the very least, but really should have been 256kbps. If they want to lead the industry and other bands to a new solution, then LEAD. . . . There's no revolution here, folks, at least not yet. It's details like these that could have taken this band from simply 'doing something different' to actually setting an example for others to follow. What should have been done? A tiered structure. Cheap, low-bitrate MP3s (the ones we're getting) for 'whatever price you want' followed by loss-less FLAC files, then a low-priced single CD in minimal packaging, a vinyl option, the double CD in nice packaging for a higher price, and the ridiculously expensive 'Disc Box.'"

The criticism made Jonny Greenwood's head spin.

"Bit-rate talk and any references to FLACs are just hi-fi nerds being hi-fi nerds," he says. "It's like megapixel talk with digital cameras—interesting to tech people, but it says nothing about the photography itself."

Maybe so, but Radiohead's critics had a point. Somebody should have put Tom Johnson in charge of the band's marketing department. Three months after making *In Rainbows* available on digital download, the band released it the old-fashioned way: as a high-fidelity, beautifully packaged CD, manufactured and distributed by an independent record label, ATO.

In the first week of 2008, it debuted at number one on the *Billboard* charts, the fourth consecutive Radiohead album to debut in the top 5 during the digital era. The sales figures weren't gaudy: 122,000 units sold in the United States, down from the band's 2003 peak of three hundred thousand for its previous studio album, *Hail to the Thief*. But the numbers were still impressive, given that most of the band's fans had already downloaded the music.

What they heard was Radiohead once again making like Pink Floyd. It still believed in the old-fashioned album, and *In Rainbows* was constructed as one. In reclaiming its music from the whims of the peer-to-peer marketplace, Radiohead was making less an economic statement than an aesthetic one.

Like all of Radiohead's albums, *In Rainbows* was meticulously structured; remove one song, and the whole thing might collapse. The ten songs created a loose narrative about intimacy, its allure and its traps. They explore humanity's essential contradiction: the desire to be loved, no matter what the cost, no matter how painful the heartbreak. For a band often accused of being cryptic, that's about as direct and universal as Radiohead has ever gotten.

By Radiohead standards, *In Rainbows* was downright warm, the chilled beauty of earlier albums melted by transparent emotion, sparse song structures, and unusually direct lyrics.

"House of Cards" suggests Radiohead doing Jobim, a long-distance nod to bossa nova with pensive guitar and a relaxed soul-singer vocal. "I don't want to be your friend / I just want to be your lover," Yorke sings.

That sense of yearning—often unrequited—is the album's central theme. Whereas on past albums Yorke and his bandmates inhabited a world that sounded cut off from human connection, *In Rainbows* positively pines for it.

"Videotape" says as much. It's a stately voice-and-piano elegy undercut by off-kilter percussion. The narrator finds himself being judged at the gates of heaven. Mephistopheles claws at his heels. But his thoughts are with the one he left behind: "You are my center when I spin away."

Inside rainbows, there's nothing but thin air, the song suggests. But still we keep chasing them.

For the band, there was gold at the rainbow's end. A year after the release of *In Rainbows,* the big numbers started to roll in. The album had sold 3 million copies, including downloads from radiohead.com, according to the band's publisher, Warner/Chapell. The sales from the band's website alone exceeded the total sales for the band's previous album, *Hail to the Thief.* The figures included one hundred thousand limited-edition box sets, sold at the U.S. equivalent of $81—an $8 million haul, with the band keeping most of the profits. The publicity windfall helped ensure one of the most successful tours of 2008, with the band playing to 1.2 million fans.

It was an impressive accomplishment, if only an intriguing first step in a new direction for the business as a whole. This revolution, as successful as it was, could have used a few tweaks: the low-bit-rate digital release was slipshod; after two months, the Radiohead website stopped offering the name-your-price MP3 files; and the band ended up tying its fate to a traditional record label (albeit an independent one) rather than pioneering a new marketplace dynamic. Perhaps that was too much to ask of any band.

How, exactly, would the band proceed? As Jonny Greenwood said as 2008 wound down, "By the time we finish the next record, everything will have changed again anyway, so we'll decide then."

The author doesn't want to relinquish power. There are no good hypertext novels because writers want to have complete control of their world. Musicians are the same way. It's a test for us to see how willing we are to let the audience have more control. I don't mind doing that. I started playing music because I loved it, and playing it made me more involved in the process. This gets people more involved in the process. It's a good thing. The Dismemberment Plan's remix record (the 2004 release *A People's History of the Dismemberment Plan*), where they had their fans remix the songs, that kind of stuff is amazing. I'd like to see more of that, where listeners are participating more in the music, where there is more of a conversation between the creator and the audience. The line gets more blurred, and I don't see that as a bad thing.

—Rick Valentin, singer-guitarist of the indie-rock band
  Poster Children, born 1966

20

"Steal, Steal, and Steal Some More"

Radiohead's *In Rainbows* strategy got at least one guy thinking "I can do this better."

Trent Reznor initially was impressed by the British band's flexible-price digital release strategy, but was disappointed by the follow-through.

"I think the way [Radiohead] parlayed it into a marketing gimmick has certainly been shrewd," Reznor said in a March 2008 interview with the Australian Broadcasting Corporation. "But if you look at what they did, though, it was very much a bait and switch to get you to pay for a MySpace-quality stream as a way to promote a very traditional record sale."

Reznor, who long had praised Radiohead as one of his favorite bands, saw the quintet's efforts to meet the file sharers halfway as "insincere" because of the digital release's subpar sound and lack of accompanying artwork. "It relies upon the fact that it was quote-unquote 'first,' and it takes the headlines with it."

Only a few days before the interview, Reznor had pulled off a digital-distribution coup of his own, and made more than $1 million, without the help of any record label. If Radiohead opened the door to a new future, Reznor ran through it with guns blazing.

It was a moment he had been awaiting for nearly two decades. During that time, he had released five studio albums as Nine Inch Nails. The first two made him a star. *Pretty Hate Machine* (1989)

and *The Downward Spiral* (1994) merged the aggression of indus-
trial rock with gothic introspection and arena-sized choruses. *Spiral* sold 4 million copies, punctuated by an indelible performance at
Woodstock 1994, when Reznor and his band took the stage at the
rain-soaked festival caked in mud.

Yet those successes were tainted by his dealings with his first
label, TVT. The relationship was so toxic that he agreed to a deal in
which he would continue to share royalties with TVT in exchange
for being allowed to move to a new label.

His contract was sold to Interscope Records, which in 1999
released his third album, *The Fragile.* It arrived at the height of the
teen-pop sales boom, with 'N Sync and Britney Spears dominating the charts. It spread twenty-three widely varied, scrupulously
detailed, yet unusually spacious songs across one hundred minutes
on two CDs. For the first time, Reznor sounded like something
more than just a rubber-suited, death-tripping gargoyle. For the first
time, Reznor opened up the sound, his trademark claustrophobia
pierced by interludes of disquieting softness and subversive beauty.
Cellos, violins, pianos, even a ukulele broke up the doomy assault,
and Reznor sometimes sang with quiet conviction, even tenderness,
rather than the unrelenting scream of old.

The arrangements pulsed with surprises: the uplifting orchestra-
tion that salvages the suicidal "The Great Below," the Prince-like
techno-funk (circa "Controversy") of "Where Is Everybody," the
sinister junkyard percussion of "I'm Looking Forward to Joining You, Finally." Even more striking were the handful of instrumental tracks, from the death-march grandeur of "Pilgrimage" to
the anxious piano ripples of "Ripe (With Decay)." Reznor blended
instruments and sounds in previously untested combinations: using
cardboard boxes and bicycle chains as a drum kit, tinkering with
detuned mandolins and rusted synthesizers, and subverting even traditional instruments such as guitars and pianos until they sounded
like alien intruders.

All of which added up to one of the best headphone records in
rock history. Not that anyone outside his hard-core fan base cared.

"It was a great record released at the wrong time," says Jimmy Iovine, the chairman of Interscope Records, Reznor's label at the time. "It was a very singles-driven era, and there was too much information on that record. His old fans couldn't digest it. And a new audience just didn't get it."

Like Radiohead, Reznor was all about the sanctity of the album, a body of interwoven songs, artwork, and imagery.

"I realize that maybe I've let some people down because *The Fragile* wasn't more extreme, more dark, and excessively evil, and I didn't come out with fangs and wake up in a coffin," he said a few months after the album was released and its fate as a commercial dud had been sealed. "*Downward Spiral* hit a nerve in popular culture. Now I don't know if I'm becoming obsolete or if the generation I came from doesn't exist anymore. It was a generation of music lovers who wanted some depth, who treated the music as art, and I include myself in that. I was a fan who loved the imports and wanted to get the B side, and listened to an album twenty times to get something out of it. But if you put a gun to my head and said name ten great bands that have come out in the last five years, you'd be wiping my brains off the wall. The climate right now supports disposability."

Reznor can come off as a whiny prima donna. But he was locked into a long-term contract with an industry still beholden to commercial radio and MTV airplay, and he didn't see a way out. "It's tougher now than a few years ago, because there are fewer avenues to get music to the public," he said. "And those that are available seem to have taken the ball and run with what's easily digestible."

Two years later, Reznor was counting the days to his emancipation from the label system. He could see viable alternatives for getting his music to his fans, but he was still under contract to Interscope, which in turn had been swallowed by Universal. Internet distribution offered a glimmer of possibility, but he wasn't sold on it yet.

"Artwork isn't that big a factor for the kid being exposed to music through his hard drive," he said. "But for me it still comes down to appreciating this as an art experience. That's what I am still fighting for. I don't think the digital delivery method is together right now.

To me, listening to something I downloaded on the Internet, usually at a shitty bit rate, is not the same as the experience of listening to a record. So as much as I think the idea of eliminating the record labels from the equation is a good one, I would still like to see a physical record in the store in some capacity."

Nonetheless, he knew those ideals would no longer suffice as a business practice. "I need to risk failure through other presentations," he said. "I'm just now coming to terms with what those things might be."

In 2007, Reznor embraced that reality by entering into a creative partnership with his fans. That year, he transformed his final Interscope album, *Year Zero,* into a new-media phenomenon.

With its novelistic scope and labyrinthine musical detail, *Year Zero* fit with Reznor's grandiose vision of what an album could and should be; it suggested a digital-era response to operatic classic-rock albums such as Pink Floyd's *The Wall* and the Who's *Quadrophenia.* Set fifteen years in the future, the album was a dystopian soundtrack for a world in which religious zealots control the government, drugs sedate the populace, and a mysterious "Presence" drifts through a landscape of terrorism, global warming, and nuclear war.

It was every bit as ambitious as *The Fragile,* but this time Reznor devised a marketing campaign as inventive as his musical ideas. Weeks before its official release, Reznor's operatives scattered clues about the album's themes on a proliferating network of websites, MP3 music files, videos, phone lines, tour T-shirts, even USB drives planted in bathrooms in Portugal, Spain, and England during Nine Inch Nails concerts.

The fans did the rest. They swapped files and information on message boards and via e-mails, gradually piecing together a story line for the album that continued to unfold over the next year. *Year Zero* wasn't just any old concept album. It was a multimedia experience that empowered the listeners, making them part of the creative process.

All told, twenty-seven websites were involved, generating 2.5 million visits in ten weeks, fifty thousand e-mails, and one hundred thousand video streams. Fans had streamed the album more than four hundred thousand times on Nine Inch Nails' MySpace page, with the single "Survivalism" drawing nearly 1 million streams and five hundred thousand YouTube views. In addition, Reznor leaked several songs to music blogs and encouraged fans to trade them.

The Recording Industry Association of America was not amused. It sent cease-and-desist e-mails to blogs hosting the files. The story brought an avalanche of media attention and confirmed Reznor's determination to break with the mainstream labels. At a September 16 show in Sydney, Australia, he urged fans to rip off his new album rather than pay the retail price: $34.99 in Australian dollars, or $29.10 U.S.

"Last time I was here I was complaining about the ridiculous CD prices . . . and now my record label all around the world hates me because I called them out and called them greedy fucking assholes," he said. "Has the price come down?"

The crowd answers: "No!"

Reznor: "Well you know what that means. Steal it. Steal away. Steal, steal, and steal some more and give it to all your friends and keep on stealing. Because one way or another these motherfuckers will get it through their head that they're ripping people off and that's not right."

The rant, videotaped by a fan and then posted on YouTube, became a viral hit, drawing four hundred thousand views and four hundred comments.

A few weeks later, he announced that his deal with Interscope had expired. "I have been under recording contracts for eighteen years and have watched the business radically mutate from one thing to something inherently very different," he posted on the Nine Inch Nails website. "It gives me great pleasure to be able to finally have a direct relationship with the audience as I see fit and appropriate."

The next day, Radiohead made *In Rainbows* available as a free download. And a few weeks later, a Reznor-produced album, Saul Williams's *The Inevitable Rise and Liberation of Niggy Tardust*, was released in similar fashion on Williams's website. Fans were given an option to download the album for free or pay $5 for the same songs at a higher bit rate.

The album was as ambitious as its marketing plan. A dense collage-style mixture of grimy grooves and Williams's fiery, politically tinged rapping, it explored issues of racial identity in the same way that its inspiration, David Bowie's 1973 concept album *The Rise and Fall of Ziggy Stardust,* plumbed gender and sexual identity. Though it was promoted on Nine Inch Nails' website, the initial sales figures disappointed Reznor: After little more than two months, 154,449 fans had downloaded Williams's album, but less than 19 percent paid for it.

"I thought if you offered the whole record free at reasonable quality—no strings attached—and offered a hassle-free way to show support that clearly goes straight to the artists who made it at an unquestionably low price, people would 'do the right thing.' . . . [Yet] less than one in five feels it was worth $5," Reznor wrote on his website. The sales figures were "disheartening."

"Add to that: we spent too much (correction, I spent too much) making the record utilizing an A-list team and studio . . . an old publishing deal, sample clearance fees, paying to give the record away (bandwidth costs), and nobody's getting rich off this project."

But the numbers kept on rising, abetted by Williams's incendiary tour and an unlikely TV ad. Williams's 2004 song "List of Demands" became the soundtrack for a Nike gym-shoe commercial in the spring of 2008. With its strident vocal demanding reparations for slavery over a slamming beat and a synthesizer screaming like a teakettle, the song never stood a chance of commercial radio airplay. But it found an audience through the sixty-second ad: the YouTube video of the original full-length video was viewed four hundred thousand times, and the digital single started selling at a pace of ten thousand per week.

By mid-April, the downloads for *Niggy Tardust* had topped 225,000, and sales hit sixty thousand—double Williams's previous best for his 2004 self-titled release on Fader Records.

"I know that a lot of people who spent time with the album were like, 'I gotta get this dude some money,'" Williams says. "We got a slew of people who were starting to feel guilty about the amount of time they were spending dancing to the album and looked back and gave their $5. So I feel like it's been wonderful, a marvelous result for me. And at the end of the day, it's been about the exposure. Not only the exposure to me and my music, but for me, who always falls in the category of being a 'message writer,' there are a lot of people being exposed to perhaps a new way of thinking, some new ideas, and that really excites me."

Reznor learned from the experience, and offered a more refined version of the pay-what-you-can-afford model for his next release, a four-part album, *Ghosts I-IV*, containing thirty-six instrumental tracks spanning nearly two hours. On March 2, 2008, he announced on his website that the music would be available immediately in five configurations at five price levels: as a free download of nine tracks in a high-fidelity MP3 format (320 kilobits per second), a $5 download for all thirty-six tracks, a $10 double-CD set, a $75 hardcover book containing two CDs and a DVD, and a $300 limited edition box set that included two CDs, a DVD, an optical disc containing a slide show, and four vinyl albums.

Business was brisk. The next day, Reznor posted an announcement asking fans to be patient after the high volume of downloads crashed his website.

"We quietly released this album last night without any warning, and without any press," Reznor wrote. "Because we know how devoted our fans are, we planned for an overwhelming response, and expected heavy traffic. To our surprise, the traffic was more than three times what we anticipated, and has only been getting heavier throughout the day. The response has been absolutely phenomenal, and we couldn't be happier, but our servers have taken a beating, causing numerous problems with the download site."

Reznor also made the tracks available through various rogue file-sharing sites, including piratebay.org. He attached no digital-rights restrictions to the music and encouraged listeners to share and remix it as extensively as possible.

The music, a product of a ten-week recording binge that included collaborators such as producer-mixer Alan Moulder and guitarist Adrian Belew, ranged from contemplative piano-based nocturnes to percussive assaults. As usual, the heavily processed mix defied listeners to identify individual instruments in the swirling, gray-sky collages. Sheet-metal percussion that conjured German noise terrorists Einsturzende Neubauten and eerie *Blade Runner* synthesizers cozied up alongside bursts of guitar. Track fifteen sounded like someone hammering nine-inch nails in the apartment next door.

Though the tracks were relatively concise, none of them remotely sounded like anything on the commercial radio landscape in the late winter of 2008. Had Reznor still been a vassal in the major-label system, an elaborately packaged four-CD set of instrumentals would've been deemed an unnecessary extravagance at best, a career-killer and deal-breaker at worst.

Certainly, it was the kind of self-indulgent release that only a committed fan would need. But that was the beauty of an Internet-focused release with a five-tier pricing system. It allowed listeners to determine their level of commitment at a price of their choosing. Like Radiohead, Reznor had used his newfound freedom to empower his fans. But he'd also taken that empowerment several steps further.

A week after releasing *Ghosts I-IV*, Reznor reported that he amassed more than $1.6 million on 781,917 transactions, including free and paid downloads and orders of physical product. The $300 box set sold out of twenty-five hundred copies within a day.

In a week, Reznor had instantly rendered the traditional outlets for determining the popularity of music—SoundScan, commercial radio airplay, MTV exposure—irrelevant. To those institutions, *Ghosts* didn't exist. But it was the most popular album in America by a wide margin.

Reznor then called on fans to upload music videos for *Ghosts* on a special section of YouTube. A few days later, Radiohead announced a similar strategy, in which fans were encouraged to submit music-video concepts via video or storyboard. The best ones would receive budgets ranging from $1,000 to $10,000 to follow through on their ideas. The band later solicited remixes of the *In Rainbows* track "Nude" and drew 6 million unique visitors to its website and collected twenty-two hundred fan remixes.

Radiohead had played its hand, Reznor raised the ante, and now both bands were coming up with new ways to engage their fans, with no one in between to muck up the conversation. In their view, the customer was not only always right, the customer was a coconspirator, a creative partner. The future of the music industry was still being shaped, but there was no longer any question that it had arrived.

ACKNOWLEDGMENTS

"What the hell is that?"

Those were the first words I heard from a certain major-label executive after he read a story I had written for the *Chicago Tribune* in the midnineties containing references to "MP3 files." The concept was so new that this otherwise fairly knowledgeable music-biz lifer called me to demand further explanation. I couldn't fault him. No one really understood the implications of file sharing back then, but as the story developed, it soon became apparent that the music world would never be the same.

I was thrilled to cover the story for a great newspaper, a story that presaged our own industry's difficult transition into the digital era. That reporting became the springboard for this book, and I thank my editors at the paper for their role in guiding and sharpening my coverage. In particular, I have Scott Powers, Emily Rosenbaum, Kevin Williams, Carmel Carrillo, Tim Bannon, and Jim Warren to thank for their professionalism, skill, and high standards.

The same holds true of my colleagues on *Sound Opinions.* Nearly every week since its inception in 1999, the radio show reported on some new development in online music and interviewed many of the key players in the transformation. Our producers were invaluable in spotting stories and trends before they became national news, particularly Jason Saldanha, Robin Linn, Todd Bachmann, and Matt Spiegel. I also benefited from the informed and always provocative perspective of my cohost and *Chicago Sun-Times* counterpart, Jim DeRogatis.

For research assistance above and beyond: Andy Downing and Rachael Liberman. They helped me wade through hundreds of hours of interviews, and their journalistic skills were invaluable. Emma Martin, Eric Grubbs, and Maggie Schultz shared their insights into

251

peer-to-peer file sharing and hooked me up with dozens of contacts. I ended up interviewing more than a hundred file sharers, and I thank all of them for their time and knowledge.

David Dunton's counsel as my agent and friend once again guided me through this process from start to finish. A writer couldn't ask for a better ally and sounding board. My editor at Scribner, Brant Rumble, gave this project a vision and helped hone the story. His enthusiasm never wavered, and his perceptive and careful edits made it a better book.

My parents, Len and June, told me from an early age I could accomplish anything in life, even write a book. That my fondest wish since grade school has been realized three times is in no small measure due to the values and confidence they instilled in me. My parents-in-law, Dan and Pat Lyons, graciously allowed me to take over their home office many times so that I could hammer away at my manuscript, and always made me feel like I was doing something worthwhile (even if I sometimes had my doubts). My wife's uncle and aunt, Denny and Cathy Coll, cheered me on, if only to give me incentive to finish the damn thing.

My daughters, Katie and Marissa, indulge me. They lose me to writing for days at a time and always welcome me back to the real world with open arms. My wife, as usual, gets the last word. Not because she demands it, but because she deserves it. Deb, thanks for seeing me through another one with grace, selflessness, and love.

—Greg Kot

INDEX

ABOUT THE AUTHOR

Greg Kot has been the music critic at the *Chicago Tribune* since 1990. With his cohost, Jim DeRogatis, Kot cohosts *Sound Opinions*, "the world's only rock 'n' roll talk show," nationally syndicated on public radio and available worldwide via the Web. Kot has written for *Encyclopaedia Britannica* as well as *Rolling Stone, Details, Blender, Entertainment Weekly, Men's Journal, Guitar World, Vibe,* and *Request.* Kot's biography of Wilco, *Wilco: Learning How to Die,* was published in 2004. His *Tribune*-hosted blog, "Turn It Up," debuted in 2007. A longtime basketball junkie, he coauthored *Survival Guide for Coaching Youth Basketball* in 2008. He lives on Chicago's Northwest Side with his wife, two daughters, and far too many records.

For more information, or to contact the author, visit gregkot.com.